C. G. Jung and the Archetypes of the Collective Unconscious

American University Studies

Series VIII
Psychology

Vol. 7

PETER LANG
New York · Bern · Frankfurt am Main · Paris

Robin Robertson

C. G. Jung and the Archetypes of the Collective Unconscious

PETER LANG
New York · Bern · Frankfurt am Main · Paris

Library of Congress Cataloging-in-Publication Data

Robertson, Robin
  C. G. Jung and the archetypes of the collective unconscious.

  (American university studies. Series VIII,
Psychology ; vol. 7)
    Bibliography: p.
    Includes index.
    1. Archetype (Psychology) 2. Subconsciousness.
3. Psychology—History. 4. Gödel's theorem.
5. Jung, C. G. (Carl Gustav), 1876–1961. I. Title.
II. Series.
BF175.5.A72R63   1987   150.19′54   86-21117
ISBN 0-8204-0395-4
ISSN 0740-0454

CIP-Kurztitelaufnahme der Deutschen Bibliothek

Robertson, Robin:
C. G. Jung and the archetypes of the collective unconscious /
Robin Robertson. — New York ;
Bern ; Frankfurt am Main; Paris : Lang, 1987.
  (American university studies : Ser. 8,
  Psychology ; Vol. 7)

ISBN 0-8204-0395-4
NE: American university studies / 08

Cover illustration: Charon accepting his fare to take a
passenger across the river Styx.

© Peter Lang Publishing, Inc., New York 1987

All rights reserved.
Reprint or reproduction, even partially, in all forms such as
microfilm, xerography, microfiche, microcard, offset strictly
prohibited.

Printed by Weihert-Druck GmbH, Darmstadt (West Germany)

Contents

Acknowledgements xi

Foreword xiii

1. Introduction 1
   A Prelude to Jung's Psychology 1
   Twentieth-century Science 3
   The Renaissance Ideal 5
   Cracks in the Mirror 7
   The Twentieth Century's Dilemma 8
   New Paradigms 9

PART I: THE BIRTH AND DEATH OF THE RENAISSANCE IDEAL

2. The Renaissance Ideal 13
   Man the Creator 13
   Copernicus and the Observational Method 14

3. The Birth of the Scientific Method 17
   Isaac Newton 17
   Indivisible Particles, Absolute Space and Time ... 18
   Great Theories 19
   Empiricism 20

4. Immanuel Kant's Legacy 23
   Leibniz' Categories of Judgement 23
   Berkeley and Hume 24
   Kant's Answer to Hume and Berkeley 26
   Science's Pragmatic Response 28

5. The Precursors of Experimental Psychology 31
   Founders of Associationism 31
   Parallelism 32
   John Stuart Mill's Creative Syntheis 34

6. Experimental Psychology's Founders 37
   Gustav Fechner and Weber's Law 37
   Hermann Von Helmholtz and the Conservation of Energy 41
   Wilhelm Wundt 42
   Limiting the Psyche to Consciousness 43

7. The History of Hypnosis 47
   Paracelsus 47
   Animal Magnetism, Mesmerism, and Hypnotism 49
   Current Academic Evaluation of Hypnosis 50
   Gestalt Psychology vs. Associationism 51
   The Value of Subjective Experience in Psychology .. 52

8. Clinical Psychology's Founders 55
   Jean Martin Charcot 55
   Pierre Janet 56
   What Led to the Discovery of the Unconscious? 57
   Philosophy and Its Children 58

9. Sigmund Freud 61
   Freud's Early Work 61
   The Interpretation of Dreams 63
   Three Essays on the Theory of Sexuality 67
   Summary of Early Freudian Ideas 70

PART II: THE PSYCHOLOGY OF C. G. JUNG

10. The Background for Jung's Ideas 75
    Nature and Mind/Science and Poetry 75
    Ghosts and Spirits 76
    The Emergence of Consciousness from The Unconscious 77

11. Jung's Model of the Psyche 81

      Personal Conscious and Unconscious 82
      The Collective Unconsious 85
      The Nature of Mathematical Proof 86
      An Example of an Archetypal Image 89

12. **The Creativity of the Unconscious** 93
      The Computer Model 93
      An Anecdote About Dolphins 95
      Hypnotism and the Unconscious 97

13. **A Dynamic Model of the Psyche** 101
      How Archetypes Emerge into Consciousness 101
      Archetype and Experience 103
      Complex and Archetype 104
      The Emergence of Ego 106

14. **The Shadow** 109
      Actual and Potential 109
      The Shadow 111
      Projection and Transference 113
      The Shadow as Archetype 116
      The Expanded Ego 118

15. **The Anima/Animus** 121
      Body, Soul, Mind, and Spirit 121
      Mandalas 124
      Repression and Integration 125
      The Masculine/Feminine Syzygy 128
      Cultural or Biological? 130
      Anima and animus 131

16. **The Self** 137
      The Confrontation with the Unconscious 138
      The Symbol 141
      Eastern Spiritual Traditions 146
      The Self as the Transcendent Function 146
      Abraham Maslow and Self-actualization 149
      The Self and the Mystical Experience 150
      Pascal, Lao Tzu, and Holograms 151

17. Alchemy as a Model of Psychological
    Development 153
    Jung's Rediscovery of Alchemy 153
    A Short History of Alchemy 155
    Bringing Order Out of Chaos 158

18. The Mysterious Union 161
    The Conjunction of Opposites 162
    The Personification of Opposites 165
    The Nature of the Conjunction 165
    The Alchemical Creation Myth 167
    The Three Unions 167
    The Unio Mentalis 168
    The Union of the Mind and Body 170
    The Union with the Unus Mundus 173
    Summary 175

PART III: GÖDEL'S PROOF

19. The Roots of Modern Mathematics 179
    Philosophy from the Renaissance to Kant 179
    The Problem Passes from Philosophy to Science 181
    Analytic Geometry 183
    Calculus 186

20. Mathematical Formalism 191
    Peano's Postulates 192
    Non-Euclidean Geometry 195

21. Self-referential Systems 199
    The Barber Paradox 199
    Self-referential Systems 201
    Principia Mathematica: Mathematics' Tower of Babel ... 203
    Transfinite Numbers 205

22. Gödel's Proof 211
    Summary: Mathematics Before Gödel 211
    Gödel's Insight 212
    Further Readings on Gödel 213

    Mapping Arithmetic and Logical Signs onto
       Numbers 213
    The Amazing Code 216
    Mapping Meta-Mathematics onto Mathematics 217
    The Significance of Gödel's Proof 222
    Gödel and Jung 224

Bibliography 231

Index 242

Acknowledgements

To "Win" Sternlicht. Over the five years of our work together, his knowledge and interests have paralleled mine in an amazing way. As psychologist, scientist, independent thinker, editor, and friend, he has provided a constant mooring which has kept my ideas from drifting off into space. Without my dialogs with him, this book would never have come into existence.

To Dave Moonitz. Our friendship began thirteen years ago with a discussion of Gödel's Proof. That discussion was the first of many which would ultimately lead to this book. The quality of his ideas is only matched by the constancy of his friendship.

Finally, to my wife, Katherine Esmela. When I decided that my life as a business executive was killing me, she encouraged me to find a new life as a psychologist and writer. When that new life left us broke and desperate, she continued to tell me how proud she was of the life I had chosen to lead. She's an amazing woman; the great miracle of my life is that she chose to marry me.

Foreword

For a long time we have needed a new model or way of perceiving ourselves, and through that new perception of ourselves gain a different perspective of the world around us. The old ways of looking at both ourselves, and the world no longer provide us with appropriate answers to the questions we are being forced to ask, if we are going to survive. Clearly, the arrival of that critical time seems to be upon us in the second half of the twentieth century. The manner in which we think about the problems of pollution, crime, war, hunger, population density, disease, use of earth resources, relationship between individuals, and collective groups, all indicate the fragmented, inadequate fashion by which we attempt to solve these problems.

Just as Galileo changed the long held Aristolean ego-centric and geo-centric view of the universe, the nature of the work in modern physics, biology, chemistry, mathematics, and depth psychology (particularly of) C.G. Jung, all add up to the expectation of a similar radical change in our perspective.

We live in the time of that emergent paradigm, that new model or principle of thought. That is what this book is about. It describes and illustrates a process of synthesis, of bringing together divergent thoughts, of the connection between widely separated ideas. After all, what could seem more distant from the world of abstract, pure mathematics than the world of the self-referent, subjective, depth psychology of C.G. Jung. Yet, as this book illustrates, these worlds are much closer than they seem at first glance.

I was vaguely aware for many years, quite intuitively, that

the formalism of logic and the process of thinking were intimately associated with the irrationality of intuition, along with emotion, and the rationality of the feeling process. However, I never did articulate, refine, and make more explicit all those vague, intuitively derived concepts beyond what Jung developed in his description of psychological types and the four functions. Namely, that our epistemology, the assumptions concerning the source of our knowledge was based on the irrational functions of intuition and/or sensation, while what we did with that information was processed by the rational functions of thinking and/or feeling. Even now, as we increase our experience with psychological typology, the original formulations by Jung are undergoing modification, and our understanding of the reality of the human condition is also modified.

It was Robin Robertson who began to weave the pattern together for me. When we first met, it was immediately apparent that Robertson and I shared many interests and mutual values; including a connection to the work of C.G. Jung, and extending out to an interest in a variety of scientific areas as well as philosophy and art. While in discussion, Robertson expressed dissatisfaction with the predominant attempt in our culture to solve our problems rationally, it was some time before this interest took on more practical meaning. This was in the form of a series of papers illustrating the futility of solely pursuing the rational explanations for our experiences at the expense of the irrational, yet real world, that is both inner and outer.

I found his position particularly unusual since he brought to the discussion his training as a theoretical mathematician and his experience as a computer systems analyst and an actuary, which I also found unusual as a point of genesis for arguing the value of the irrational.

The broad comparative view that he adopted of the evolution of the sciences, of mathematics, philosophy and the arts led to insights and an understanding of the intimate relationship among the various disciplines that comprise the knowledge we have of ourselves and the universe. Since we are self-reflecting creatures, our view is dependent upon such fundamental assumptions as to whether the world is entirely a material, rationally structured entity, or there are other non-material, irrationally based forces that are valid as well.

In that light, it is not surprising that Jung's work becomes an important cornerstone in the exploration of the emergence of that new paradigm, one that was not bound to a rational, material tradition. Robertson observed that while Freud was the discoverer of the unconscious, he was also one of the last great exponents of the materialist position. Freud was still in the unfortunate position of being . . . "part of both the receding and the emerging paradigms" (page 2). Robertson continues:

> "Freud's realization that dreams spoke in a symbolic language was deeply important. However, his reduction of dreams to wish fulfillment, and dream symbols to sexual signs, was an ill chosen attempt to over-simplify their complexity" (page 84).

Through the examination of later work related to the symbolic process by Piaget in child psychology, Noam Chomsky in linguistics, Konrad Lorenz in ethology, Mircea Eliade in mythology and religion, Robertson weaves the fabric of the role played by the non-verbal, the physical, the irrational as well as rational forces at work in, for example, the complexity of symbolic meaning.

We have only begun to appreciate the consequences of the long struggle that started in earnest with the questions asked by Hume, Berkeley, Liebniz, and Kant concerning the nature of human thought, and subsequently the nature of the cosmos. However, these questions about material reality, cause and effect, a priori and a posteriori judgement could only be answered by philosophers until the developments of modern psychology and related science became available for us to examine them critically. For example, it was through Benjamin Whorf's field studies of linguistics among the Hopi Indians of the southwestern U.S. that Kant's assumption that everyone experiences time and space in the same fashion was demonstrated to be untrue.

The struggle has continued long and hard; for when psychology, the youngest of philosophy's children came into existence, it prided itself on following the methods of its siblings, physics and chemistry, the "hard" sciences. Psychologists were anxious to disavow any "philosophy" in their methods. However, the fundamental problems have not gone away by either wishing them away or ignoring them into non-existence. The problems faced by Immanuel Kant are still with us, and we may speculate that one of the reasons for the emergence of psychology as a science was to explore the re-union of man and the nature from which he has been so alienated. The union that can only occur in the psyche.

Another cornerstone to western thought process is the assumption we make concerning causality. We assume, for example, that the laws of nature are based on a series of causal occurences. We generally examine events in terms of cause and effect. However, a critical examination of those 'causal' laws of nature reveals the statistical quality of those truths which only approximate the idealized, Platonic view of nature. As pointed out by Jung in his Foreword to *The I Ching*, we need scientific laboratories with their controlled, restricted environments to support the idealized, abstract image of cause and effect. We strive to eliminate chance and thus eliminate the understanding of the reality of the moment, and its meaning, which Jung termed 'synchronicity', the acausal connection between events. The ancient Chinese in their discovery and development of the principles of the I Ching must have recognized the validity of the fact that anything that happens in a given moment belongs to the situation as an indispensable part of the event. Therefore, the fall of the yarrow stalks, or the throwing of the coins is assumed to be part of the moment of consulting the oracle.

While this is not a process that appeals to a critical western mind used to experimental verification of objective facts, it is the process arrived at to describe the cosmos by modern twentieth century physicists who also recognize the outer, objective world as a psychophysical entity.

Fred Alan Wolf, in an easily understood book entitled, *Space-Time and Beyond*, explores current nuclear theory. He concludes that the physical universe does not exist independent of the thought of the participators, but is the construction of the mind. It is but a short step to understand that as consciousness changes so does the universe. Obviously, this change does not occur instantly, but usually over a period of time. The work of Nobel Laureate Eugene Wigner demonstrated that consciousness (I would add "meaning") modifies the quantum wave and thereby changes the physical universe.

As I indicated in a commentary in *Psychological Perespectives* some years ago, (1972) modern science now recognizes the influence between the "knower" and the "known". Heisenberg's discovery of the uncertainty principle described at the nuclear level, that the simultaneous knowledge of the velocity and the position of a particle was not possible to obtain in physics, is a limitation of objective observation.

W. Pauli's Nobel Prize winning work on the principle of acausility in nuclear physics bears a kinship to C.G. Jung's work on the principle of synchronicity in the realm of psychological phenomena in that each refers to reality in terms of meaning, each points to the significance of the 'knower' in the process of the simplest observation.

The assumptions of the old paradigm concerning the objective order of the-universe, as understood through the theoretical models of behavioral psychology or even psychoanalysis, are not consistent with the observations of the rest of current science, with our experience, or the current appreciation of reality and its potential. In *Symmetries and Reflections* (1967) Wigner comments, "The recognition that physical objects and spiritual values have a very similar kind of reality. . .is the only known point of view which is consistent with quantum mechanics."

Despite the discovery of the relationship by physicist John Bell (now called 'Bell's Inequality') which showed conclusively that the experimental results predicted by quantum theory contradicted the principle of separability, the paradox remains and the validity of quantum mechanics stands unchanged.

The principle of separability, briefly stated, holds that things no longer in contact or in communication with each other cannot effect one another. In other words, whatever happens to one of these isolated things cannot influence the behavior of the other thing. Yet, the quantum wave seems to violate that principle. The operation of quantum mechanics points to a connection which Fred Wolf has dubbed the 'Einstein connection'. Physical experiments have shown that observations performed on one object have influenced another object even though these objects have no known physical connection. This all sounds similar to the psychological principle of synchronicity described by Jung.

One of the more important of Jung's contributions to psychology has been the introduction of this very principle of the participant-observer. It forms an important basis for the therapeutic process in Jungian psychology. The issue, long espoused by most schools of psychology, especially the behaviorists, concerning the validity of the purely "objective" observation no longer has any real support. Psychology, as a science, including depth psychology, can now join the twentieth century as a respected member of the family of sciences. In his book *The Phenomena of Man*, (1959) Pierre Teillhard de Chardin summarized it succinctly:

> That an interpretation of the universe-even a positivist one-remains unsatisfying unless it covers the interior as well as the exterior of things; mind as well as matter. The true physics is that which one day will achieve the inclusion of man in his wholeness in a coherent picture of the world. . .

and, indeed, it is that more complete inner wholeness that Jung has brought to depth psychology in order to bridge the gap between the inner and the outer, the material and the non-material world.

The American Indians of the southwestern United States

have a mythology and a religion which holds that the existence of Earth, wind, water, the stars depend on man's thought about them. The well-being of humanity, then depends on the relationship between man and the self, and his care of Mother Earth with all she provides by way of plants and animals in the total scheme of things. How very different from our own western way of thinking about our world with our alienation from the self, the environment, with our attitudes toward pollution and our attempts to control the earth for our own narrowly defined benefit at the expense of everything else, including our own inner reality, the unconscious.

We find in the "new physics" a general trend toward what is known as "field theory", whether in the form of the quantum field, the electromagnetic field or the gravitational field. Each of these field theories is an attempt to relate matter and/or its process to the environment in which it finds itself. It is an attempt to discover the unifying principles that govern the myriad interactions found in the universe. While all of the interactions of all of the known particles that make for the process and the matter in the universe seem to fall into four categories, scientists do not know why.

The most familiar are gravitational interactions and electromagnetic interactions, mainly because they are experienced in the every day world such as things that fall to the ground, as in the case of gravity, or in the form of heat in the case of electromagnetic interaction. The other two interactions are simply called strong and weak and are not at all obvious to casual experience. The weak interactive force describes the process found in chemical processes and accounts for the formation of atomic and molecular structures. The strong interactive force is responsible for the structure of the nucleus of the atom. The force of the nuclear bind is at least one million times as powerful as the weak molecular binding force.

Indeed, the current search for a unified field theory to describe and explain the operation and interactions within the physical universe is reminiscent of Jung's description of the work of the medieval alchemist. I am reminded of Edward

Edinger's description of the alchemical process of the 'coniunctio' in his *Anatomy of the Psyche* (1985) as the expression of the ultimate unifying process to the medieval alchemist. Each of the major processes within alchemy, of solutio, calcinatio, coagulatio, sublimatio, and mortificatio play a role in the achievement of the coniunctio. This, of course, must be understood symbolically as the work of the psyche on the path of what Jung called individuation, the process of becoming a whole (unified) individual.

As Edinger and Marie Louise von Franz a close associate of C. C. Jung, have pointed out, the imagery of alchemy with its focus on what is process rather than a static description, permits us to view the objective psyche and the archetypal elements contained within the unconscious in a new light, in order to gain further understanding of the functioning of the human condition.

For me, among the many ideas bequeathed to us by Jung that remains to be explored for its underlying connection to the complexes and to the archetypes is the dynamic condition of psychological types. Jung indicated that an understanding of the types was essential to individuation, that is the process of becoming whole. The problem of psychological types, at least in terms of type function, even if not in terms of type attitude, remains, however, unsettled and perhaps controversial as to its usefulness. By that I mean, in a number of surveys taken among Jungian analysts, many have indicated that they seldom use the concept of type function (thinking, feeling, sensation, intuition) in their analytic work. Certainly there is disagreement and confusion among analysts in describing the identifying quality for the same person. It is, clearly, a subjective reaction. There is much less disagreement in dealing with type attitude, that is the introversion and extraversion dimension. Perhaps, the initial assumptions concerning the basis of type function must be reexamined. The tools of consciousness and understanding available to us, in this subjective realm, are already personally biased in terms of our own particular orientation as a thinking type, or a feeling type, and so on, to the world. Until we can recognize more clearly the nature of the interaction between the 'knower' and the 'known', or how the 'participant-observer' is influenced in this very subjective field, we shall probably continue to experience confusion and disagreement. Perhaps type function is not only not static from birth, but oscillates between a dominant function and an auxillary function depending on the demand of the environmental circumstances. The continued exploration of the type problem would, I feel, be entirely within the spirit of Jung's work, and consistent with the broader span of the scientific paradigm. An early edition of Volume 6, of the Collected Works, *Psychological Types*, Jung had sub-titled "The Psychology of Individuation". I felt sorry when subsequent editions eliminated the sub-title, for it took away some of the meaning which Jung obviously intended as highlighting the significance of types, and type function. Aside from the advantages of becoming conscious of a critical set of functions involved in our perception and the meaning of what we perceive, the study of types also offers an additional facet to the unifying principle. Professor C.A. Meier, one of Jung's early associates, expressed those same ideas in an article in the *Journal of Analytical Psychology* (1978). However, that is the subject of another work.

In conclusion, Robertson's approach to the synthesis of the disciplines of knowledge is worthy of attention and the application of further effort. It is time to seek for the relationship between ideas and events. It brings about a new, wholistic, refreshing, and productive way of looking at what we know concerning ourselves and our relationship to the universe.

April, 1986; Palm Desert, California
Win Sternlicht

1

Introduction

A Prelude to Jung's Psychology

The purpose of this book is to examine the key elements in the psychology of C. G. Jung, and to examine to what extent they are supported by scientific research and personal experience. The author will attempt to show that a new view of the world began in the Renaissance, a view that regarded man as an observer and the physical world as the proper object of man's observation. That new view eventually developed into the rationalist/materialist position that separated mind and body, and alienated man first from the world, then from his fellow men, and finally from himself.

In the seventeenth century, modern science developed as a logical extension of the materialist position. With the boost of science's achievements, the rationalist position reached its peak in the nineteenth century. As the twentieth century began, problems inherent in the materialist position appeared in virtually all the sciences and arts. Physics especially found it necessary to develop a new rationale for science, one that recognized that there is an inherent connection between the observer and the observed. However, at this same point in time, experimental psychology came into existence, proudly espousing all the materialist values physics was discarding.

As early as the high Renaissance, a second viewpoint appeared, a view that stressed the harmony between mind and matter rather than the separation. Because materialism was the dominant world-view, this holistic view could only express itself through fringe phenomena, such as astrology, alchemy, or hypnotism. Hypnotism lived a life at the edges of "science" for fully three hundred years before, at the end of the nineteenth century, at Charcot's clinic in France, it became one of clinical psychology's first tools. In the hands of Sigmund Freud, it led to the discovery of the body of unconscious thoughts, feelings, and memories which Freud called the unconscious.

Though the discoverer of the unconscious, Freud was also one of the last great exponents of the rationalist position. Thus Freud found himself in the uncomfortable position of being a part of both the receding and the emerging paradigms. In such times, great thinkers are forced, despite the lack of sufficient information, to speculate on the nature of the new world they see ahead. Freud did just that. If some of his successors have since converted Freud's hypotheses to dogma, it doesn't detract from the greatness of Freud's achievements.

In contrast to Freud, who enjoyed theorizing, Jung was a descriptive scientist. He observed and described rather than theorized. He constructed provisional models that fit his observations, and always sought to find superior models. Since he did not believe that modern psychologists were the first to observe and describe the psyche, Jung examined earlier models, both in the Western and Eastern traditions.

Because Jung observed rather than theorized, he observed much that Freud missed. Initially, Jung tried to explain all the elements in his patients' dreams in terms of Freud's theory of dream interpretation. But Jung found that the dreams were far richer than the theory. In particular, Jung found that his patients' dreams contained collective symbols, symbols that occurred in the dreams of many patients, symbols that had been documented in other cultures in other times. This discovery was the result of observation, not theory.

Having noted the existence of these collective elements, Jung continued his observations, in an attempt to see if the collective symbols formed any patterns. When they did, indeed, fall into patterns, Jung attempted to construct models that fit the patterns. But he always remained dissatisfied with the inability of such models to capture the complexity he observed. That is why he remained open to any models, regardless of their source, that could better fit this strange world of the psyche. This led him to study fields as diverse as medieval alchemy and modern physics.

Over a life-time of research into the nature of the psyche, Jung came to believe that the unconscious was the connecting point between matter and psyche. Jung saw that the mere existence of the collective unconscious implied a world far different from that proposed by either materialists or idealists. It appeared that mind and matter, rather than being separate, distinct entities, were merely two aspects of a single, interconnected reality. They appeared to be separate because of the limitations inherent in observation. Jung's analytic psychology provides a record of one man's systematic study of that unitary reality. If his findings appear strange, it is only because reality itself is strange.

Twentieth-century Science

Twentieth century physicists and, more recently, some key biologists and chemists, have reached similar conclusions. While searching for the building-blocks of nature, which was the great goal of the materialist position, the physicists discovered that matter is inseparable from psyche. They found that matter and energy have twin faces, a particle face and a wave face, and neither can be reduced to the other. They found that observation affects the observed. In order to understand these strange findings, physicists (and other scientists) have turned to depth psychologies, such as Jung's, or to Eastern mysticism, and other such sources, for some clue to the nature of reality (see examples that follow).

Spurred by these clues, several key new models of reality have emerged; e.g., neuro-physiologist Karl Pribram's Holographic Brain model proposes that the human brain stores information like a hologram; i.e., that each localized group of brain cells contains the same information as is contained in the entire brain (Pribram,1981:90–103). Quantum physicist David Bohm has presented a model of an Implicate Order [Bohm's phrase for a unitary reality] beyond time and space from which and into which the world we know is constantly unfolding and enfolding (Bohm,1980).

Biologist Rupert Sheldrake proposes that all biological order is created by morphogenetic fields, which exist separately from the individual organisms which display the order, and which have a memory of previous order (Sheldrake,1981). Chemist Ilya Prigogine received the Nobel prize for his discovery of chemical compounds which reverse entropy and create order out of disorder. Prigogine proposes that such order-producing systems are not freak occurrences, but rather the norm in nature (Prigogine,1984).

These new viewpoints are scientific hypotheses open to experimental verification. Sheldrake in particular has suggested several lines of experimental research which could help prove or disprove his hypothesis. However, from the literature, it appears that these theories are so radical that there is yet very little research to verify or deny their validity.

The history of modern physics and, to a lesser extent, modern biology and chemistry, have been well-recorded in books like Frijof Capra's *The Tao of Physics* (Capra,1975) or Gary Zukav's *The Dancing Wu Li Masters* (Zukav,1979). However, it is not as well-known that a mathematician named Kurt Gödel developed a proof in 1931 whose implications are more significant than those of relativity or quantum physics or the discovery of DNA. Gödel proved to the satisfaction of mathematicians and logicians that logic itself is limited. Gödel demonstrated that no logical system can ever fully explain reality. Gödel appears to have been unaware of Jung or his discoveries in psychology. But Gödel's own discoveries in mathematics have deep implications for psychology, implications that corroborate Jung's own conclusions. This book will attempt to record how discoveries in mathematics led ineluctably to Gödel's Proof, and to describe the significance, beyond mathematics, of this great discovery.

Jung's model of the psyche is also a scientific hypothesis open to verification. It is based on careful observation and detailed description. It presents a model of reality which is internally consistent, and which leads to conclusions about the physical world as well as the world of the psyche. As an example, Jung proposed that there is an acausal ordering system in nature which exists as a complement to causality; he termed this principle synchronicity. Jung discovered synchronicity through his explorations of his own and his patients psyches. However, if such acausal ordering does exist in the world, physical experiments should be able to be designed which can test its existence. Several such experiments in modern physics, though designed for other purposes, have in fact seemed to confirm Jung's theory of synchronicity. Much of Jung's theories are open to such physical experimentation. All are open to psychological study and verification. But very little such study and verification has been done, perhaps because very few experimental psychologists, other than those involved with depth psychology, are aware of Jung's conclusions, or his reasons for reaching them.

However, long before Jung discovered the collective unconscious, long before Gödel turned logic topsy-turvy, philosophy was forced to confront the same issues. This book will initially trace the development of the rationalist position and the counter-development of the holistic position. In tracing the development of these positions, the emphasis will be on philosophy, since philosophy saw the problems inherent in the materialist position long before they emerged in other fields. The philosophical history begins in the Renaissance.

The Renaissance Ideal

Man has always asked ultimate questions: what is the nature of the world, the nature of man? What is the relationship of man to the world? The great changes in world-view revolve around new ways of asking those eternal questions and new answers to the same questions. During the thousand years of the Middle Ages, between the fifth and the fifteenth centuries, Western man largely accepted that God created the world and asked: What is the nature of God? What is the relationship between God and man? Most medieval thinkers started from the presumption of a static world over which man had little or no control. Their curiousity centered around God, not the world.

According to medieval historian Etienne Gilson, there were two kinds of medieval thinkers, those who believed that "since God has spoken to us it is no longer necessary for us to think", and those who believed that "the divine law required man to seek God by the rational methods of philosophy" (Fremantle,1954:xii). Both types proceeded from fixed premises; the idea that a thinker should repeatedly check his premises and his conclusions against experience was alien to the main stream of Medieval thought.

During the fourteenth, fifteenth and sixteenth centuries, Renaissance Man suddenly looked at the world with new eyes and asked a different question: What is the nature of the world? Renaissance Man continually turned to the world and described what he saw. When that description led to questions, he proposed solutions, then turned once more to the world to check the validity of his conclusions. However, just as few Medieval thinkers thought to question their premises and check them against reality, few Renaissance thinkers thought to question the validity of the act of observation itself. They largely took for granted that their observations were accurate representations of the world.

During the Middle Ages, the world was accepted as God's creation and, therefore, eternal and immutable. During the Renaissance the world became a mystery to be examined and explained, but the mind doing the examining and explaining was unquestioned. There was an implicit belief that "the human mind is, in effect, a mirror that reflects without distortion the indwelling structure of the external world" (Aiken, 1956:31). This Renaissance attitude led to the creation of modern science during the seventeenth century.

Science has continually tried to construct experiments carefully enough that the mind doing the observation did not have to be accounted for in the experiment. This book will try to demonstrate that this is an impossible condition, that all observations of reality ultimately are, in part, observations of the mind of the observer as well. This is not to say that there is no validity in a properly constructed scientific experiment. It is just an acknowledgement that the world is a whole and that any system or experiment which separates that whole into parts is provisional; a different separation will tell us different facts about reality.

Cracks in the Mirror

As early as the seventeenth century, philosopher John Locke tried to describe human thought. Locke attempted to reduce human thought to a string of sense perceptions of the physical world. These sense perceptions were single, indivisible units, patterned by Locke on the idealized physical bodies Newton used in his *Mechanics* to explain the material world. During the eighteenth century, Bishop George Berkeley and David Hume took Locke's ideas to their natural conclusions and arrived at paradoxical results. For example, Berkeley agreed with Locke that all thought is made up of units of sense perception. However, Berkeley said, if all we can ever experience are such perceptions, we are totally unjustified in assuming there is any world outside those thoughts. Hume attacked science's most cherished tool: causality. He argued that there is no logical necessity to presume that one event "causes" another; all we can ever really assert is that two events occurred at the same place, and one just preceded the other in time.

In the late eighteenth century, Immanuel Kant tried to resolve the problems raised by Berkeley and Hume. Kant agreed with Hume that knowledge of the outer world can never have a logical necessity. Kant agreed with Berkeley that all we can know are our thoughts. But Kant went further and proposed that there are certain active, organizing principles, which exist in the human mind and whose function is to organize perceptions of the physical world. He called these organizing principles "categories"; causality was one such "category" of thought.

Kant said that while we think we are passively experiencing sensations from the outer world, we are really actively organizing those sensations into humanly acceptable categories. Thus, when we think we are experiencing the outer world, we are really experiencing the "categories" of our own minds. If the human mind is a mirror, it is a mirror that reflects itself. Kant felt that we can never experience "das ding an sich" ("the thing in itself", which was Kant's phrase for the underlying physical reality), only the categories of the human mind (Aiken,1956:27–50). Carl Jung and Kurt Gödel were to advance the issue of the mind as a "self-referential" system far beyond Kant.

Philosophy normally deals with problems long before they emerge as issues for other fields. Though Kant's ideas changed the direction of philosophy, they took over a hundred years to have their full impact on the arts and sciences. Only with the birth of the twentieth-century did the necessity of resolving this dichotomy between the inner and outer worlds begin to dominate all fields of human thought.

The Twentieth Century's Dilemma

The ancient Chinese prayed not to be born in "interesting times", because "interesting times" were times of upheaval and uncertainty. The twentieth century has surely been an "interesting time". Medieval man asked: What is the nature of God? Renaissance man asked: What is the nature of the world? From the Renaissance to the end of the nineteenth century, that question seemed sufficient to all except a few philosophers. Man in the early twentieth century asked a new question: What is the relationship between the world inside and the world outside man?

Of course, coming at the culmination of the long development of rationalism/materialism, the question could never be articulated that clearly. Instead, physicists asked what matter might be once it ceased to display any qualities we might associate with matter. Artists asked what they were to paint once they realized that they could only paint what they perceived and could never capture the outer world itself on their canvas. Writers asked what the subject matter of literature could be if men were eternally separated from one another.

Twentieth-century art, music, literature, physics, biology, and philosophy have all tried in their various ways to deal with the same dilemma: if the mind and the world are separate, and we are locked inside the mind, how can we ever find a bridge back to the world? Many brave attempts have been made to resolve this seemingly insoluble problem. Some of these have been premature attempts to achieve a new synthesis, but some seem to be fore-shadowings of a new way of viewing reality in which this dilemma would not exist.

All of these fore-shadowings seem to revolve around the belief that there is a single transcendent reality, of which the material world outside us, and the psychic world inside us, are both representations. Kant felt that because man was condemned to experience only the "categories" of the mind and not the world itself, the mind and the world were eternally separated. But upon deeper reflection, that position is untenable. For if the "categories" of the mind had no correspondence to the physical, then how could these "categories" organize our sensory perceptions of this world? That question is only beginning to be answered in our time.

New Paradigms

Thomas Kuhn's classic book *The Structure of Scientific Revolutions* (Kuhn,1970) examines both "normal science" and the processes that accompany a major shift in scientific thought. "Normal science" is done during times when there is a paradigm that is sufficiently encompassing that most scientists within a given field can design experiments and extend science without having to question the underlying paradigm. By a paradigm, Kuhn implies not only the explicit set of rules espoused by a science, but also the vague, underlying sense of how reality is constituted and what "proper science" should examine. "Normal science" doesn't challenge the paradigm because it isn't necessary. It limits itself to better explaining the paradigm, and to extending the paradigm in directions that are accepted within the paradigm.

When anomalies occur, which don't fit into the paradigm, they are either explained away or ignored. When they become so numerous that there is a need for a new paradigm, then "normal science" ceases and a "pre-paradigm" period begins. In such a period, nothing can really be taken for granted. A number of models emerge, each of which has to explain its ground rules before it can even begin to communicate its theory. Eventually, one of the new models triumphs, a new paradigm emerges, and there is a return to "normal science" (Kuhn,1970).

Kuhn doesn't extend his argument beyond revolutions in scientific theory, but it is hard not to see the same process at work in all revolutions of thought. We appear to be in the midst of a "pre-paradigm" time. The old paradigms no longer seem to satisfy us. A bewildering variety of new theories abound, no two of which can seem to agree on much of anything. The Renaissance belief in man's ability to rationally explain the world seems to underlie most of the old paradigms. This book will try to show that the psychology of Carl Jung is one expression of a new paradigm, which believes that the world of matter and the world of the psyche are ultimately manifestations of a unitary cosmos.

A new view of the cosmos always looks very strange when viewed from the standpoint of the old. To make Jung's ideas easier to understand, this book will attempt to do three things: (1) trace the development of ideas in philosophy which finally led to Jung's psychology; (2) describe the psychology which Jung developed; and (3) trace the development of ideas in mathematics that led to Gödel's Proof, and show how Gödel's ideas support Jung's position.

Part I:

The Birth and Death of The Renaissance Ideal

2

The Renaissance Ideal

Man The Creator

When a new world-view captures man's imagination, a rich outpouring of creativity occurs in all areas of life. The Renaissance was such a time. Western man first began to realize that man was not only a creation of God, but a creator himself. With this realization man was free, in a way he hadn't been free since the golden age of Greek philosophy. The growth of Christianity was the greatest unifying force in the history of the Western World. But it effectively brought an end to speculative thought. Throughout the Middle Ages, Scholastic Philosophy, which started from religious dogma, not from observed fact, dominated Western thought. When the Renaissance was born in the fourteenth-century, the world was once again open for man's examination, and he gloried in his freedom.

During the Middle Ages, God's word was considered a better guide than man's experience or reason. The Renaissance ideal was better expressed in statements by Leonardo Da Vinci such as "Experience never errs; it is only your judgements that err by promising themselves such as are not caused by your experiments", or "all our knowledge has its origin in our perceptions" (Richter,1970:288).

Da Vinci was able to combine this belief in the power of experience with a belief in God by a changing view of God. Da Vinci addressed his God with "O admirable impartiality of Thine, Thou first Mover; Thou hast not permitted that any force should fail of the order or quality of its necessary results" (ibid:285). Thus, for the educated man of the Renaissance, God had created a world of necessity and it was man's responsibility to use his reason to discover the rules that governed that world. Da Vinci said that: "the senses are of the earth; Reason stands apart in contemplation" (ibid:287).

This new combination of freedom and responsibility produced a flourishing of genius that was unprecedented in European history. Da Vinci, Michelangelo, Erasmus, Luther, and Copernicus were all born within the twenty-five year period between 1450 and 1475. Erasmus and Luther each fought the intellectual domination of the "Holy Mother the Church" in his own characteristic way. Erasmus, a man of the mind, fought against the limits of doctrine, pleading for man's ability to pursue truth to its logical conclusions regardless of church dogma. Luther, "that most unphilosophical of characters" (De Santillana,1956:143), broke the domination of the Church and created the Protestant movement. Each was attempting to give man a central place in the scheme of things; each was deeply religious.

Michelangelo and Da Vinci made man the central subject of art. Medieval art dealt with man only in generalities; its real subject was God. Michelangelo created art that pictured not only a particular man, but more than that, a heroic man. Michelangelo's art cried that man could be as the gods. Da Vinci, the quintessential Renaissance man, created art that captured ordinary reality so extraordinarily that the viewer began to realize what a mystery lay within each person, each object. Again both were, in their characteristic styles, bringing God down from the heavens, and placing divinity in the world in which man lives, and within each man himself.

Copernicus and the Observational Method

Copernicus made a similar statement about a very dissimilar subject: the nature of the universe. Before Copernicus, the earth was regarded as the central object in the universe, eternally fixed and unmoving. Ptolemy had decreed that a series of clear, perfectly-formed, nesting spheres surrounded the earth, and on those spheres were the sun, the planets, and the stars. Since astronomical observations are critical for agriculture, medieval man knew a great deal about the actual positions and movements of the heavenly bodies. But observations had to fit theory, not theory to observations. Unfortunately, calculations based on Ptolemy's perfect spheres didn't fit those observations; more and more complex rationalizations had to be made in order to preserve earth's central position.

Copernicus had the brilliant realization that perhaps the movement was, in part, the perception of the viewer. Perhaps the earth was moving around the sun. His view seemed sacrilegious to sixteenth-century churchmen, who were convinced that God had created the world and everything in it in six days. From that time on, the world was static and unchanging, with the known exceptions, such as the Flood, which were recorded in the Bible. For them and for most educated Europeans, Ptolemy's views were merely a scientific explication of what they already knew from the Bible. Knowledge of the world didn't need to come from observation; that knowledge was already contained in the Bible.

The scientific method is so taken for granted now that it is hard to realize that it is not self-evident. It seemed self-evident to Aristotle that heavier objects fall faster than lighter objects. For the next nineteen-hundred years (!), Aristotle's statement was regarded as so self-evident that it was never tested. It was only in the seventeenth-century that Galileo tested the theory and found that it was false. Now it is also true that without accurate clocks, which only came into existence in Europe in the seventeenth-century, testing Aristotle's theory would have been difficult. But more central is the fact that no one cared enough to try to overcome that difficulty. It just never occurred to anyone that such self-evident facts might be wrong and need to be tested. Without that realization, observation had to be subsumed within theory and dogma.

Copernicus' theory was the first intimation that perhaps the nature of reality depended on the position of the observer, a view that Einstein was to make so central in his Theory of Relativity. In a Copernican world, man's observations and conclusions became central, because in a world of flux and movement, everything depended on the observer (De Santillana,1956). Interestingly, some modern physicists have taken this concept to its natural conclusion; i.e. they assume that the world only exists if it is observed. This view was anticipated by the eighteenth-century philosopher Bishop Berkeley. In chapter four, we will discuss why Berkeley proposed such a startling view, and how it was answered by Kant.

This emphasis on the central position of man, and the importance of his observations, was the great break between Renaissance and Medieval thought. The Scholastic thought of the Middle Ages dealt only with the consequences of a priori principles; it never found it necessary to compare its conclusions with observations in the outer world. This new method of thought led to the accumulation of more detailed information about the outer world than had been added in the previous eighteen hundred years, since the end of the Golden Age of Greek philosophy.

The need to deal with this new data in a systematic way led to the creation of an explicit scientific method in the seventeenth century. The scientific method gave man a generalized tool for examining the world. Renaissance man gathered data about the world with the ingenuous enthusiasm of a child reaching for a leaf. The scientific method demanded data in much the same way as a furnace demands coal. Because of this demand, the rate at which data was gathered further increased. The data, once processed through the techniques of the scientific method, led to changes in the world of normal men. As the rate at which data was gathered increased, the changes in the world increased. Today that rate of change is so extreme that stability is the rarity and change the norm.

3

The Birth of the Scientific Method

The Renaissance was an age dominated by genius. The number of outstanding personalities was incredible by the standards of previous ages. But with the development of the observational method, soon to be dignified by the title of the scientific method, creation was no longer restricted to individual geniuses. This new tool enabled men to pool their observations about the world so that ordinary men could extend the work of genius in a way that was new to the world. But first one more genius, perhaps the most influential of all time, was to make his mark on the world.

Isaac Newton

When Isaac Newton was born in 1642, science as we know it was just coming into existence. It was still a small thing, exciting to those who could see its possibilities, but little known otherwise. When Newton died in 1727, science was the dominant force in human thought, and Newton was the primary cause for that change in status. In poet Alexander Pope's famous words:

> Nature and Nature's laws lay hid in night;
> God said, Let Newton be! and all was light
> (quotation in Gamow,1961:51).

The seventeenth century was a time in some ways like our own, an "interesting time", a time of change and unpredictability, when many contradictory ideas fought for supremacy. The new Renaissance view of man as observer and creator brought an end to the absolute dominance that religion and the "ancients" (the Middle Ages' most characteristic term for the great Greek thinkers) had previously had over Western man's thought. With that displacement, a vacuum was left, waiting to be filled by a new total explanation of reality, an explanation which could compete with the authority of religion and the "ancients". Newton, with his *Opticks* and *Principia*, seemed to his contemporaries to have explained all of nature. Not even religion or the "ancients" had ever subsumed so much of reality under a single umbrella. Before Newton, there were speculations; after Newton, there were Laws!

Newton conceived most of the ideas he would develop over the rest of his life during a single eighteen month period. Newton was 23, and had just received his B.A. "without particular distinction". The plague was roaring through Europe and Newton retired to his parent's home until the University was reopened. During that period, he discovered differential and integral calculus, his Theory of Colors, and the concept of gravity as a force that held the universe together. These were to form the core of his life's work in science (Gamow,1961:52–53).

Indivisible Particles, Absolute Space and Time

Newton's Laws explained Motion, Force, and Light in straight-forward ways that lent themselves to practical application. Newton's Laws concerned material particles, their motion and their interaction. He even regarded light as composed of particles and resisted to his death the idea that light was a wave phenomenon. Newton's world was a world of absolutes: absolute space and time, and perfect, indivisible particles moving in that absolute space and time. In Newton's words from the *Principia*:

> Absolute space, in its own nature, without relation to anything external, remains always similar and immovable. Absolute, true, and mathematical time, in itself, and from its own nature, flows equably without relation to anything external.
> (quoted in Gamow,1961:174).

Great Theories

It should be obvious that such a world is a construct of thought. Neither Newton nor any one of us has ever experienced absolute space or absolute time. All human experiences of space and time are of a particular space and time. Absolute space and time are concepts that Newton used in order to develop general theories of nature. Those general theories could then be applied to particular cases. The power of Newton's concept of absolute space and time is less in its possible truth than in its broad utility. In short, it was a "scientific" theory in the best sense of the term.

In "interesting", "pre-paradigm" times theorists express new visions of reality, trying to replace the old ineffectual visions. The mark of a great theorist is the extent to which his vision captures the imagination of others. The fact that so many can respond to the new description of reality implies that it was "in the air", but the great minds are there first. And they see the vision in both broader perspective and finer detail than the others around them. Frequently their vision will be too far ahead of its time, and rejected. But the visions of the greatest theorists eventually triumph.

A great theory, whether in science or the arts, has to express the main outlines of a total picture of reality. There is little room in it for caveats and exceptions. A great theory necessarily explains both what the previous theory already dealt with, and the problems that caused the original theory to be called into doubt. However, as time passes, and lesser men apply the theory, little problems are found. Since the theory explains so much of reality so well, these exceptions are explained-away with sophistry, or ignored. Labyrinthean corollaries are added to the theory; overly subtle definitions are applied to show why a straight-forward understanding of a concept is inadequate. It is only when the exceptions can no longer be ignored that still another new theory emerges. It in turn is likely to be absolute and total because it reflects a new vision. This is the cycle of creativity. Such great new theories are rare. The discovery and formulation of Newton's Laws marked the shift from the religious view to the scientific view of the cosmos.

Great new theories reflect the Zeitgeist ("spirit of the times"). Most often, a great new theory develops because there is a need for such a theory. If the need is not great enough, the energy to produce such a massive rethinking of reality is just not present. Newton's vision of indivisible particles, of absolute space and time, was not only Newton's vision, but the vision of his time. Medieval man had been stuck in a world where everything was meant to serve God's purpose, where everything was joined in a static whole. Renaissance man desperately wanted change and separation. He wanted to be free to pursue his own vision unhampered by religious limits. This is not to say that Renaissance man was irreligious, far from it. But he wanted to separate his thoughts from his spiritual needs, to pursue his thoughts wherever they would take him. That was the Zeitgeist that Newton expressed (see Kuhn, 1970 for more on the nature of scientific revolutions).

Empiricism

Influenced by his comtemporary, Isaac Newton, philosopher John Locke first voiced the empiricist's creed, a philosophy still espoused by many scientists. He described the human mind as a sort of empty vessel containing separate and distinct particles called ideas. All ideas were either simple or complex. The simple ideas came directly from experience; the complex from the mind operating on simple ideas. All ideas thus came directly or indirectly from experience; experience could be either external sensory experience or internal experience of the mind's own states. Though full of difficulties, Locke's views are representative of the main-stream of thought prior to the twentieth-century (Berlin,1956:30–112).

As the author has pointed out, even Newton, with his profound impact on the later course of the world, was more a representative of his time than its creator. The development of the scientific method and its application to astronomy, physics, and philosophy can be arguably attributed to Galileo, who died the year Newton was born. A half a century before Newton, Descartes had his prophetic dream and announced that "cogito ergo, sum" ("I think, therefore I am"). Descartes' contemporary Hobbes reduced the mind even more than Locke would fifty years later; Hobbes saw no need for anything mental that couldn't be reduced directly to sense perceptions (Hampshire,1956).

The Renaissance had created man the creator, standing in the center of the world, observing all that went on about him. This separation of observer and observed was a necessary step to advance beyond Medieval thought patterns, but it inevitably also led to alienation from the world. And with alienation came an increased tendency to view not only the world, but man himself, as still another object to be observed.

Leonardo da Vinci exclaimed that "instrumental or mechanical science is of all the noblest and the most useful" (quoted in Richter,1970:289). There was a power in this vision that is too often either accepted without question by materialists, or dismissed as dehumanizing by idealists. European man had been static for nearly thirteen hundred years, from the end of the Gnostic Christian movement to the beginning of the Renaissance. The separation of observer and observed led ineluctably to the four steps that became the scientific method: (1) observe dispassionately; (2) record those observations accurately; (3) propose hypotheses to explain them; (4) design experiments to test their validity; and repeat those four steps as often as necessary.

The mastery that man began to acquire over his environment was intoxicating. Though that mastery was to lead man to arrogance and hubris, the vision was still necessary for man's further development. In our own century, the limits of man's intellectual aspirations have become all too apparent, but the denial of the majesty of man's intellect is no answer at all. A way has to be found that honors the greatness of Da Vinci, and Descartes, and Newton, without losing the sense of community and spirituality that were taken for granted before the Renaissance. There always has to be a new vision, not a turning back of the clock.

4

Immanuel Kant's Legacy

Leibniz' Categories of Judgement

Seventeenth-century philosopher John Locke perfectly expressed the spirit of the new age of science. Another major philosophical voice in the seventeenth century was the mathematician and philosopher, Gottfried Wilhelm von Leibniz. Leibniz, often called the last universal man because of the extreme breadth of his knowledge, was the first philosopher to separate judgements systematically into two categories: analytic and synthetic, also called a priori and a posteriori. This separation was the first advance in logic since the time of Aristotle, whose logic implicitly assumed all judgement was analytic.

Analytic, or a priori, judgements are those where the conclusion is known prior to experience, such as "all wives are women." The conclusion is already contained in the definition of the subject, since a wife is a married woman. All mathematical logic is analytic. An example of a synthetic, or a posteriori, judgement would be "most women over the ages of twenty-one are wives." In order to determine if this is true, the world has to be observed. That observation might prove that most such women were in fact not married (Hampshire,1956:142–182).

> The strength of analytic judgements lies in their necessity, and the weakness of such judgements in that they tell us nothing new. The strength of synthetic judgements lies in their ability to tell us something new; and the weakness of such judgements in their having no necessity. If we could have judgements providing us with both information and necessity, we should have the best of both worlds.
> (Reese,1980:277).

Berkeley and Hume

As the eighteenth century dawned, Leibniz' categories of judgement awaited a genius who could put them to proper use. That genius was to be Immanuel Kant. But before Kant came a pair of philosophers, each of whom would influence Kant: Bishop George Berkeley and David Hume. Berkeley was the exact counter-point to the empiricism of John Locke. He voiced what has come to be called philosophical Idealism. Briefly, his position was that ideas are all that can ever be experienced.

Locke asserted that all our ideas are directly or indirectly derived from sensory experience. Berkeley agreed, but further asserted that it was nonsense to speak of a physical world separate from our perceptions of it. Descartes had asserted that "I think, therefore I am"; Berkeley now realized further that all that men ever experience are their thoughts. As far as any man is concerned, there is no world unless he thinks of it. Now Berkeley was deeply religious, and he explained that since the World always exists in God's mind, therefore it does exist. That argument didn't have much impact on other philosophers, but they didn't know how to deal with Berkeley's initial argument that we can never prove the existence of an outer world (Berlin,1956:115–161).

While Bishop Berkeley denied the existence of the material world, David Hume denied causality. Hume stressed the importance that the assumption of causality plays in normal life. If we see (A) a billiard ball strike a second ball, and then we see (B) the second ball move, we say that the first event (A) caused the second event (B). It is the assumption of such necessary causality that forms the core of all of Newton's Laws, of all science. Hume drew attention to what is actually experienced in a so-called cause-and-effect relationship. Hume pointed out that all that is really known is that two events (A) and (B) are contiguous in space, and that (A) preceded (B) in time. In order for (A) to cause (B), there also needs to be some necessary connection between the two events.

Hume insisted that there is no such necessary connection that can be logically demonstrated.

> The sole criterion of necessary truth, according to Hume is the law of non-contradiction. If a proposition cannot be denied without contradiction, it is necessarily true.
>
> (Aiken,1956:32).

In other words, the "sole criterion of necessary truth" is what Leibniz called analytic judgement, where the conclusion is contained in the subject. But the conclusion that (B) follows (A) is only a synthetic judgement; i.e., an observation about the outer world. As Leibniz pointed out, these are separate types of judgement. A synthetic judgement can never have the necessity of an a priori, analytic judgement. But all that can be known of the world is a posteriori, derived from experience.

In considering the collision of the two billiard balls, many alternate, though improbable, assumptions could be made without logical contradiction. It could be assumed that the second ball was alive and jumped for joy, or that a flying saucer shot a ray gun at the ball and that's why it jumped. Neither of these assumptions may seem very likely, but there is no *logical contradiction* in asserting them. It is only experience that causes us to conclude that (A) caused (B). We conclude that because we have seen objects strike other objects, and the second object moves. All cause-and-effect is the same. What actually happens is that if two events are observed to be contiguous in time and space often enough, a necessary connection is assumed to exist between them and we say that one event caused the other (Berlin,1956:115–260).

Hume's argument seemed unassailable. If there could be no logical necessity in any judgement about the outer world, anything could happen at any time. Hume's argument had to be answered by philosophers, or philosophy was at a dead end. Immanuel Kant inaugurated modern philosophy with his answer in his *Critique of Pure Reason* in 1781. Kant said that there existed a category of judgements that were inherently true, of which causation was an example. Kant said that in addition to Leibniz' a priori and a posteriori judgements, there existed a third category of judgements which were neither analytic nor synthetic.

Kant's Answer to Hume and Berkeley

Kant said that there were "synthetic a priori" judgements, such as "2 + 2 = 4" or "a straight line is the shortest distance between two points", or "every event has a cause". Berkeley asserted that the outer world can never be experienced, only the inner world of man's thoughts and feelings; Kant agreed. Hume said there can be no logical necessity in any conclusions about the world; Kant agreed. But Kant saw deeper than Berkeley or Hume. Kant argued that synthetic judgements were not really about the world around us, but rather about the world as filtered through the sensibilities of a human being.

For example, he argued that we never experience raw sensory data; all our experiences are in a certain time and place. Time and space, Kant argued, are examples of inherent categories, contained in all humans, through which we experience reality. Kant said that judgement consisted of taking sensory data in through these inherent structures, and applying logic to reach a conclusion. In Kant's words "thoughts without content are empty, and intuitions without concepts are blind" (Reese,1980:276–280).

Benjamin Whorf and other linquists have discovered that Kant was wrong in his assumption that everyone experiences time and space in the same way. Whorf found that the Hopi Indians, among others, have a very different sense of time and space than the normal Westerner. To quote Whorf:

> ... the Hopi thought world has no imaginary space ... it may not locate thought dealing with real space anywhere but in real space, nor insulate space from the effects of thought.
>
> (quotation in Hall,1966:92).

> Many of Kant's particular analyses are no longer acceptable to analytical philosophers; nor is his general scheme, with its profoundly dualist conception of human nature, its unknowable thing-in-itself. . . . But Kant still represents the ideal of what the philosophical mind at its best can be.
>
> (Aiken,1956:273).

Why then, if the particulars of Kant's ideas are no longer accepted, is Kant so important? Kant saw the profound truth that there are inherent structures in the human mind (regardless of whether he was correct in describing those structures), and that those structures mediated between the physical world outside man, and the psychic world of his thoughts. He realized that those inherent structures were something more than groupings of sensory experience, as Locke had tried to insist. While fully accepting Berkeley's argument that only ideas can be experienced, Kant refused to accept the solipsistic conclusion that therefore there is no physical world. Kant insisted that both inner and outer worlds existed and that they conjoined in these inherent structures.

With the Renaissance, man was free once more to think what he would. But there was no examination of what thought itself was. When Descartes established that, for himself, he knew he existed because he thought, he was expressing the Zeitgeist of a time intoxicated with its power to think. Newton turned his immense intellect to the world and saw a world that was convenient for thought: composed of separate and distinct particles in some absolute, unchanging space and time.

Locke was the first to examine the nature of thought itself. Under the sway of Newton's ideas, he asserted that thought consisted of separate and distinct sensory experiences that corresponded one-to-one with the physical world. Berkeley and Hume found that materialism, taken to its logical conclusion, produced idealism; i.e., man knows no world except the world of his thoughts, and there was no logical necessity in any assertions about the world outside his thoughts.

Finally, Kant saw that humans inherently organize reality; thoughts are not just atoms of sensory experience or closed logical chains. He argued that physical reality is experienced only through inner structures which organize the "world of a thousand things" (a Chinese phrase for the multiplicity of details the world contains, which they then contrast with the oneness inside, which is much like Kant's organizing principle). The fact that human beings are able to structure physical reality sufficiently to process sensory perceptions at all argues strongly that there are inborn, identical psychic structures in all of us.

Of course, like all highly original ideas, Kant's categories present a more straightforward picture than we find in reality. Current research shows that our sense organs themselves organize reality. Further organization goes on as sensory data is presented to the mind. But the full chain of operations is far from understood at this point in time.

Regardless of this complexity, the point remains that if Kant was right, then an understanding of the nature of the human mind was critical in determining truth. The study of the human mind, psychology, needed to become a field in itself, and not just an adjunct to other fields. However, the time was not yet ripe, and modern psychology wasn't to begin until the second half of the nineteenth century, when the twin poles of experimental and clinical psychology came into existence. Kant had the most profound effect of any philosopher since Plato, but the world of the late eighteenth century was not yet ready to accept the full impact of his teachings.

Science's Pragmatic Response

Instead of grappling with the problem, the eighteenth century regarded it from a pragmatic point-of-view. Newton's Laws seemed an effective counter-argument to Berkeley and Hume by their very existence. Though Berkeley and Hume denied that man could ever speak with necessity about the physical world, Newton seemed to have done just that. Meanwhile, within the framework of Newton's Laws, it was sufficient for scientists to propose provisional theories about the world. As evidence came along that the theories didn't answer, well then, modify the theories. It was a wonderfully pragmatic way to deal with reality. And since it was so inordinately successful, who was to argue.

In the seventeenth-century, along with the development of science itself, a new tool appeared in mathematics: probability theory. It was to remain an interesting, but peripheral, mathematic genre until science started dealing with larger and larger quantities of things, in physics and chemistry at first, but then increasingly in more and more fields. As the number of things under consideration grew, it became impractical to apply Newtonian methods.

For example, while Newton's laws enabled scientists to much more accurately calculate the positions of the planets, it was beyond science's ability to explain fully even the behavior of three gravitational bodies (the "three-body problem"). Scientists believed that with enough knowledge, the positions of every planet at every point-in-time could be predicted, but this was in practice beyond their means. So increasingly they used statistical methods.

It was only with the discoveries of twentieth-century physics that the world of Newton's Laws, the world of cause-and-effect, broke down even for science, and scientists had to deal with the issues that Berkeley and Hume raised two centuries earlier. However, the primary battle field was to be neither in philosophy nor science, but in a field where the two met: psychology.

5

The Precursors of Experimental Psychology

In the discussion of Kant, the author said that psychology, as a separate field of study, did not come into existence until the second half of the nineteenth century. But several trains of thought did develop that would later lead to psychology as we know it. Kant attempted to provide a solution to the disturbing problems posed by Berkeley and Hume. Berkeley denied the existence of external reality, and reduced the material world to ideas. Hume denied the existence of the human mind that experienced the ideas, and any structures like causality which gave order to the ideas. Kant restored the physical and psychic worlds, and the structures of the mind (of which causality was an example) which formed a bridge between the two worlds. The natural next step would have been to do research to see if such structures actually existed and, if so, to describe them accurately. But instead, a quite different path was taken.

Founders of Associationism

In Scotland, a contemporary of Hume's, Thomas Reid, founded a school of philosophy, called appropriately the "Scottish School". Reid and his followers, advocating "common sense" and "instinct", threw out the whole argument. If Berkeley and Hume denied the existence of physical reality, then their arguments weren't worth considering. However, a quote attributed to Dr. Thomas Brown, one of Reid's followers, shows that Reid's and Hume's views were more similar than Reid would have liked to believe.

> Yes, Reid bawled out we must believe in an outward world; but added in a whisper, we can give no reason for our belief. Hume cries out we can give no reason for such a notion; and whispers, I own we cannot get rid of it.
>
> (quotation in Heidbreder,1933:52).

But though at base their philosophical beliefs were more similar than they knew, Reid's common-sense position led to an emphasis on empirical research, which would eventually culminate in experimental psychology. However, Associationism proper can be traced less to a reaction against Hume than to an acceptance of Locke's empiricism. Locke believed that the mind was a "tabula rasa" (a blank slate) upon which the history of our sensory experience was written. David Hartley founded a school of thought based on Locke's ideas. In the words of Boring (1929:193–194):

> David Hartley took Locke's little-used title for a chapter, 'the association of ideas,' made it the name of a fundamental law, reiterated it, wrote a psychology around it, and thus created a formal doctrine with a definite name, so that a school could repeat the phrase after him for a century and thus implicitly constitute him its founder. It is apt to be thus with 'founding.' When the central ideas are born, some promoter takes them in hand, organizes them, adding whatever else seems to him essential, publishes and advertises them, insists upon them, and in short 'founds' a school . . . origination and founding may be very different matters.
>
> (quotation in Schultz,1969:26).

> The general law of association is that if sensations have often been experienced together, the corresponding ideas will tend to occur together . . . association may be either successive or simultaneous. The former determines the course of thought in time; the latter accounts for the formation of complex ideas. These few principles form the basis of associationism.
>
> (Heidbreder,1933:54).

Parallelism

Implicit in associationism is the idea that the physical and psychic worlds are separate but parallel, and that somehow there is no contradiction in such a separation. This idea of "parallelism" was first explicitly discussed by seventeenth-century philosopher Baruch Spinoza. Spinoza asserted that there is a single, underlying reality. He felt Descartes, with his separation of mind and matter, to be wrong.

> ... thought and the system of things in space are only two aspects of a single reality, and are at every point inseparable.
> (Hampshire,1956:101)

In other words, for Spinoza, mind and matter were parallel only because they were particular manifestations of a single reality. Without the assumption of a "unus mundus" ("unitary world", see Jung,1963:759–75), parallelism makes no sense whatsoever. If mind and matter are separate and distinct substances, then there can be no connection between events in one and events in the other. Yet it is just this parallelism that is implicit in associationism. Since associationism led to much of modern experimental psychology, this is a critical point to understand.

The idea that reality is inter-connected is either explicit or implicit in many of the contemporary scientific and psychological paradigms which will be examined later in this paper. Jung felt that there was a single underlying reality, the "unus mundus", of which both the physical world and the mental world were manifestations. Man possessed an inborn unifying structure which Jung called the "Self", through which he could experience that underlying reality (see Chapter 16). In contrast, Spinoza's single reality, which he called interchangeably God or Nature, was a cold mechanical realm, much like the clock-like universe that was later developed out of Newton's ideas (Hampshire,1956). For Spinoza, as for Kant, man and nature were eternally separate. This is a far cry from the organic, creative, feeling unity that Jung described, and which other holistic thinkers of recent times seem to be arriving at, but Spinoza was writing in the seventeenth-century, not at the dawn of the twenty-first.

John Stuart Mill's Creative Synthesis

Difficulties developed in trying to describe exactly how association operated. It is one thing to believe that complex ideas all derive ultimately from simple, sensory perceptions. It is quite another to show how this actually operates in even the simplest situation. This is much the same dilemma behaviorists currently have experienced in trying to reduce complex operations to a simple reflex-arc, but that is getting ahead of our story.

Dr. Thomas Brown, who provided the earlier quotation comparing Reid and Hume, tried to find under what specific circumstances association operates. "The laws of recency, frequency, and intensity—that much-used trio—are among them" (Heidbreder,1933). This "much-used trio" form the core of current behavioral psychology.

John Stuart Mill was convinced that there was more to the mind than mechanical combination. He argued that the mind has an active role in acquiring sensory data and assimilating it not merely through association, but also through a "creative synthesis". In Mill's words:

> When many impressions or ideas are operating in the mind together, there sometimes takes place a process of a similar kind to chemical combination. . . . those ideas sometimes melt and coalesce into one another, and appear not several ideas but one . . . the Complex Idea, formed by the blending together of several simpler ones, should . . . be said to *result from*, or be *generated by*, the simple ideas not to *consist of* them [Mill's emphasis].
> (quotation in Boring,1929:230).

It is in the combination of many of these ideas, which have already been presented in this book, that some approximation to Jung's views begins to emerge. Assume, like Spinoza, that there is a single inter-connected reality, a "unus mundus", and that matter and psyche are only two aspects of that reality. Assume, like Kant, that the human mind contains inherent structures that are part of that underlying reality. Sensory data is experienced relationally, then categorized and processed using those inherent structures of the mind.

That set of assumptions, which developed in philosophy out of necessity, begins to approximate the starting point for Jung's psychology. Of course, the great part of Jung's work is his detailed descriptions of those structures and of the dynamics of their interrelationship with consciousness. This is also the world at which modern physics and biology are arriving. But that world-view remained for the twentieth-century to discover. It was apparently too early for someone to put together such a synthesis of ideas in the seventeenth-century when Spinoza wrote of a single reality; or in the eighteenth-century when Kant wrote of "synthetic a priori" judgements; or even in the nineteenth-century when John Stuart Mill wrote of "creative synthesis". Mill's idea was again, in the same spirit, one more idea whose time was not yet ripe.

6

Experimental Psychology's Founders

Up to now, this book has only discussed the precursors of psychology. The story of psychology as a separate field begins in the second-half of the nineteenth-century with the experimental research of Fecher, von Helmholtz, and Wundt in Germany, and the clinical research of Charcot, Janet, and Bernheim in France. Most of current academic and experimental psychology can be traced back to the three Germans. The clinical psychology line that began with the three Frenchmen would lead to Jung, but Jung was also an experimental psychologist.

For example, Jung did pioneering work in word association and work with Galvanic Skin Response that anticipated biofeedback research. Jung was well-read in philosophy and was well aware of the philosophical roots that underlay both clinical and experimental psychology. That allowed Jung to put both sides in perspective, and pick and choose from both camps, though he was always first and foremost a healer. This book's discussion of experimental psychology's three pioneers will begin with Fechner, who was the only one of the three who shared Jung's broad erudition.

Gustav Fechner and Weber's Law

Fechner was an interesting study in contrasts, and his work reflects those contrasts. Throughout his life he was pulled between the twin poles of mind and matter, in his case expressed by his interest in both metaphysics and science. His early work was first in physiology, then in physics. He experienced a crisis in mid-life, where he became ill and withdrew from the world. His earlier work had no meaning for him unless he could find some way of reconciling the science he practiced with the spiritual world in which he believed. After a dozen years as a reclusive invalid, he suddenly recovered.

> The primary result of [the crisis] was a deepening of Fechner's religious consciousness and his interest in the problem of the soul . . . his philosophical solution of the spiritual problem lay in his affirmation of the identity of mind and matter and in his assurance that the entire universe can be regarded as readily from the point of view of its consciousness.
> (Boring, 1929:278).

Here is the first statement of the position Jung was later to express. However Fechner, with his emphasis on experimental science, took a much different route than Jung in his attempts to justify his position. Fechner felt that if the mind and body were two manifestations of a single consciousness, then there should be physical constants that reflected the connection between the two.

As has already been discussed, Kant said that there were psychic constants which he called inherent structures or categories; Jung called them initially "primordial images" (Jung, 1966:101) and later "archetypes" (Jung, 1960:270) (from the Greek, meaning "prime imprinter"). And, of course, long before either, Plato proposed the existence of idealized patterns of which the objects of the material world were but pale copies. The key addition of Kant was the explicit recognition that these eternal patterns existed in the human mind, and that it was the human mind that formed the meeting ground for the material and the spiritual.

But Fechner, the experimental scientist, wanted to find some way to actually quantify physical relationships between the mental and physical realms. Fechner found just such quantification in the work of Ernst Heinrich Weber. Weber conducted a series of experiments in which he tried to discover the threshold of sensory awareness. He had a subject hold a weight, then a second weight which was slightly heavier. He kept increasing the difference between the weights until the subject could detect a difference. He found that:

> ... the smallest perceptible difference between two weights can be stated as a ratio between the weights, a ratio that is independent of the magnitudes of the weights.
>
> (Boring,1929:113).

Weber also found the important extension that the ratio was constant for all subjects. Finally, the results were similar in his experiments with visual and auditory response.

That may sound commonplace. After all, it merely says that the heavier the weight, the larger the difference between it and the second weight before any difference can be detected. In other words, the sensory world is experienced through relationship, not absolute difference. However, remember that the laws of mental association see the mind as nothing more than a "tabula rasa" on which is recorded an endless chain of associations to sensory experiences. Man's experience of the world should then be absolute, not relational.

The fact that sensory experience is relational should have been exciting enough to open up whole new directions for research. For example, does this relational ordering of sensory experience occur in the mind or at the level of the sensors themselves (more recent research seems to show the latter to be the case)? If our sensory experience is relational, do we have hierarchies of relationship proceeding from the sensory to the psychological? Do such relational perceptions occur in all species? Is there some lowest level of animal development at which they cease to occur? Do different species order reality in markedly different ways? Within humans alone, how does pathology affect this ordering, and at what levels? The questions are endless.

To Fechner, Weber's experiments were a revelation, and he called the results Weber's Law. Actually, it might better be called Fechner's Law since Weber never saw the full significance of his discoveries, nor did he develop the general form of the law. As Fechner stated Weber's Law, sensation (which

Fechner felt to be a purely mental process) varied with the natural logarithm of the stimulus (which Fechner felt was purely physical). Another way of expressing Weber's Law is that response varies arithmetically as stimulus varies geometrically. Fechner spent the next decade extending that research.

In the course of that research, he developed many of the techniques of experimental psychology. He felt satisfied that he had accomplished his goal: to quantify the relationship between mind and body. Few experimental scientists since then have agreed with his self-assessment. William James, for example, stated:

> ... in the humble opinion of the present writer, the proper psychological outcome [of Fechner's research] is just *nothing* [James' emphasis].
>
> (Boring,1929:294).

Despite James' negative opinion of Fechner's work, Fechner's belief in quantifiable results created experimental psychology, and his methods are still in use today. The author finds it disappointing that Fechner's vision of a unity (which Fechner thought to be consciousness) underlying mind and matter has been almost totally ignored. The identical result has occurred several times since.

For example, Gestalt psychologists conducted extensive research in the first half of the twentieth century which further demonstrated that sensory experience is relational, not absolute. Their research demonstrated that our perceptions divide the world into "figure" and "ground"; that is, at the sensory level, the world is perceived relationally. Their research is accepted by physiologists, but the implications seem to be often overlooked outside their field (Köhler,1947).

The same scenario has been repeated in our own time in the new field of bio-feedback. Barbara Brown, one of the pioneers in the field, thought that the relationship between mind and body could now be quantifiably examined in a new way that had almost unlimited potential to resolve old epistemological problems. Instead, she feels that those who work in the field have totally dismissed such possibilities because they feel uncomfortable with the idea of "mind". Therefore, the work, in her opinion, has degenerated into trivia (Brown,1983).

Hermann Von Helmholtz and the Conservation of Energy

To return to the trio of great German experimental psychologists, the second was Hermann von Helmholtz. Helmholtz was far and away the greatest of the three as a natural scientist, but the least interesting as a precursor of modern psychology. He did outstanding physiological research on vision and hearing, and measured the speed of the nerve impulse.

> Psychology was for him an exact science, dependent upon the use of mathematics . . . and upon experiment.
> (Boring,1929:303).

Von Helmholtz' greatest impact on psychology was from his work as a physicist! Today, physicists, who work with the deepest levels of matter, and depth psychologists, who work with the deepest levels of psyche, are increasingly turning to each other's discipline for answers. But von Helmholtz was a representaive of his time, a thorough materialist who scoffed at psychic processes. However, he did not dismiss energy as an occult concept, even though in many ways it is the least materialistic of all concepts. Von Helmholtz was the first to formulate the Law of Conservation of Energy, which hypothesized that the sum total of energy is constant. As modified by Einstein to include transformations between matter and energy, it remains one of the two primary assumptions of physical science. The other is the Law of Entropy: which proposes that organization always decreases.

But as stated by von Helmholtz, the Law of Conservation of Energy was a freeing concept for scientists of many different fields, including psychology. It meant that transformation was possible without occult explanations. Without such a law, any dynamic science is impossible. Both Freud and Jung were to draw on this law as a cornerstone of their thought. In fact, it was their differences on the nature of psychic energy, or libido, that caused their split.

The word "energy" has become so common-place that energy is thought of as a "thing", a material object. We talk glibly of electrical energy or atomic energy. But energy is not a "thing"; it the only the possibility for transformation. Energy is the concept of an intermediate undefined state between two defined states. It is frequently a useful heuristic device to think of energy as a "thing" and discuss "electrical energy" or "magnetic energy", but it is only a device. For example, Freud's concept of "libido" or "psychic energy" was enormously useful, but only a device. From his writings, it appears that Freud viewed "libido" as limited to sexual energy, which casts some doubt on the extent to which he understood this more general concept of energy. From his writings, it appears certain that Jung did (see "On Psychic Energy" in Jung:1960).

Wilhelm Wundt

Wilhelm Wundt, the last of the trio, is frequently called the founder of psychology. It would be more accurate to split the title of founder of "experimental" psychology among Wundt, von Helmholtz, and Fechner, and reserve the title of founder of psychology itself for Freud. Wundt founded a psychological laboratory in Leipzig in 1879, and it was his work, and the work of his pupils in this laboratory that led to the wide-spread development of experimental psychology.

Wundt was an encyclopedist rather than an originator. He brought together, classified, and published the many psychological facts that had already been discovered, and continued this process throughout his life. He called his method of research "introspectionism"; it is now a relic of the time, accepted neither by the behaviorists and other experimental psychologists, nor any of the other varied clinical disciplines.

While the name "introspectionism" might bring to mind deep, and perhaps fuzzy, thoughts, that was hardly Wundt's territory. Rather he studied the simple reactions that behavioral psychology has mapped so well, but did it by experiments with trained human subjects who made simple discriminations. He felt there was no place in experimental psychology for animal, child, abnormal, or applied psychology, which limited his field of study tremendously. It was this narrowness that led to the counter-development of behavioral psychology.

Though Wundt's vision was narrow, his impact was great. The time was ripe for a quantitative, experimental psychology, and Leipzig became the gathering place for all the bright young men of the 1880's and 1890's. An Englishman, Edward Tichener, became an enthusiastic convert and brought Wundt's psychology to Cornell University. Largely through Tichener's autocratic presence, experimental psychology became the major psychological force in America at the end of the nineteenth-century. While, like Wundt, Tichener's own views are largely forgotten, experimental psychology still dominates American psychology.

Limiting the Psyche to Consciousness

Experimental psychology patterned itself after the physical sciences. It wanted to avoid anything that could be termed mystical or even philosophical at any cost. Eventually that attitude would lead to behavioral psychology which limits psychology to physical behavior, thus taking the "psyche" totally out of psychology. At the time of experimental psychology's founding, it was still the order of the day to point to consciousness as man's distinguishing attribute, so the time was not yet ripe for the full reductionism of behavioral psychology. However, the idea that there might be psychic processes that were not conscious was abhorrent to Wundt and his followers.

In "On the Nature of the Psyche", Jung quotes "a representative of the Wundt school" as saying that ". . . a psychic state cannot be described as psychic unless it has reached at least the threshold of consciousness" (Jung,1960:349). Jung continued later:

> In this connection, a philosophical opponent of the unconscious makes the very illuminating remark: 'Once this is admitted, one finds oneself

at the mercy of all manner of hypotheses concerning this unconscious life, hypotheses which cannot be controlled by any observation.' It is evident that this thinker is not out to recognize facts, but that for him the fear of running into difficulties is decisive. And how does he know that these hypotheses cannot be controlled by observation? For him this is simply an a priori . . . Wundt himself is of the opinion that, as regards the so-called unconscious processes, it is not a question of unconscious psychic elements, but only of more dimly conscious ones' . . . This attitude implies a clear rejection of the unconscious as a psychological hypothesis.

(ibid:350f).

Unlike some later psychologists and biologists, who could accept instinctual behavior yet deny unconscious psychic processes, Wundt realized that his rejection of the unconscious also implied a rejection of instinctual behavior. Jung quotes Wundt on this subject:

If the new-born animal really had an idea beforehand of all the actions it purposes to do, what a wealth of anticipated life-experiences would lie stored in the human and animal instincts, and how incomprehensible it would seem that not man alone, but animals too, acquire most things only through experience and practice!

(ibid:352).

Of course, Fechner stood outside this orthodoxy. Fechner felt that "the idea of a psychophysical threshold is of the utmost importance because it gives a firm foundation to that of the unconscious generally" (ibid:354). Unfortunately, Fechner's experimental techniques were adopted while his ideas were ignored. Experimental psychology was a new discipline and its members patterned themselves on stern, no-nonsense physicists like Von Helmholtz, not those they regarded as dreamy romantics. Experimental science requires just such discipline in order to be effective, but it is unfortunate that the "zeitgeist" had little room for any non-physical phenomena like the psyche.

If early experimental psychologists had to deal with the psyche at all, they wanted it reduced to consciousness, and consciousness reduced to tiny little elements that could be experimentally "introspected", as Wundt taught. Again, that was a sensible beginning approach to a complex area; however, in time, it became too limiting. A strange borderline phenomenon currently known as hypnotism was to lead clinical psychologists to recognize that consciousness was not the be-all and end-all of the psyche.

7

The History of Hypnosis

Paracelsus

Experimental psychology can trace its origins to the Renaissance rediscovery of the power of the conscious mind. Clinical psychology originated in the study of unconscious processes. This could have occurred through the study of dreams or myths, but in fact hypnotism was the first bridge to the unconscious mind. Boring says:

> Write in order the words *magnetism, mesmerism, hypnotism, hysteria, suggestion*, [Boring's emphasis] translate them into proper names, writing Van Helmot, Mesmer, Braid, Charcot, Bernheim, and you have the outline of (clinical) psychology . . . before Freud.
> (Boring,1929:694).

But that chain can be extended back still further. This book has already shown that an unbroken train of thought can be traced from its beginning in the Renaissance to its culmination in experimental psychology. A second train of thought also began in the Renaissance and eventually led to clinical psychology. This line began with a mysterious figure of the high Renaissance, sixteenth-century physician Philippus Aureolus Bombast von Hohenheim, more commonly known as Theophrastus Paracelsus. Paracelsus was both renowned and reviled, the most famous physician of the sixteenth century and one of its most prolific authors. Both his fame for his incredible skill as a physician, and the angry dismissal by many of his colleagues, were products of his vision of man and the universe.

The author has said many times already that the Renaissance

was a time when "man the observer" came into prominence. That observation could be turned outward toward the macro-world or inward toward the micro-world. In 1543, for example, both Andreas Vesalius' *Concerning the Structure of the Human Body* and Copernicus' *Concerning the Revolutions of the Heavenly Bodies* were published. Paracelsus, like Jung four centuries later, was interested less in one or the other of the two worlds than in the necessary connections between the macro and micro-worlds.

Jung said "there can be no doubt that Paracelsus was influenced by the Hermetic idea of 'heaven above, heaven below' " (Jung,1942:31). The alchemical dictum "heaven above, heaven below" implied that reality was an inter-related whole, each of whose parts reflected the totality. This concept has already been mentioned in the discussion of Fechner's theories. It will arise over and over in the pages to follow. In Paracelsus' words:

> ... in every human being, there is a special heaven, whole and unbroken ... for heaven is man and man is heaven, and all men are one heaven, and heaven is only one man.
>
> (quotation in ibid:31).

Interestingly, Paracelsus felt that love was the connection between the seemingly separate worlds inhabited by each human being. "First of all it is very necessary to tell of the compassion that must be innate in a physician." "Where there is no love, there is no art." "The practice of this art lies in the heart: if your heart is false, the physician within you will be false" (quoted in ibid:42). The idea that love, or eros, is the supreme principal of relationship will resurface in the twentieth-century, first with Eros reduced to sexuality by Freud. Later Jung would restore Eros to his full dignity in his exploration of the connections between the conscious mind and the outer world on one side, and the unconscious mind on the other. However, before we can turn to Jung and his views, this paper has yet to follow the twisting path that led from Paracelsus to Freud and Jung.

Animal Magnetism, Mesmerism, and Hypnotism

Paracelsus, with his desire to find the connections between the micro-world of the human, and the macro-world of the universe, was interested in astrology and alchemy, and the effects of magnetism.

> Paracelsus established the doctrine that magnets, like the stars, influence human bodies, and Van Helmot [a century later] inaugurated the doctrine of animal magnetism.
>
> (Boring,1929:695f).

Van Helmot taught

> ... that a magnetic fluid radiates from all men and may be guided by their wills to influence the minds and bodies of others.
>
> (ibid:116).

Mesmer, late in the eighteenth century, caught the imagination of all Europe with his startling cures using "animal magnetism." The scientific community refused to accept such a concept and either denied Mesmer as a fraud, or attributed his success to some personal power that Mesmer alone possessed.

> It is interesting to see just what factors were at work in this rapid rise and decline of mesmerism, especially because the little drama was reenacted more than once afterward. The affair was a conflict between radicalism and conservatism in science and in the medical art. Mesmer was seeking something new, just as his scientific contemporaries were engaged in discovery; but the new thing that he found was very new in that it appeared, as Mesmer incorrectly formulated the principle, to break with the accepted scientific tradition and medical practice.
>
> (ibid:118).

It was only in the first half of the nineteenth century that James Braid was able to present the phenomenon of hypnotism in a form acceptable to the scientific community. Thus hypnotism came to be marginally accepted three hundred years after Paracelsus revealed it to the Western World, two hundred years after Von Helmot popularized the term "animal magnetism", fully fifty years after Mesmer demonstrated its efficacy to all of Europe.

When a concept does not readily fit into the framework of science, the scientific community denies the concept if it can, ignores it if it cannot. There is a sense in which this is appropriate; a general world model which can be usefully applied to many cases is more useful than a collection of exceptions that have only partial application. But it is always the great discoverers who sense when an exception is important and when a new model, which includes the exception, needs to be developed. Our own century is filled with such exceptions, all begging to be included in some wider explanation of reality. The author's presumption that Jung provides one such model is, of course, the reason for this book.

Prior to Braid, it was felt that animal magnetism resided in the "mesmerist". The key shift in Braid's presentation, which made it acceptable to science, was to shift the responsibility from the physician to the patient. In Braid's early views, patients were mesmerized because they fixated on something until they paralyzed themselves.

> Later he came to recognize more clearly the importance of the factor of suggestion in inducing the phenomena, and his emphasis shifted even more from the physiological to the psychological aspect of the state.
> (Boring,1929:128).

Current Academic Evaluation of Hypnosis

It is interesting to speculate what would have happened if Braid had initially presented suggestion as the cause of hypnosis. Would this have been dismissed as occultism in the same way as animal magnetism was dismissed? Was it only because Braid first presented a physiological explanation that hypnotism acquired any validity whatsoever?

Currently, most of the academic experimental research on hypnotism is performed by behavioral scientists, and it is once again common to dismiss hypnotism. They largely ignore the vast body of clinical hypnotic case studies as irrelevant. J. P. Sutcliffe, for example, dismisses Milton Erickson (who is considered the father of modern hypnotism, and whose views will be discussed more later) as "credulous". Sutcliffe feels that all of hypnotism can be explained as either (1) simulation of a hypnotic state by the patient; or (2) delusion on the part of the patient (Hilgard,1965:14–20). Once again, experimental and clinical psychology go very different directions.

Gestalt Psychology vs. Associationism

The power of scientific experimentation lies in the ability to separate the observer and the observed and limit the parameters under consideration. This is an incredibly powerful method, but an essentially artificial one. It is never truly possible to eliminate extraneous factors. Good scientists recognize this and design their experiments accordingly. Unfortunately, when the object under observation is a human being, there is a tendency to view a human subject as an object like other objects regardless of the humanism of the scientist. Again the best scientists avoid this trap, but it is a trap nevertheless.

Over and beyond this danger, lie the dangers inherent in the materialist position itself, the dangers of dismissing the psyche as an epi-phenomenon. As has been shown earlier, this is a point of view that existed from experimental psychology's beginnings, and which was implicit in philosophy at least back to Locke, with his origination of associationism. If the human mind is only a jumble of associations of units of sensory experience, then why not ignore the inner experience and concentrate on the sensory stimulus itself and the physiological response to the stimulus? In chapter 6, we discussed Weber's law and its implication that the human mind perceives relationships, not simple sensory units, and that this relational perception appears to be inborn. Later in this paper many more examples of this will be given, but one appears appropriate to be given at this point.

In a series of classic experiments by Gestalt psychologists K. F. Lashley and Wolfgang Köhler, chickens were taught to distinguish two different shades of gray; let's call them Gray-1 and Gray-2, with Gray-2 the darker of the two shades. If the chickens correctly identified Gray-2, they received a reward of food. With the chickens trained to pick Gray-2, the psychologists brought in Gray-3, which was darker than either Gray-1 or Gray-2. They exposed the chickens to Gray-2 and Gray-3.

Now, if associationism was correct, the chickens should once more have picked Gray-2, because they had made a straightforward association of Gray-2 with a reward of food. But, in fact, the chickens picked Gray-3, the darker shade. In other words, the chickens had associated a relationship, "darker", with getting a reward (see Köhler,1947:118f).

It is important to stress that the chickens were not exposed to a series of situations in which they had to pick the darker shade of gray. They were only trained with the one pair of grays, yet they learned from that one situation to pick the darker shade. In these experiments, stimuli did not lead immediately to response; "between the stimuli and the response, there occurs the processes of organization" (ibid:119). Thus, even at the sensory level, experience is structured relationally.

The Value of Subjective Experience in Psychology

This, and many similar experiments, seem to show that not only humans, but animals also organize sensory perception. As has been pointed out earlier, the question of how much organization goes on at various levels between the original sensory perception and the eventual complex organization in the psyche is an open question. In order to get a better picture of that complex organization, subjective information supplied by the subject becomes as important to the scientist as his own observation of behavior. Both are equally important sources of data.

The recognition that subjective experience was worthy of consideration was of central importance to those physicians who founded clinical psychology. Their job was not disinterested research into the nature of human psychology; their job was curing desperately ill fellow human beings. Clinical psychologists had no hope of helping the patient without acknowledging the importance of his subjective experience. Frequently, they would try to discount the subjective experience as the ravings of a madman. But they were far more likely than an experimental psychologist to at least be interested in the experience.

Thus the lines were initially drawn between Experimental and Clinical psychology. Interestingly, today those walls are coming down more and more to the mutual benefit of both sides. Behaviorists have moved into clinical psychology and many have broadened their stance to include subjective responses, and even more importantly, the need for humanism to temper scientific objectivity. Clinical psychologists have learned the power of the scientific method, have realized that it does not have to be dehumanizing in the right hands.

8

Clinical Psychology's Founders

Before Braid, hypnosis had to exist on the fringe of scientific respectability. It was an interesting curiousity, but hardly something with which a respectable doctor or scientist would dirty his hands. But Braid's limited initial assumption that hypnosis was simply a physiological phenomenon made the study of hypnosis acceptable to the scientific community.

Jean Martin Charcot

Jean Martin Charcot was appointed at the Saltpetriere clinic in France in 1862. Shortly after his appointment, he established a neurological clinic there, soon to be the most famous clinic in Europe. He specialized in patients who would now be classified as neurotic. As in our own time, there was hardly a short supply. The majority of the patients at that time were women, and therefore their condition was dubbed hysteria (from the Greek for uterus: "hystera"). Psychologists are now quite aware that males are as prone to neurosis as females, but are more reluctant than women to discuss their emotional problems.

In any case, Charcot treated these patients with the new tool of hypnosis, with some success. He ignored Braid's later theory, that hypnosis was caused by suggestion, and preferred to consider both hysteria and hypnosis as physiological conditions of women.

> The similarity between the symptoms of hypnosis and hysteria led Charcot to think that hypnotizability is characteristic of hysteria and in a sense a symptom of it. That was a mistake.
> (Boring,1929:698).

Charcot was in the ideal position to discover what Freud was later to term the "unconscious". By "unconscious", Freud meant literally that portion of a person's thoughts, feelings and memories of which he has no conscious awareness. Charcot was treating hysteric patients in whom unconscious material was constantly coming to the surface of their minds. He was using hypnosis, which cut past any conscious prohibitions and gave him the opportunity to explore deep unconscious material. But because he regarded hypnosis as merely another evidence of hysteria, and because he considered hysteria to be a physiological complaint of women, he never took advantage of his opportunity.

Pierre Janet

Pierre Janet and Freud both studied under Charcot at his neurological clinic, though Freud only briefly. Janet was not only Charcot's student, but his successor as head of the clinic. Janet had several advantages over Charcot in furthering the study of the unconscious mind. First, he had Charcot's work on which to build. But second and more important, Janet was a much broader thinker than Charcot, with a background not only in medicine but also in academic psychology and philosophy. He became interested in hypnosis, not as a symptom of hysteria, and not only as an individual phenomenon, but as one of a number of processes that seemed to bypass conscious control. His life's work was, to use the title of his great youthful work, "L 'autotisme psychologique" (the psychology of automatic responses).

> In 1892 Janet's main argument about hysteria was that it is a splitting of the personality, caused by a concentration of consciousness on one system of ideas and its retraction from others.
> (ibid:700).

Many clinical psychologists could attest to the accuracy of Janet's description of the state; neurosis is indeed often characterized by a withdrawal of energy from normal areas and over-concentration in neurotic areas. For example, in a sexually repressed time, such as the Victorian era when Freud and Janet saw hysteric patients, neurosis centered around sexuality. In the current time, where there is an excess of sexual freedom and far too little outer stability, neurosis centers on problems of self-definition (see May,1969:38f).

Much of Jung's work described exactly how such shifts of energy occur. He realized that the area in which neurosis chooses to operate is a product of the culture and the time. The over-concentration of attention is a symptom, not a cause. Charcot used hypnosis to release unconscious processes, but interpreted them as physiological. Janet realized that hypnosis provided an example of a phenomenon involving not merely physiological processes, but also unconscious psychological processes, and that there were a number of such unconscious processes.

However, it was still left to Freud to discover the unconscious mind. Freud himself never realized the full scope of the unconscious because he assumed that the repressed sexuality he found in his patients was a universal condition, not a culturally determined one. Jung, able to build on each his great predecessors, was able to explore further than any. Jung would surely have echoed the words of Newton: "If I have achieved anything of greatness, it is because I have stood on the shoulders of giants."

What Led to the Discovery of the Unconscious?

In the discussion of Newton, the author contended that Newton was as much a representative of his times, as he was an innovator. The ideas that would lead Newton to his great theories of light and gravitation were "in the air." Similarly, at the beginning of the twentieth-century, the idea of the unconscious was also "in the air." With the birth of the "Renaissance Ideal" of man as observer, a chain of thought came into existence which would increasingly alienate man from the world around him. This paper has traced that chain from Da Vinci's and Michelangelo's heroic model of man, to Descartes elevation of the intellect, to Newton's Laws of Motion and

Opticks, to Locke's Associationism, and on to Wundt and experimental psychology. This line of thought equated man with his mind, and the world with matter, and separated the two.

The Renaissance had hardly dawned when Paracelsus grew interested not in man's separateness, but in the relationship between man and nature. This paper has traced one of Paracelsus' ideas, the idea that magnetism affects the human body, through Van Helmot's animal magnetism, Mesmer's mesmerism, to scientific respectability as hypnotism with Braid. Charcot then used the technique with hysteric patients. Janet generalized the concept beyond hypnotism alone and studied many such processes. Clearly, over this long period, the idea of the separation of man's intellect from the matter of the outer world, was the dominant idea. Paracelsus' conviction of the inter-connection between the macro-world of nature and the micro-world of man's psyche was ignored through most of this period. It only found expression through phenomena at the fringes of science, such as hypnotism.

In chapter 4, we saw how the dominant chain of thought led, in philosophy, to its own downfall. Rationalism and materialism led to associationism. That then led ineluctably to the deadly arguments of Hume and Berkeley that seemed to deny the very existence of either a material universe or a human intellect. Kant solved the dilemma with his formulation of a transcendent realm of universal categories that united both matter and psyche. The particular categories Kant identified are now assumed to be merely products of his culture. His pessimism at there being any way for a human to bridge the two worlds, and attain conscious access to these categories, is also dismissed today. But his concept of inborn, universal "categories" presented philosophy with the potential for a solution to its dilemma.

Philosophy and Its Children

Issues become critical for philosophy long before they impinge on other fields of thought. The dilemma presented by

Hume and Berkeley, and Kant's solution to the dilemma, were of little interest to physics or chemistry or biology. Philosophy is the mother of the other sciences. Each was initially merely an area of interest for philosophy. Each in turn grew independent enough to call itself a separate field: first mathematics, then physics, later chemistry and biology. Each disavowed any philosophic under-pinnings. Of course, despite their disavowals, each of the sciences has an unspoken, underlying philosophy.

For example, mathematicians divide themselves into two major categories: "pure" and "applied". "Pure" mathematicians regard mathematics as an abstract science that has no god to serve except mathematics itself. They state, with pride, that their field of study has absolutely no practical application. Yet, interestingly enough, new concepts in pure mathematics do inevitably find their way into applied mathematics, then into the sciences and, finally, into the everyday world that affects all of us. That this should occur at all is a profound mystery. Albert Einstein perfectly expressed the mystery in these words:

> How can it be that mathematics, being after all a product of human thought, is so admirably appropriate to the objects of reality?
> (quotation in Brain/Mind Bulletin, 6/18/84).

For approximately two thousand years, Euclidean geometry was accepted as representing reality itself. Several nineteenth-century mathematicians simultaneously developed new geometries with different assumptions from Euclidean geometry. Surely nothing could have seemed less likely to affect anything beyond mathematics itself. Yet, when Einstein presented his theories of relativity, one of these geometries turned out to better represent a relativistic universe. It was this geometry that was used in the exacting calculations that launched the rocket that put man on the moon.

When psychology, the youngest of philosophy's children, came into existence, it prided itself on following the methods of its siblings, the "hard" sciences; it was especially anxious to disavow any "philosophy" in its methods. But psychology as a separate science appeared just as the "hard" sciences were forced to deal with the conflict that Kant faced in philosophy a century earlier. One might say that psychology's reason for existence was to explore that union of man and nature that can only be found in the psyche. The first man to fully realize the importance of that exploration was Sigmund Freud, the subject of our next chapter.

9

Sigmund Freud

Freud's Early Work
Freud began his long career as a scientist, not a physician. His specialty was the nervous system. It was only after fifteen years of work as a research scientist that he turned to clinical medicine in order to earn more money for his growing family. Though Freud always regarded himself as a scientist first and foremost, science is founded on careful observation and description; Freud was more of an "explainer" than a "describer". The entire body of his work is characterized by a repeated pattern. Freud would make careful observations initially, then develop a theory to explain the facts. So far, this is exactly the scientific method. However, the theories he developed were far too often impossible to verify because they involved metaphysical models.

It is ironic that Jung has often been accused by dealing in metaphysics, not facts. In actuality, Jung was always careful to confine himself to a description of what he actually found in the dreams and visions of his patients or himself. He then constructed limited models from these observations that were open to scientific investigation. Freud created theories, not models, and those theories still elude scientific examination.

However, Freud had no theories when he began his clinical work. He just wanted techniques that could help him deal with his patient's problems. Initially, under the guidance of Charcot and his colleagues, Freud used hypnosis.

> When Freud began the practice of medicine it was natural, in view of his scientific background, that he should specialize in the treatment of nervous disorders. . . . Freud spent a year in Paris (1885–86) learning

Charcot's method of treatment. However, Freud was not satisfied with hypnosis because he felt that the effects were only temporary and did not get at the seat of the trouble.

(Hall,1954:14).

Freud, by his own admission in letters to his friend Fliess, was not a very skilled hypnotist, and wanted a method that he could use with more success. Freud found that method when he began his cooperative work with an older colleague, Joseph Breuer. Breuer had already developed an alternative to hypnosis which interested Freud a great deal: the cathartic or "talking" cure. Breuer found that if hysteric patients were encouraged to talk about whatever came to mind, they felt relief and their symptoms decreased.

Freud experimented with patients and found that Breuer's talking cure, or free-association, as Freud came to call it, was preferable to hypnosis. He also turned to his patients' dreams as a source of unconscious material. When he began to have the patients free-associate about their dreams, Freud had the general method he was to most use in the years to come. Using these new methods, Freud discovered that, far from being meaningless anomalies, neurotic symptoms expressed an underlying dynamic. More and more, Freud began to believe that there was a whole system of unconscious thoughts, feelings, and memories that underlay conscious behavior.

Up to a point, Freud was a careful scientist. He methodically recorded the unconscious material that patients brought up in their dreams and free-associations. At the same time:

> . . . in the 1890's, with characteristic thoroughness, Freud began an intensive self-analysis of his own unconscious sources . . . by analyzing his dreams and saying to himself whatever came into his mind, he was able to see the workings of his own inner dynamics.
>
> (ibid:15).

It was a common-place observation among the many therapists who worked at Charcot's clinic that the problems usually turned out to be sexual. Freud immediately sensed that this was a central concept and tried to convince Charcot and Breuer of its importance. Both were proper European gentlemen who were too embarrassed to deal with sexuality and, therefore, turned to other explanations. Though Freud was a thoroughly proper Victorian gentleman himself, equally embarrassed at addressing such a forbidden topic, he grew more and more convinced that sex was the key that opened the door to the unconscious mind. In actuality, sex was only one such key, a key more characteristic of Victorian Europe than of man in general.

Freud's life was a long one, and he continued to change his theoretical system up to the end of his life. However, there were two key ideas that Freud formulated in the early years of his career that formed the initial core for all his later work, though both were to be extensively modified in later years. It is important to remember that his theories were to be revised only by Freud himself; he brooked no heresy from his followers. The first was the idea that underlying our conscious thoughts lies a huge reservoir of unconscious thoughts, feelings, and memories.

His initial, justly famed exploration of the territory of the unconscious came in *The Interpretation of Dreams*, which he developed during the 1890's and first published in 1900. The second concept was the primacy of the sexual instinct in human development. The initial statement of his sexual theories came in 1905 with the publication of *Three Essays on the Theory of Sexuality*. Each concept is important enough to discuss briefly below.

The Interpretation of Dreams

In the opening chapter of *The Interpretation of Dreams*, Freud presented a history of "The Scientific Literature of Dream-Problems (up to 1900)".

> The peoples of classical antiquity . . . took it for granted that dreams were related to the world of supernatural beings. . . . it appeared to them that dreams must serve a special purpose in respect of the dreamer; that is, as a rule, they predicted the future.
> (Brill,1938:184).

Freud moved on to Aristotle, with whose views he clearly felt more at home. Freud continued:

> In the two works of Aristotle in which there is a mention of dreams, they are already regarded as constituting a problem of psychology. We are told that the dream is not god-sent . . . the dream is defined as the psychic activity of the sleeper.
>
> (ibid:184).

Freud was thus clear from the outset that dreams told us only about the dreamer, and that he would have little patience with any theories of dream interpretation that seemed at all mystical or religious. In the body of the book, Freud then developed his own theory of dream interpretation, the theory that "every dream is the fulfillment of a concealed wish" (Lazun,1962:48). Calvin S. Hall summarized Freud's view as "we dream about what we want" (Hall,1954:25).

Freud felt that dreams revealed all the urges we repressed during waking consciousness. As civilized beings we can't allow ourselves to consciously acknowledge our primitive feelings of lust, hatred, greed, etc. During sleep, our ability to suppress such forbidden thoughts is weaker and they emerge into a shadow consciousness. However, as a last protection, some internal "censor" twists the undesireable thoughts into symbols that hide their meaning from us.

The author's experience is quite different; he has found that when people begin to record and study their dreams, the dreams exercise a fascination that far exceeds the manifest content of the dream. The elements of the dream seem to contain an energy of their own. That would accord well with Freud's view, since the dream elements should be about our deepest desires. Frequently, the dreamer feels ambiguous toward the dream, just as he would if it was actually discussing "forbidden fruit". But this ambiguous response is hardly universal. Frequently, the response is totally positive. In fact, certain dreams exercise such an intense fascination for the dreamer that they seem like messages from the gods, as the "ancients" believed them to be.

The concept of the "censor" seems unlikely at best. Dreams seem to speak a language of their own, not to conceal, but to reveal. All cultures which have honored dreams have noted this and realized that dreams speak in symbols. It is critical to realize that a symbol is not merely a sign, standing in one-to-one representation with something else. in Jung's words:

> . . . a symbol always presupposes that the chosen expression is the best possible description or formulation of a relatively unknown fact, which is none the less known to exist or is postulated as existing.
> (Jung,1971:814).

Freud viewed dream symbols as simple signs that could be reduced to a sexual interpretation. For the origination of this concept, Lauzun claimed priority for Freud's disciples Stekel and Rank, stating that:

> . . . it was under the influence of two other future dissenters, Stekel and Rank, that Freud wrote the chapters of *The Interpretation of Dreams* which deal with symbolism and compare dreams with poetry and myth . . . the supposed symbolism in which anything long is a penis and anything hollow is a vagina.
> (Lauzun,1962:51).

Regardless of priority, the reduction of all dream symbols to sexual images is a terrible impoverishment of the rich palette of dreams. It is only with very recent research in some quite disparate fields that we begin to realize why dreams speak in symbols. For example, linguist Noam Chomsky has developed a model of a "deep structure" which he asserts underlies all language; he argues that this "deep structure" is an inherent, inborn structure of the human mind (see Chomsky,1968).

Biologist/psychologist Jean Piaget has carefully studied children's behavior and development. He has argued, in opposition to Chomsky among others, that language develops out of motor actions (see Piaget,1955). The synthesis that seems to be emerging among many linguists and psychologists is that both are right, there is a "deep structure" that underlies language, and that this "deep structure" is inborn, but it is evidenced first in motor actions and only gradually develops into a spoken language. Anthropologist Edward T. Hall has shown how large a part of language is non-verbal (see Hall,1959).

Ethologists like Konrad Lorenz have shown how animals also possess inborn "symbolic" responses which will be triggered by specific cues in their environment, at different points in their development. When the correct situation occurs at the correct time, the animal will "imprint" their inner pre-disposition onto the actual event (see Evans,1975).

For example, when Lorenz was studying the behavior of geese, one orphaned baby goose "imprinted" its inner concept of a mother onto Lorenz. All that was necessary was for Lorenz to be the first creature that the baby goose saw at a certain key point in its development. The baby goose, having "imprinted" the inner concept of mother onto Lorenz, took to following Lorenz wherever he went, just as baby geese always follow their mother. Clearly, the inborn symbol that corresponded to mother wasn't an actual picture of a mother goose, because Lorenz could hardly qualify (see Lorenz,1952).

Mircea Eliade's studies of primitive religious mythology offer still another source of information on archetypal structures. Eliade has found that common symbols occur in the myths of cultures at similar stages of development. For example, the belief in a time when everything was perfect, such as the Garden of Eden episode in the Hebrew/Christian Bible, seems universal. Another universal example is the belief that there is a central axis that connects the world of man with the world of the gods.

Like the symbols in our dreams, these mythological symbols reappear in all cultures in all times with remarkable similarity. They are filtered through the particulars of a given culture just as the symbols in our dreams are filtered through our particular memories. Thus the Norse myths show the central axis mentioned above as a great tree, while the Bible speaks of it, in Jacob's great dream, as a ladder stretching up to heaven (see Eliade,1959).

The above examples from varied fields point once again to the likely existence of Kant's "categories" and Jung's "archetypes". Chomsky's work points to a deep underlying structure that eventually shows itself as language. Piaget's work demonstrates that language exhibits itself first in motor actions, not words. Hall supports Piaget in showing the extensive amount of non-verbal language. Lorenz' work shows that man is not alone, that animals possess similar inborn, instinctual, symbolic responses. Eliade's studies reveal that whole cultures express their deepest beliefs in terms which are also symbolic and, in large part, independent of the particular culture that expresses them.

Freud's realization that dreams spoke in a symbolic language was thus deeply important. However, his reduction of dreams to wish-fulfillment, and dream symbols to sexual signs, was an ill-chosen attempt to over-simplify their complexity. To quote Eliade on the need to include a place for religious symbolism:

> . . . the *sacred* is an element of the *structure* of consciousness. . . . religious symbols constitute a prereflective language. As it is a case of a special language, sui generis, it necessitates a proper hermeneutics [Eliade's emphasis].
>
> (Eliade,1977:313).

Three Essays on the Theory of Sexuality

In *Three Essays* Freud examined whether so-called sexual perversions were innate or developed. By perversions, Freud meant:

> . . . sexual activities which either (a) extend, in an anatomical sense, beyond the regions of the body that are designed for sexual union, or (b) linger over the intermediate relations to the sexual object which should normally be traversed rapidly on the path towards the final sexual aim.
>
> (Strachey,1962:16).

He found that neurotics revealed all the sexual perversions in the course of psychoanalysis. Since neurotics were "a numerous class of people and one not far removed from the healthy," he felt that the perversions were innate and that normal sexuality was developed (ibid:97). If perverse sexuality was innate, Freud theorized that it should be found in infants, and that is exactly what he did find.

> There seems no doubt that germs of sexual impulses are already present in the newborn child and that these continue to develop for a time, but are then overtaken by a progressive process of suppression . . . the sexual life of children emerges in a form accessible to observation round about the third or fourth year of life.
>
> (ibid:42).

According to Freud, the child passed through three transitional stages, usually by age five: the oral, the anal, and the phallic. Each took its name from the erogenous zone stressed during that stage of development. During the oral phase, sexuality expressed itself through taking in with the mouth. Thumb-sucking is the example most would think of, but every young child goes through a phase where everything is put in the mouth during the course of a child's ever-curious examination. In the anal stage, the child discovered, and gloried, in its first creation, its feces. The phallic stage marked the child's discovery of its genitals; during this stage the child rubs itself in a masturbatory fashion.

Freud termed this tendency of sexuality to take on multiple expressions and objects "polymorphous perverse" sexuality. After the three transitional stages, a period of latency followed wherein the infant's polymorphous perverse sexuality is forced to adapt to the demands of society. Finally, at adolescence, the child's genitals once more became the main erogenous zone but this time a proper sexual object was found in a person of the opposite sex.

The adult personality was determined by the child's manner of dealing with these developmental stages. If the child failed to deal successfully with each of the stages, adult sexuality would fail to find its full development in hetero-sexual genital sexuality. It was because of such psycho-sexual developmental problems that sexual perversions existed in adults. The perversions were not developed; instead, they marked an absence of proper development. The infant's sexuality was originally "polymorphous perverse" and remained that way in the adult because the child was not successful in dealing with one of the three early stages.

Freud was later to examine the psychological implications of the three psycho-sexual developmental stages at great length. He felt they were sufficient to explain all differences in personality. For example, psychologist Calvin S. Hall said concerning the oral phase:

> Tactual stimulation of the lips and oral cavity by contact with and the incorporation of objects produces oral erotic (sexual) pleasure, and biting yields oral aggressive pleasure . . . the mouth, therefore, has at least five main modes of functioning, (1) taking in, (2) holding on, (3) biting, (4) spitting out, and (5) closing. Each of these modes is a prototype or the original model for certain personality types . . . the child, having learned to make a particular adjustment, uses the same adjustment when similar situations arise later in life. If taking things in through the mouth is pleasurable, as it is when the child is hungry, then taking in or incorporating knowledge or love or power when one feels empty may also be pleasurable.
>
> (Hall,1954:103f).

Freud came full-circle in his examination. He began by considering where sexual perversions originated, and found they were innate, that infants are "polymorphous perverse". He traced the developmental stages that lead to adult sexuality, and found that the failure to successively deal with any stage left the adult with the original childish sexual perversion. More importantly, Freud now had a developmental scheme that could be used to reduce any adult problem to an infantile developmental problem. Any adult achievement, from art to religion, could also be reduced to a failure to develop a full adult sexuality.

The same strengths and weaknesses are seen here as in Freud's work on dream analysis. Freud's analysis in each case was incomparably brilliant, very like the sort of argument used in medieval scholastic philosophy. Unlike scholastic philosophers, Freud tried to be a descriptive scientist, describing what he had actually observed in patients before he made intellectual generalizations from his observations. But very unscientifically, Freud tended to see what he wanted to see. Very few others would be willing to accept so readily that all instinctive behavior was only a manifestation of sexual behavior.

A child turns to its mother's breast not merely for food and nourishment, but equally for love and tenderness. Experimental psychologist Harry F. Harlow's research with chimpanzees demonstrated that an infant chimp has as strong a need for nurturing as for food. In one experiment, two "mothers" were constructed for an orphaned chimp. Both "mothers" were roughly shaped like a mother chimp. One was a wire cage that provided milk; the other was warm and furry but gave no milk. The chimp would cling to the furry "mother" and only go to the wire "mother" long enough to get its hunger satisfied (see Bylinsky, 1973).

Yet Freud was satisfied to see a child's thumb-sucking, for example, as a purely sexual satisfaction. Jung disagreed with Freud and said [in 1912, just at the point when he was beginning to split with Freud]:

> . . . if we take the attitude that the striving for pleasure is something sexual, we might just as well say, paradoxically, that hunger is a sexual striving, since it seeks pleasure by satisfaction. But if we juggle with concepts like that, we should have to allow our opponents to apply the terminology of hunger to sexuality.
>
> (Jung,1954:241).

Summary of Early Freudian Ideas

Through his work with neurotic patients, Freud came to realize that an unconscious dynamic underlay their conscious actions. He tried to use hypnotism to tap that unconscious well, in the manner of Charcot, but found it an unsatisfactory method. Breuer's "talking cure", which Freud came to call "free association", gave Freud a tool to get beyond the conscious mind. Dreams were a rich source of unconscious material. Freud decided that dreams were wish fulfillment; their complexity was due to an inner "censor" who made a last attempt to prevent forbidden thought from coming into consciousness.

This unconscious material appeared overwhelmingly sexual to Freud. He found that his patients were invariably sexually disturbed; they exhibited all the sexual "perversions" in their desires. Freud theorized that this was because sexuality is originally "polymorphous perverse"; i.e., it will take any object. It is only by going through a proper sexual development, before age five, that proper adult sexuality develops. Freud felt that all human problems, and even all human achievements could be traced to problems in childhood sexual development.

Freud thus stood at the end of the long line of thought that we have traced from its beginnings in the Renaissance. That line began by glorying in man the observer. With Descartes, man became synonymous with his intellect; the great split between man's mind and body was now explicitly stated. Man developed an ever-greater ability to stand separate from the world around him, dissecting the world into ever smaller parts. Science grew from this ability, and science brought man a new power to dominate his world. Man increasingly turned this power onto himself, separating his rational mind from his body and emotions. His body's needs and wisdom were increasingly hidden from man's consciousness, which saw itself as a disembodied intellect.

As this separation grew over hundreds of years, hidden away from consciousness, a counter-balance also developed. This was a pull toward harmony, relationship, connectedness, rather than separation. Since the prevailing rationalism was unsympathetic to this mode of thought, it exhibited itself largely through fringe phenomena. One such phenomenon was hypnotism, which we have followed from Paracelsus to Freud. However, Freud himself stood firmly in the materialist camp, resisting any encroachments of "the black mud of occultism" (as Freud described it to Jung) (Jung,1965:150).

> ... reason, so Freud felt, is the only tool—or weapon—we have to make sense of life, to dispense with illusions (of which, in Freud's thought, religious tenets are only one), to become independent of fettering authorities, and thus to establish our own authority.
>
> (Fromm,1959:2).
>
> ... for him reason was confined to thought. Feelings and emotions were per se irrational, and hence inferior to thought.
>
> (ibid:7).

How ironic that Freud, an exemplary product of the rationalist tradition, should discover the unconscious mind. Freud was led to its discovery by rationalism itself; it explained so much. But because the mind and the body had long ago been split, and the body relegated to an inherently inferior position, Freud was confronted with a dilemma. On the one hand, he saw that our conscious lives are largely controlled by unconscious motivation. Yet this unconscious motivation was a primitive, instinctive unreasoning force.

The picture was a gloomy one and one that Freud never resolved. At first, he even hoped that the mere knowledge of the unconscious motivation would be enough to restore the rational mind's dominion over the primitive instincts. But he soon found that was an empty hope. He decided that the best man could do was understand this split inside himself, and hold to the side of rationality when faced with the void of the unconscious. Freud held to this pessimistic view of man's possibilities, while he continued to develop his system of thought, continuing to hope for some way out of this dilemma.

The way out lay in a synthesis of conscious and unconscious, of mind and body. It lay in relationship, not separation. It could be found not in nineteenth-century ideas, standing at the end of the rationalist tradition, but in twentieth-century ideas, which had been only embryonic in the centuries before.

Part II:

The Psychology of C. G. Jung

10

The Background for Jung's Ideas

Nature and Mind/Science and Poetry
Jung's father was a minister in a rural region near Basel, Switzerland. Jung's long-time co-worker Marie-Louise von Franz wrote that

> Jung loved animals and plants, not only when he was a child but all his life, and he could never see enough of the beauty of lakes, forests and mountains. Nature was for him of prime importance and striking descriptions of nature are scattered through all his works.
> (von Franz,1975:27)

This "earthy" quality always remained an integral part of Jung. He was more interested in the reality he observed than in theoretical discussions that had no roots in the world.

> He remained faithful all his life to the conviction that the facts of nature are the basis of all knowledge...for him nature is not only outside but also within.
> (ibid:32f).

Jung was well-educated in literature and philosophy, in contrast to Freud and most of the early clinical and experimental psychologists, whose education was almost entirely scientific. He gloried:

> ...in Goethe's *Faust*, which his mother brought to his attention when he was in the Gymnasium. 'It poured into my soul like a miraculous balm'...For the rest of his life, and despite certain moral criticisms of the character of Faust, Jung kept his great admiration for Goethe and, indeed, loved him as one loves a kindred spirit.
> (ibid:34f).

Jung was convinced that an accurate description of reality required both scientific precision and poetic understanding.

> [This made it] difficult to find a form in which to communicate his innermost convictions. . .he tried to assume the scientific style of the contemporary psychological works, but he was never able entirely to give up poetic language.
>
> (ibid:36).

In an attempt to be "scientific", his early experimental work was written in a turgid style that is reminiscent of "scientific" papers to this day. But his later work abounds in poetic passages that better capture the majesty of their subject. This combination has scared off many readers, just as a similar combination has made Hegel suspect as a philosopher, and C. P. Snow as a novelist. The latter has argued convincingly that our time needs people and thoughts that bridge the "two cultures" of science and the arts (Snow,1959; also see Snow,1960). C. G. Jung's work does just that.

Ghosts and Spirits

The farmers who lived in the region near Jung's childhood home accepted the reality of the earth that fed them; equally, they accepted that there were other, un-earthly aspects to reality. As a boy, Jung heard tales of ghosts and spirits, of poltergeists and possession. Unlike most intellectuals, he didn't dismiss these out-of-hand as superstition. If they were experienced as "psychic" realities, Jung wanted to know why, and he wanted to explore them. His first scientific paper was a study of a young female cousin who had become locally acclaimed as a medium for a short time (Jung,1902:37–155).

It was Jung's curiousity about phenomena dismissed by his colleagues that led him to his greatest discoveries, and which has also prevented many from accepting Jung's ideas. He was never able to dismiss experience because it didn't fit his view of reality. In his spiritual auto-biography, *Memories, Dreams, Reflections*, Jung spoke of his interest in psychic phenomena as a student, and the reaction of his fellow students.

> I read virtually the whole of the literature available to me at the time. Naturally I also spoke of these matters to my comrades, who to my great astonishment reacted with derision and disbelief or with anxious defensiveness. I wondered at the sureness with which they could assert that things like ghosts and table-turning were impossible and therefore fraudulent, and on the other hand at the evidently anxious nature of their defensiveness.
>
> (Jung,1965:99).

Jung never lost his earthy roots; he was always content to describe the reality he found. He left it to others to theorize about that reality. Of course, like all good descriptive scientists, he was a superb model-maker. However, as opposed to theoreticians, he realized that models were only partial. His whole career was an attempt to find ever better models to express the inexpressible.

In dealing with Jung's ideas, it's important to understand this stolid, earthy side to his personality. Jung always stressed that he considered himself a descriptive scientist. When Jung described concepts his colleagues regarded as mystical, such as his concept of the collective unconscious, Jung was describing something that he had personally experienced so many times that he could not justifiably ignore it. If Jung erred at all in spreading his ideas, it could be that, like Darwin, he collected evidence far beyond the point most would regard as necessary. Jung once said that he had analyzed over 80,000 dreams! It was only within such an enormous background of experience that Jung proposed his concepts.

The Emergence of Consciousness From the Unconscious

Jung felt that psychology was too young a science to develop a theoretical super-structure, so he tried to content himself with describing what he encountered. However, as a clinical psychologist, he was also concerned with the practical problem of how to resolve these polarities as he encountered them in his patients. It was in his attempts to resolve their problems that Jung encountered a world that had been previously unknown to Western science. It was through his resolution to confine himself to description that he was able to produce such a detailed and accurate picture of the deepest levels of the human psyche. Finally, it is through Jung's enormous erudition that he was able to relate what he encountered in the dreams and fantasies of his patients to the art, literature, philosophy, mythology, and religion of the world.

Jung found that his neurotic patients' conscious resources were always inadequate to their problems. He felt that neurosis reflected an attempt at a resolution from a new direction: the unconscious. Like Freud, Jung turned to the unconscious of his patients in an attempt to find a solution to their problem. Since Jung was a descriptive scientist, rather than a theoretician, he found a much different world than Freud. Jung's 1935 lectures at the Tavistock clinic in London summarized his ideas at approximately the mid-point of his career. During these lectures, Jung commented that:

> [Freud] derives the unconscious from the conscious. . .I would put it the reverse way: I would say the thing that comes first is obviously the unconscious. . .in early childhood we are unconscious; the most important functions of an instinctive nature are unconscious, and consciousness is rather the product of the unconscious.
>
> (Jung,1968:8).

This is one of the key distinctions between Jung's and Freud's views of the unconscious. Freud initially felt that the unconscious was merely the repository for consciously repressed thoughts and feelings. Due to Jung's early research, Freud acknowledged that there were elements in the unconscious that seemed to be some sort of "race memory". But because Freud had already developed his theory of the unconscious, he didn't consider those "race memories" anything more than curiosities.

As a young doctor just beginning his life work, Jung was enormously impressed with Freud's ideas. Accordingly, Jung began his own exploration of the unconscious of his patients with the assumption that he would encounter only repressed products of consciousness. But the descriptive scientist won out as Jung continued his exploration. It was impossible to retain Freud's theories and deal adequately with the full contents of his patients' dreams. So he gradually discarded Freud's theories and just described what he found.

> . . .we cannot directly explore the unconscious psyche because the unconscious is just unconscious, and we have therefore no relation to it. We can only deal with the conscious products which we suppose have originated in the field called the unconscious.
>
> . . .we do not know how far the unconscious rules because we simply know nothing of it. You cannot say anything about a thing of which you know nothing. When we say the unconscious we often mean to convey something by the term, but as a matter of fact we simply convey that we do not know what the unconscious is.
>
> (ibid:6f).

Jung's remarks recognize that, in dealing with the unconscious, we are encountering a world that can only be viewed indirectly, through its by-products. This is the same world encountered by particle physicists, who are forced to deal with sub-atomic particles which can only be viewed indirectly, through their by-products. Particle-physicists record the interaction of sub-atomic particle in a "bubble-chamber". To a layman, a picture of a bubble-chamber just shows a bewildering complexity of lines. Just so, the bewildering, non-logical, seemingly incoherent picture of dreams. But both bubble-chambers and dreams can imply a great deal to those who observe, with openness and understanding, enough of either. Nineteenth century science still assumed it could directly observe nature; the twentieth century has learned otherwise. Jung was a thoroughly twentieth-century man, while Freud was a nineteenth century man; the difference is profound.

Freed from the strait-jacket of Freud's pre-formed schemata, Jung found a very strange world indeed, equally as strange and totally parallel to the world of particle physics. It was an undifferentiated world, seemingly free of the restrictions of time and space that define consciousness. Again, from the Tavistock lectures:

...the conscious mind moreover is characterized by a certain narrowness. It can hold only a few simultaneous contents at a given moment. All the rest is unconscious at the time, and we only get a sort of continuation or a general understanding or awareness of a conscious world through the succession of conscious moments. We can never hold an image of totality because our consciousness is too narrow...the area of the unconscious is enormous and always continuous, while the area of consciousness is a restricted field of momentary vision.

(ibid:8).

The next chapter will present Jung's model of the psychic world that he discovered.

11

Jung's Model of the Psyche

In the following, the author is presenting what he understands to be Jung's model of the psyche. It has already been stressed that Jung was never satisfied with the models he found or constructed. Therefore, many different models are presented over the vast body of his work. As a clinical psychologist, his first interest was in a dynamic model of the psyche which adequately dealt with the clinical problems he encountered in psycho-therapy. However, as we will see later in this paper, he came to believe that the course of individual human development, which he called "individuation", was not random and meaningless, but purposeful. He developed two major models to help describe the dynamics of "individuation": (1) through the archetypes of Shadow, Anima/Animus, and Self; and (2) through a psychological interpretation of the stages of alchemy.

The author has already stressed that Jung was a descriptive scientist, not a theoretician. Both models developed slowly over long periods and information on both is spread over numerous works written at different points in time. Because of this, Jung never presented a theoretically complete version of either of the two models, and inconsistencies can be found between different presentations of the same material. The model based on the archetypes of Shadow, Anima/Animus and Self was earlier and never fully developed once Jung discovered the alchemical mode. However, it was never discarded and, even in his last works, he still made reference to the earlier model.

Beyond this, Jung's more general thoughts about the nature

of the psyche and the relationship between consciousness and the unconscious, which form the foundation on which each of the above two models are constructed, are spread over thousands of pages and scores of years. Many of the more explicit descriptions are early in his career and would clearly have been modified if he had ever returned to re-edit them in later years, as he did with several of his major works. Therefore, there can be a wide difference of opinion on what Jung actually intended.

For example, a great deal of literature by analytic psychologists deals with the psychological interpretation of various archetypes found in mythology and fairy tales. This work was begun by Jung himself in several classic monographs, but has been vastly extended by later psychologists. A strange recent book contended that such work reflects a total mis-understanding of Jung and that Jung's work was intended to stress the biological roots of archetypes, not their psychological interpretation (Laughlin,1982).

To the author's reading, and to most major interpreters (such as James Hillman, Marie-Louise von Franz, Edward Edinger), Jung's work stressed both. But it is easy to see how, in the enormous reaches of Jung's thought, one can find evidence to demonstrate many points of view.

Therefore, the author's presentation of Jung's model of the psyche should be read with the understanding that other sound interpreters might disagree. To the extent possible, the author will attempt to combine Jung's early and late works to present a coherent whole. He will also attempt to show where there may be inconsistencies in Jung's thought, and where he feels Jung implied ideas which he never bothered to present explicitly.

Personal Conscious and Unconscious

Jung proposed that the totality of the human psyche (actual or potential) breaks-down into three categories: (1) personal consciousness, (2) the personal unconscious, and (3) the collective unconscious. Personal consciousness, of which modern man is so rightly proud, is a very transitory affair, consisting of whatever occupies our conscious awareness at a given moment of time. There is nothing which we retain permanently in consciousness, including our sense of identity or ego, which comes and goes. Consciousness is only a sliding frame which moves along, sometimes lit by awareness, sometimes not.

> Consciousness . . . is an intermittent phenomenon. One-fifth, or one-third, or perhaps even one-half of our human life is spent in an unconscious condition. Our early childhood is unconscious. Every night we sink into the unconscious, and only in phases between waking and sleeping have we a more or less clear consciousness. To a certain extent it is even questionable how clear that consciousness is.
> (Jung,1968:6).

Everything passes into consciousness by way of the unconscious first. Even sense perceptions, which many still regard as primary, are processed somewhere inside us, in a way of which we are largely unaware, and then pass into consciousness. Objects and events become conscious momentarily then pass out of consciousness again, as our awareness either shifts to something else, or turns itself off for awhile. Those things that were conscious are either recorded in some fashion or lost.

> . . . the *sum total of unconscious contents* [Jung's emphasis] falls into three groups: first, temporarily subliminal contents that can be reproduced voluntarily (memory); second, unconscious contents that cannot be reproduced voluntarily; third, contents that are not capable of becoming conscious at all. Group two can be inferred from the spontaneous irruption of subliminal contents into consciousness. Group three is hypothetical; it is a logical inference from the facts underlying group two.
> (Jung,1959:4).

Jung was deliberately simplifying the extremely complex relationship between conscious and unconscious material in order to stress that consciousness is not the whole of the psyche. As examples of the first group, we can all recite the alphabet or the multiplication tables. Consider, however, the fact that a great deal of unconscious material can be accessed without ever passing into conscious awareness. For example, we don't have to be conscious of tying our shoes in order to correctly tie them; however, we can make ourselves aware of how we tie them if necessary. We can even do so in our minds without actually touching shoe or shoelace. The relationship between conscious and unconscious is clearly complex.

Or consider the huge gray area that lies between Jung's first two categories, all that material which can be recovered into consciousness, but only with difficulty. We can all recall into consciousness events of emotional significance in our lives. The amount of conscious recall of such events largely varies with the significance of the event; in his early work, Jung presented this in energetic terms. Emotion was psychic energy. Memories passed into consciousness when the energy level was high enough (Jung,1960:1–130).

There are many memories that are at the borderline of conscious recall for us. These might have been originally too insignificant to pay close attention to. We could try mental tricks of association in order to try to recall these hazy memories. If the tricks are clever enough, such as being put into a deep hypnotic trance, we can usually recall every detail of these borderline events. The energy model helps explain all this quite well.

Other memories are also not easily recoverable, but not because they have too little emotional significance, but because they have too much. For example, if an event was too painful for us to accept, we may have recorded the memory fully, but erected psychic barriers to prevent our reexperiencing the pain. This could be a physical pain, such as a broken bone, or an emotional pain, such as an incident when we were deeply humiliated. These are what Freud means by "repressed" memories.

Another example would be an event that was too threatening to deal with. If, while crossing the street, we suddenly saw a car coming at us, we might block out the perception even before it caused us pain. Our conscious memory would end with the sight of the car coming at us. We might also have no conscious memory of an event that threatened our view of reality. For example, if a person had constructed a rigidly rationalistic view of life, they might not see a ghost, if there was such a thing, even if it appeared to them. The sight would be too threatening, in that the whole view of reality on which they had constructed their life would be in jeopardy. So they wouldn't consciously see the ghost, nor would they be able to bring that memory into consciousness. However, it might be accesible by special techniques such as hypnosis.

All of these memories are part of what Jung calls the personal unconscious. They constitute the totality of Freud's unconscious (with the exception of the small place he allotted to vestigial race memories after Jung pointed out inescapably collective images in dreams). But Jung contended that there remained a much bigger entity than the personal unconscious, which he termed the collective unconscious.

> While the personal unconscious is made up essentially of contents which have disappeared from consciousness through having been forgotten or repressed, the contents of the collective unconscious have never been in consciousness and therefore have never been individually acquired, but owe their existence exclusively to heredity.
> (Jung,1969:88).

It is clear from quotations such as this that Jung was indeed convinced of the biological roots of archetypes. But he stressed over and over that instincts and archetypes were two sides of the same coin.

The Collective Unconscious
> . . . there exists a second psychic system of a collective, universal, and impersonal nature which is identical in all individuals. This collective unconscious does not develop individually, but is inherited. It consists of pre-existent forms, the archetypes.
> (ibid:90).

In our time, the study of the relationship between learned and instinctual behavior has become the cornerstone of the new fields of ethology, best-known to the public through the popular works of Nobel prize winner, Konrad Lorenz (see

Lorenz,1952;Evans,1975), and socio-biology, whose best-known representative is its founder, biologist Edward O. Wilson.

There are also some pioneering animal researchers, like Jane Goodall, who, unsatisfied at the results previously obtained by observing animals in laboratory settings, have begun to observe animal behavior in its natural setting over long periods of time. This research has shown just how much behavior hitherto assumed to be exclusively human is also exhibited by animals and has implied that much of human behavior seems to be affected by inherited genetic patterns. Jung would have strongly supported all of this research.

> Instincts are impersonal, universally distributed, hereditary factors of a dynamic or motivating character, which very often fail so completely to reach consciousness that modern psychotherapy is faced with the task of helping the patient to become conscious of them. Moreover, the instincts are not vague and indefinite by nature, but are specifically formed motive forces which, long before there is any consciousness, and in spite of any degree of consciousness later on, pursue their inherent goals . . . there is good reason for supposing that the archetypes are the unconscious images of the instincts themselves; in other words, that they are patterns of instinctual behaviors. . . . The hypothesis of the collective unconscious is, therefore, no more daring than to assume there are instincts. . . . The question is simply this: are there or are there not unconscious, universal forms of this kind? If they exist, then there is a region of the psyche which one can call the collective unconscious.
>
> (ibid:91f).

The Nature of Mathematical Proof

Mathematicians like to prove something by a technique they call a "reductio ad absurdum." Basically, that technique is to assume the opposite of whatever proposition they want to prove, follow the logical implications of that assumption, and eventually arrive at a contradiction. Since the contradiction follows in a single logical chain from the original assumption, the original assumption must be wrong. But since the original assumption was the opposite of what the mathematician was trying to prove, and since this opposite assumption was proved to be incorrect, then the proposition is proved correct.

In effect, two wrongs do make a right in mathematics. It's an enormously powerful tool, in that a single exception can constitute a proof. To put it in simpler language, if something is assumed to be true in all cases, and even one counter-example is found, then it's not true in all cases. Stated that way, it seems so simple-minded that one wonders what use it could conceivably have. But there is a very important use.

Scientists accumulate evidence in favor of a theory in order to prove it. They try to explicitly determine the implications of a theory, then to gather evidence and see if the evidence agrees. However, it is important to realize that a theory can never be fully proved by such methods. Science is provisional. Scientists propose theories that explain reality as best they can, knowing that the theories may later prove to be inadequate. To use Leibniz' terms, which were used so powerfully by Kant, scientists deal with "a posteriori", synthetic, arguments. Mathematicians deal with "a priori", analytic arguments.

As Thomas Kuhn argued in *The Structure of Scientific Revolutions* (Kuhn,1970), in times of "normal science", when a scientific paradigm is able to deal adequately with most conditions, scientists have a tendency to ignore exceptions, under the assumption that the exceptions are either unimportant or can be somehow later subsumed into the paradigm. More importantly, most scientists in such times share a view of what constitutes reality, a view of what is or is not a "proper" subject for science.

However, when the paradigm breaks-down and more and more exceptions appear, there is a need to examine the exceptions carefully in order to find some clue to a new paradigm. But, of course, in the absence of a clear view of reality, who is to say which exceptions are important and which are trivial. And, when scientists construct new models, propose new theories, who is to say which are worth serious consideration. In such times, there is a strong tendency to stick by the older models in the hope that, somehow, they can be tailored to once more fit reality.

We are seemingly in such a "pre-paradigm" time when new theories and new models abound. Jung's concept of the collective unconscious is one such model which is still largely ignored by the scientific community. Like many other such contemporary models, it runs counter to the implicit materialist assumptions that underlie much of contemporary scientific thought. However, unlike many other such models, Jung's is the result of hard scientific research. Jung carefully observed the dreams and fantasies of his patients and described accurately what he found there. What he found was evidence of collective material. But, of course, it is difficult to prove that dream and fantasy material could not have been acquired during a person's lifetime. Therefore, clear-cut examples of collective memories are few and far between.

Let's try the mathematical method of "reductio ad absurdum". The hypothesis under consideration will be that "it is possible for the human mind to contain memories not acquired by a person during their lifetime." A mathematician would try and prove this hypothesis by assuming an opposite hypothesis and arriving at a contradiction. The opposite hypothesis would be that "the human mind only contains memories acquired by the person during their lifetime." If even one clear, unassailable example can then be given of a human memory that was not acquired by that person during their lifetime, then we have arrived at a contradiction. And that then means that the original hypothesis is proved. If so, then the question of the full extent of the human mind becomes an area for scientific exploration. Now, of course, all scientists understand this. However, in times of "normal science", there is rarely the need to consider isolated exceptional conditions. But this is not a time of "normal science" and Jung's concept of the collective unconscious needs to be carefuly explored, as Jung himself carefully explored it.

An Example of an Archetypal Image

Jung worked at the Burgholzli Mental Clinic in Switzerland from 1900 to 1909. He developed a rapport with the schizophrenic patients there by the simple expedient of listening to them. It was common practice then, as now, to ignore their dissociative speech as meaningless ravings. In contrast, Jung paid close attention to the words and tried to sort out the associational string of thoughts which lay behind the seeming nonsense.

One of the Jung's male schizophrenic patients had delusions of grandeur in which he considered himself a union of both God the Father and Christ in one person. He liked Jung and evidently decided to initiate Jung into his religion. One day in 1906, he told Jung to look closely at the sun and he'd see something interesting. He pointed out to Jung that if he looked closely he could see that the sun had a penis that hung down from it. When the penis swung from side to side, it created the winds. Jung had no idea what to make of this.

Four years later, after Jung had begun his deep studies of mythology, he came across a then recently published book by philologist Albrecht Dieterich, in which Dieterich translated a Mithraic ritual contained in a Greek papyrus. The ritual discussed the sun as a divinity and talked of a long tube coming down from the sun, which created the winds as it swung from side-to-side.

Jung remembered his patient's strange vision. The patient's working-class education and background had been far removed from such exotic topics as Mithraic rituals. He had been hospitalized since his early manhood, long before this particular manuscript was ever discovered and translated. As a patient, he had absolutely no way of acquiring this rare, scholarly book. Jung himself, at the time of the original episode with the patient, had no knowledge of mythology.

The most likely hypothesis Jung could propose was that the patient somehow tapped a collective memory. After all, the patient saw himself as a god, trying to initiate a new acolyte, Jung. The story of the sun's "penis" creating the wind was itself part of a ritual of initiation into the deeper mysteries of the Mithraic religion. To eliminate the possibility that this was an incredible coincidence of fantasies rather than an archetype of the collective unconscious, despite the centuries of separation, Jung hunted for other historical appearances of this strange symbolism.

In the author's experience with psychotic patients, he has found that during psychotic episodes they frequently expressed collective material with no filtering through personal consciousness. They simply gave up the small grasp they had on an integrated personal consciousness and were overwhelmed by the collective material. That would explain why Jung's patient's collective fantasy was exactly as expressed in the ancient ritual. However, the same collective material, when experienced by a saint or an artist, should be expressed in a much more personal way because a stable personality will manage to integrate the collective material into their personal psyche rather than just being overwhelmed by it.

Jung found that there were medieval paintings which showed a long pipe extending down from the throne of god. A dove or the Christ-child descended down it to fertilize Mary. The dove was a common medieval symbol for the Holy Ghost, who is also commonly represented as a holy wind or spirit. Thus the same collective material was expressed, though in a more individualized form since it was experienced by an artist, not a psychotic. Jung carefully checked the art in the local public art gallery in the town where the patient grew up, and found no such picture.

This example was carefully chosen by Jung, out of thousands of examples of the collective unconscious that he gathered over the years, because of the seeming impossibility of any other explanation. Provided that we accept Jung's veracity, then either the patient somehow became aware of an ancient Mithraic ritual and incorporated it into his delusions, or he is drawing on some knowledge that he didn't acquire in his lifetime. If we can open our minds to the possibility of the latter, look how much more cleanly it explains the situation.

The Mithraic ritual was an initiation into the cult of the sun god. Jung's patient also thought himself a god, and since he regarded Jung with patronizing affection, wanted to initiate Jung into the deeper mysteries. In turn, the medieval artists, wanting to show how Mary was fertilized by God drew on the same inner sources. God as a wind is carried by a tube for the medieval artists just as with the schizophrenic patient and the Mithraic ritual (see Jung,1960:317ff for details of the above case history).

The author has found numerous examples of collective material in his own dreams and the dreams of his patients. In his discussions with other therapists working with unconscious material, he has found that many of them have also found such a preponderance of collective material that they no longer doubt its existence. However, it's difficult to find an example as pure as Jung's because most of the unconscious material is mixed with personal memories.

Furthermore, it's especially difficult in these days of widespread information to prove that the dreamer could not have somehow come across the material in their reading or experience. Those who work with this collective material are convinced because they encounter it over and over, but their conviction isn't likely to sway scientists who assume that this is all nonsense. That's why Jung's example is so important. If this one example is accepted as beyond fraud, then it provides the counter-example to the current scientific view, and that view has to change. If there is a possibility that we have access to information not acquired in our lifetimes, then we have to scientifically explore just what the limits of such collective unconscious information are.

12

The Creativity of the Unconscious

The Computer Model

In the last chapter, we discussed at length Jung's patient's fantasy of the sun's penis creating the winds. It is important to recognize that the fantasy was not only collective; it was also purposeful. The patient brought up that material because he wanted to initiate Jung into religious mysteries; thus he somehow tapped into collective material about religious initiation. Just as we are able to access personal memories that fit our needs, such as how to drive a car, what the answer to an exam question is, etc., we also seem able to access collective material when it is needed.

Jung realized that everything emerges into consciousness out of the unconscious. When we call up our memories of how to drive a car, it is not our consciousness that organizes those memories and makes them available; clearly, something in the unconscious is able to organize the memories that are necessary and make them available to our conscious mind. In the example of driving a car, the remembered behaviors may never even reemerge into consciousness; we may drive the car with no conscious awareness that we are doing so. This whole process is a mystery to which we have grown so accustomed that we have come to view it as commonplace.

Behavioral psychology, for example, views behavior as a simple response to stimulus. They use the model of a reflex-arc, assuming that a stimulus leads immediately to a response. This model ignores the essential creativity that takes place in everyday life because it places all behavior at the same level; behavioral psychology sees no need for hierarchies of behavior.

Some examples that may show the complexity of the real-life situation follow.

For example, the part of our psyche that organizes and presents one with all the memories, psychic and muscular, needed to drive an auto, has to be on a higher level than the memories themselves. That is, there has to be something that organizes those memories; such an organizer is inherently at a different level of psychic organization than the memories it organizes. The unconscious is thus less a static repository of personal and collective material than an active organizational entity which serves and even anticipates the needs of consciousness.

A useful analogy can be made between the way the human mind operates and the way that a computer operates. The same computer can run many different programs, just as a human can perform many different behaviors. Both the computer and the human mind store their programs in some sort of long-term memory until they are needed. The computer also needs a special program normally called an Operating System (O/S) which operates at a higher level than any of the other programs. An O/S is like a foreman in a factory; it keeps things running smoothly. It knows which programs are running in the computer, which are waiting to run, and which have already run.

However, the O/S doesn't decide which programs need to be run, just as the foreman doesn't decide what products the factory should make. That is an executive decision; a human operator tells the computer which programs need to be run in what order of importance. The O/S then schedules the programs, locates them in its long-term memory, runs them when it has the time and resources to do so, prints the results, and stores the programs away again for later use.

Notice that there are at least three levels of operation at work here: (1) the executive level which decides which programs should be run; (2) a foreman level which keeps things running smoothly; and (3) a worker level which does the actual work we associate with the computer. By analogy, driving a car requires an executive decision on one level of the psyche, the organization and supervision of the necessary behaviors on a second level, and the actual behaviors on a third level. None of this is included in the stimulus-response model of the behavioral sciences. But even the computer model, which is more complex than the stimulus-response model, is woefully inadequate. It doesn't explain the extreme creativity of the unconscious.

An Anecdote About Dolphins

In an interview later published in an audio cassette tape, anthropologist Gregory Bateson discussed the creativity of the learning process (see Bateson,n.d.). He told of friends who had conducted research into the learning patterns of dolphins; they wanted to discover how many new behaviors a dolphin could learn and remember in succession. They taught a dolphin these new behaviors in the time-honored behavioral-science way, by rewarding it with food; in this case, the new behavior was to be some new, fancy way of jumping out of the water.

The experimenters waited until the dolphin spontaneously performed some new action, and rewarded him. When he repeated the behavior, he was rewarded again. However, once the new behavior was well-learned, they no longer rewarded him until he performed a second new behavior. This was a little frustrating to the dolphin, but it finally did something new by chance and once more got a reward.

As the experiment continued, the dolphin grew increasingly frustrated; it swam around and around its pool in an agitated fashion. Suddenly, it performed each of the behaviors it had already created in rapid succession, then immediately did a dozen new jumps and turns one after another.

Seemingly, the dolphin had extrapolated that each time it would have to demonstrate a new behavior, and hoped to cut the boring experiment short, and get all the rewards at once, by giving the scientists enough new behaviors to last them for a good while. This creative response has no place in either the stimulus-response model or the computer model.

It could be argued that the dolphin's response was a product of conscious reasoning, but the dolphin's behavior better fits what contemporary author Colin Wilson has dubbed the 'Eureka Effect" (in an interview contained on an audio cassette tape) (see Wilson,n.d.). The phrase comes from the apochryphal tale about the greatest of Greek mathematicians, Archimedes. Archimedes had brooded for weeks on the question of how to determine the volume of irregular solids. While bathing, he noticed that his body raised the level of the water. He jumped from the bath and ran naked through the streets yelling "Eureka" (literally, "I found it!").

Archimedes realized that he could put an irregular solid into a container of water, measure the increase in the volume filled by the water and that would be the volume of the solid. Colin Wilson felt that this anecdote described the key elements of the creative solution to any problem: intense immersion into all aspects of the problem, frustration when consciousness cannot resolve the issue, a moment of relaxation, then the burst into consciousness of an answer.

Arthur Koestler, in *The Act of Creation* (Koestler, 1964), discussed what is probably the most famous modern instance of the "Eureka Effect": the famous "ring-of-snakes" dream of chemist Friedrich August von Kekule. Kekule had worked for months in an attempt to discover the structure of the last remaining major organic compound: benzine. Then, one afternoon, while sitting in his study:

> I turned my chair to the fire and dozed, he relates. Again the atoms were gambolling before my eyes. This time the smaller groups kept modestly in the background. My mental eye, rendered more acute by repeated visions of this kind, could now distinguish larger structures, of manifold conformation; long rows, sometimes more closely fitted together; all twining and twisting in snakelike motion. But look! What was that? One of the snakes had seized hold of its own tail, and the form whirled mockingly before my eyes. As if by a flash of lightning I awoke . . . Let us learn to dream gentlemen.
>
> (quotation in ibid:118).

Such "ring" patterns had never previously been discovered in organic chemistry. Seemingly, Von Kekule's unconscious solved the problem for him, then presented the solution to his conscious mind in the form of a symbol which he could understand, that of a snake seizing its own tail.

Hypnotism and the Unconscious

The creativity of the unconscious can be clearly seen in hypnotic work. Earlier, it was pointed out how the use of hypnosis at Charcot's clinic led Freud to the discovery of the unconscious. James Braid's theory that hypnosis was caused by suggestion was the first Western psychological explanation of hypnotism. That has remained the accepted wisdom among most hypnotists until recently. The late Milton Erickson, generally considered the greatest clinical hypnotist of our time, thought otherwise. In one of his most important papers, "Hypnotic Psychotherapy", originally written in 1948, Erickson said that:

> Direct suggestion is based primarily, if unwittingly, upon the assumption that whatever develops in hypnosis derives from the suggestions given. It implies that the therapist has the miraculous power of effecting therapeutic changes in the patient, and disregards the fact that therapy results from an inner resynthesis of the patient's behavior achieved by the patient himself . . .
>
> . . . The therapist merely stimulates the patient into activity, often not knowing what that activity may be, and then guides the patient and exercises clinical judgement in determining the amount of work to achieve the desired results. How to guide and to judge constitute the therapist's problem, while the patient's task is that of learning through his own efforts to understand his experiential life in a new way.
>
> (Erickson,1980d:38f).

The author has used such methods in his clinical work with a variety of patients. The following case history from the author's clinical work shows how Ericksonian hypnosis taps the creativity of the unconscious to solve psychological problems.

The patient had recently made a nearly successful suicide attempt. Since then, many commonplace situations had become frustrating puzzles. She might hear the phone and have no idea what it was or what to do. Or she could be brushing her hair and then stare at the hairbrush, wondering what it was. Gradually, she was relearning the elements of her world and how to behave in that newly strange world. Meanwhile, she was vomiting dozens of times a day. She asked if something could be done to stop the vomiting.

A traditional hypnotist would put the patient into a hypnotic state, then suggest in many ways that she should stop vomiting. The hypnotist might guess from the patient's situation that she was filled with anxiety and concentrate on suggestions to relax her. The author tried instead Ericksonian techniques. After inducing a hypnotic state, he asked the patient's unconscious if it would be willing to solve the problem. Finger signals were used to get the unconscious to show that it agreed to take on the task.

A week later the patient came back thrilled. The vomiting had continued for another day. On the following day, she went to get a soft drink from the refrigerator. Without noticing it, she instead reached in the pantry next to the refrigerator and pulled out a box of noodles. She glanced at the box in surprise and decided to cook the noodles. She ate them and didn't vomit afterwards. For the rest of the week, she found herself enjoying cooking full meals rather than just grabbing snacks whenever the mood hit her. And she never vomited again.

Later in the treatment of the same patient, she began having "anxiety attacks". Again, rather than attempting to go directly after the problem, the author asked the unconscious to solve it. The unconscious agreed to substitute new behavior which would serve the same purpose as was served by the anxiety attacks themselves. Later in the week, when she started becoming very anxious, the patient spontaneously decided to clean out her fish tank.

This was something she had wanted to do for a long time. She cleaned the tank and went out and bought new fish. Not only did the purposeful action prevent the occurrence of the anxiety attack, the fish tank turned out to be a source of relaxation and tranquility to the patient. When she felt anxious, she watched the fish and grew calm. Her anxiety attacks quit entirely within weeks.

The examples in this chapter illustrate the creativity of the unconscious. They seem to imply that the unconscious is the breeding ground for the ideas and behaviors which only later become conscious. If so, then it becomes important to describe the dynamics of the relationship between consciousness and the unconscious. The next chapter begins a discussion of Jung's models of the dynamics of the psyche.

13

A Dynamic Model of the Psyche

How Archetypes Emerge Into Consciousness

As we have seen in the previous chapter, neither the behavioral model nor the computer model do justice to the complexity of the human psyche. In an important recent book, Charles Hampden-Turner presented 60 different *Maps of the Mind* (Hampden-Turner,1981). Very few of the models he described come close to capturing the dynamic quality of the human psyche; it is the dynamic relationship of conscious and unconscious that is so difficult to capture in any static model of the psyche. Jung pointed out that consciousness emerged from the unconscious rather than the other way around. His lifelong goal was to try and describe the nature and organization of the psyche in which such a dynamic could operate. It was this attempt to develop a dynamic model of the psyche that made Jung's task so difficult.

Since the unconscious itself was beyond examination, Jung could only infer its structure from unconscious material which emerged into consciousness. That's why Jung was so careful in his observation, recording and description of his patients' dream material. And that's why he was so fascinated with myths, fairy tales, primitive art and other material which he considered to contain unconscious material little changed by conscious artistic manipulation. In their primitive, untouched forms, all of these could help provide a picture of the organization and structure of the unconscious.

As was mentioned briefly in chapter 6, Jung initially referred to the "primordial images" (Jung,1966:101), and only later to the "archetypes" (Jung,1960:270) of the collective unconscious.

It is understandable that he originally thought of the archetypes as "primordial images", since it was the symbolic images that he encountered in the dreams of his patients. But he came to realize that the images were personal or cultural and that we could make no conclusions about the structure of the archetypes themselves.

> ... an archetype in its quiescent, unprojected state has no exactly determinable form but is in itself an indefinite structure which can assume definite forms only in projection.
> (Jung,1969:70).

As an example, all animals beyond a certain level of complexity appear to have an archetype for Mother. They instinctually know a great deal about what to expect from a Mother. But, as we discussed in chapter 9, Konrad Lorenz found that a baby goose's concept of "mother" could stretch to accommodate itself to the very un-gooselike Lorenz. The best way to express the situation seems to be that the archetype comes first, but it's empty until the actual experience gives it form. Of course, in saying this, we are merely saying that the actual structure of archetypes in the unconscious is beyond human observation. This is much the same as physicist David Bohm's hypothesis that there is an "implicate order" from which the "explicate order" of the physical world we know emerges (see Bohm,1980).

> It is in my view a great mistake to suppose that the psyche of a new-born child is a *tabula rasa* in the sense that there is absolutely nothing in it. In so far as the child is born with a differentiated brain that is predetermined by herdity and therefore individualized, it meets sensory stimuli coming from without not with *any* aptitudes, but with *specific* ones, and this necessarily results in a particular, individual choice and pattern of apperception. These aptitudes can be shown to be inherited instincts and preformed patterns, the latter being the *a priori* and formal conditions of apperception that are based on instinct. . . . It is not . . . a question of inherited *ideas* but of inherited *possibilities* of ideas [Jung's emphasis in all cases].
> (Jung,1969:66).

It is one thing to recognize that the psyche has both personal components and impersonal, collective components, and that the consciousness develops out of the unconscious. It is quite another to discover a process that adequately describes this complexity. As we saw in our discussion of Gustav Fechner in chapter 5, sensory perception is relational. As we saw in the discussion of Lorenz' goose, even complex relationships like that between mother and child seem to be carried in the child ready to be activated at the proper time.

> There are as many archetypes as there are typical situations in life. Endless repetition has engraved these experiences into our psychic constitution, not in the form of images filled with content, but at first only as *forms without content* [Jung's emphasis], representing merely the possibility of a certain type of perception and action. When a situation occurs which corresponds to a given archetype, that archetype becomes activated and a compulsiveness appears, which, like an instinctual drive, gains its way against all reason and will, or else produces a conflict of pathological dimensions, that is to say, a neurosis.
> (Jung,1969:48)

Let's take as an example the simplest of animals, the one-celled paramecium. A paramecium doesn't have to know a great deal to survive. It eats whatever it encounters that it recognizes as food; it runs from everything it encounters that it recognizes might eat it. The paramecium's body does not have to learn how to digest the food and how to propel itself away from danger; nor does its mind (if the term can be used that loosely) have to learn what food is and what an enemy is. Both the body's and the mind's knowledge is already stored in the paramecium because generations of its ancestors have experienced both food and enemies. Those remembered patterns are archetypes.

Archetype and Experience

Let's examine how a human baby first encounters the world through the lens of archetypal experience. Some of that archetypal experience takes visual form, some muscular; the former could be called the archetypal image, the latter instinct. But both are merely parts of the archetype itself, which cannot be other than inferred from the archetypal image and the instinctual behavior. It is the complex relationship between the archetype and consciousness that fascinated Jung.

Consider, for example, a human baby seeking its Mother's breast for nourishment. Since the breast isn't always there when the baby is hungry, the baby begins to realize that the breast is not like its own hands and feet, there to serve its needs whenever called upon. A baby's recognition that its mother's breast is separate from itself is a beginning of consciousness, a consciousness of baby as a thing separate and distinct from the rest of the world. This consciousness is the "ego", which emerges as the baby separates its concept of itself from its surroundings. And to help it in this separation are archetypal residues of the relationship between baby and Mother. As the baby experiences life, the archetype of Mother is given substance; the baby adds the knowledge of its particular Mother. But it's critical to realize that underneath that particular, personal experience is an archetype of Mother (and an archetype of "ego", but more of this later).

The recognition that the human mind has an enormous, perhaps infinite, depth of experience on which it can call, and that there is a correspondingly enormous number of archetypes, makes a crucial difference in understanding how we learn complex behaviors. For example, the capacity to learn language appears to most contemporary linguists to be inborn. It also explains why we learn so slowly when we are trying to solve a new situation, something that has never before been encountered by other members of the species. Biologist Rupert Sheldrake has shown that rat studies, the backbone of behavioral research, seems to support this view (see Sheldrake,1981).

Complex and Archetype

Above we have argued that the human psyche contains archetypes and that there are two sides to the archetype: archetypal image and instinct. We have argued further that we experience the world relationally and that the archetypes are activated in many, perhaps all, human situations. As we personally experience the world through the archetypes, the archetypes are given a particular, highly personal form. Eventually the world is almost entirely encountered through our personal memories; the archetypes lie deep within.

Jung had to discover this dynamic from the outside in. In patients, he encountered first their personal memories. In early experiments in word association, he found that patients responded more slowly to certain words. He gradually discovered that all of those words had something to do with a particular subject; e.g., the patient's personal experience of "mother." He called this grouping of memories around the experience of "mother" a "complex", in this case a "mother complex."

Since the patient's response was slower when the issue had to do with mother, Jung realized that the patient had some blockage inside around that concept. That is, there was energy trapped in the unconscious around the concept of mother. Much of the analytic task became a process of stripping away the personal memories in order to find out what lay at the core of this complex. Freud found Jung's concept of a complex extremely useful and appropriated it for his own use; he theorized that at the core of a complex was a primal sexual memory that the patient had repressed. In practice, Jung found that frequently that there was no single such memory, or that the memory wasn't sexual. More importantly, the complex still had energy for the patient after all of the personal memories were brought into consciousness. At the core of the "mother complex", for example, Jung found not a personal memory of mother but a collective, archetypal memory of the complex relationship between child and mother.

Thus archetypes are activated when necessary and accumulate personal memories around themselves to form complexes. We relate to things and people through these complexes. However, an additional element enters the picture to enormously broaden possibilities, and that element is consciousness.

The Emergence of EGO

Consciousness itself is as great a mystery as the unconscious. We think it less because we experience it directly. We are conscious of this or that, and take this mysterious relationship for granted. The core of consciousness is a sense of an "I", an "ego". All consciousness is in relationship to the ego; which thus forms the center of consciousness. Therefore, it seems that our sense of identity, and our consciousness are inseparable.

> The ego is a complex datum which is constituted first of all by a general awareness of your body, of your existence, and secondly by your memory data; you have a certain idea of having been, a long series of memories.
>
> (Jung,1968:10).

A few pages earlier, we discussed the complex relationship between archetype and experience, using the "Mother Archetype" as an example. We said that, as the baby discovers that the mother's breast is separate and distinct from itself, an awareness of self (i.e., ego) begins to take form.

> . . . [the ego] seems to arise in the first place from the collision between the somatic factor and the environment, and, once established as a subject, it goes on developing from further collisions with the outer world and the inner.
>
> (Jung,1959:5).

> . . . the ego [is] a complex of psychic facts. This complex has a great power of attraction, like a magnet; it attracts contents from the unconscious . . . it also attracts impressions from outside, and when they enter into association with the ego they are conscious. If they do not, they are not conscious.
>
> (Jung,1968:10).

The emergence of an ego appears to be the first dynamic interaction of the conscious and unconscious. The ego forms the center of consciousness and takes form at the boundaries where it experiences itself as separate from its surroundings. Like any other complex, it accumulates personal experience which grows to surround the ego archetype. As the center of consciousness it relates both to the sensory world outside and to the unconscious world inside.

With this brief description of the emergence of the ego, we conclude our discussion of the dynamic relationship between the archetypes of the collective unconscious and our sensory experience of the outer world. We are now ready to discuss the first of Jung's two models of the individuation process: that of the archetypes of Shadow, Anima/Animus, and Self.

14

The Shadow

Actual and Potential

Each of us forms our sense of identity, our ego, as much by defining what we aren't as by what we are. The baby who decides that his toes, though quite distant from his vision, are still part of his body, but the breast he suckles on, is not, is forming a sense of identity. Much of what we could be is only a potential; that potential may or may not come to be actualized and, thus, be included in our ego. For example, we might have an inborn potential for musical ability, but circumstances may never allow us to express that potential in life.

What does it mean to say that someone has an inborn potential for musical ability? It's a commonplace to say that it's "in their genes"; i.e., that someone has a genetic predisposition for musical ability in much the same way that they have a genetic predisposition toward blue eyes and brown hair. Today we realize that that genetic inheritance is a language coded with combinations of a mere four acids on helical paired chains of DNA and RNA. In fact, micro-biologists, using recombinant DNA techniques, have been able to change the DNA chains in viruses such that later generations of viruses have new properties, pre-determined by the scientists.

While the technology of such research is amazing, the critical fact is that DNA is a language of potentiality and scientific researchers are learning to read that language. It was initially thought to be a fairly straightforward language, but, with more study, researchers soon found that it was much more complex than first thought. For example, certain combinations were once thought to have unique meanings; now it is realized that they can have different meanings in different contexts. It was also once thought that DNA chains in a given organism were immutable; more recently, DNA chains with self-changing properties have been discovered. Undoubtedly, more research will reveal ever deeper mysteries in this exciting new field of science. However, it is likely to be a very long time before such research can ever say much about the question we have posed here; i.e., what does it mean to have an inborn potential for musical ability?

Different sciences normally deal not only with different fields of study, but also with different fields at different levels of organization. For example, chemistry exists as a separate science because physics cannot explain chemical interactions. Many scientists would argue that this is only because of the limitations of our present level of knowledge. Other scientists would assert that the organization of molecules, which is chemistry's domain, can never be reduced to an organization of atoms, which is the domain of physics. That is, when atoms reach a certain level of complexity those scientists would assert that something new comes into existence, which are called molecules. Correspondingly, when "organic" molecules reach a certain level of complexity, again something new comes into existence which we term cells. Again a new field of science is necessary to deal with this level of organization: biology. Since humans are conscious, we can presuppose that, at a certain level of organization of specialized brain cells, something new comes into existence once more: consciousness. Again a new field is needed: psychology.

Now perhaps the reductionists are right and science will eventually reduce consciousness to physics. Much of the point of this book's argument is that the relationship between physical and psychological is far too complex for this to ever happen. However, what is clear is that at the current state of science, physicists and chemists and biologists and psychologists are all needed, and no one field can explain all phenomena. That is why, exciting as the biological research into inherited traits and predispositions is, research like Jung's is equally necessary if we are to sort out how conscious and unconscious relate in the development of the individual human psyche.

Jung's studies indicated that some of the information which emerged into consciousness, such as his schizophrenic patient's vision of the sun's penis creating the winds, was collective. The exactness of detail of such collective memories is a far cry from a vague "inborn potential for musical ability", but both have to be included within any model that is to deal adequately with the human psyche. Instinctual behavior of even the simplest creatures is incredibly complex: the detailed, species-specific songs of birds; the intricate, species-specific webs of spiders; etc. There are seemingly very few limits on what can be passed on genetically. And, of course, humans are hardly limited to a repetoire of instinctual behavior; we have still a higher level of ability open to us: consciousness. We are only just beginning to explore the question of whether we are the only conscious beings.

We have already defined the ego as the center of consciousness, as that which we consciously "are". Since we are born with potentials that may or may not come to pass, Jung felt he needed another word to express the center of the unconscious where such potentialities lay unborn; this he termed the Self ["Self" will be capitalized in this paper to clearly separate its meaning from the more common use of "self"]. He referred to the circuitous course our lives take trying to evidence that potential as "individuation". We will have a great deal more to say about the Self in this paper, but for now it's enough to acknowledge that we are always something less than we potentially could be.

The Shadow

Ego-consciousness seems largely to come into existence at boundaries. At first there is a lack of differentiation; e.g., once more our example of baby and mother's breast. When we say "I am this", we are equally saying "I am not that", and vice-versa. Growth involves prohibitions and limitations of many sorts imposed by our physical, familial, and societal environments. A child who is praised for certain behaviors and scolded for others will soon exhibit only the approved behaviors. At first, the child needs the praise and scolding from its parents in order to remind it which are the good behaviors, which the bad. After a while, it no longer needs the parent's reminders; probably it hears them internally [note: this is Freud's Super-Ego]. Many a parent has secretly observed their child do some "naughty" behavior and then say to itself out loud: "bad girl [or boy]".

However, such an internal parent seems likely to be a transitional phase. After awhile, we "are" the person who exhibits such-and-such behaviors and doesn't exhibit other opposing behaviors. It's a more efficient state of mental organization to always behave a certain way than to have to make a decision whenever the issue comes up. Memories that we ever behaved in such "bad" ways recede from consciousness and we are no longer aware that we could ever behave any other way.

However, if that limited ego we develop deviates too far from our essential being (the Self), a compensatory figure forms in the unconscious: the Shadow. All those parts of our personal life which have been deemed unsuitable and denied collect around a single archetypal core. Everything we regard as bad, as "not us", accumulates around this center.

Like Freud, Jung used his patient's dreams as a window into the world of their unconscious. Early in analysis, a patient's dreams are frequently filled with strange, frightening Shadow figures. While the Shadow normally appears in dreams as a person of the same sex as the dreamer, early Shadow figures are less explicitly defined and frequently non-human: animals, aliens from another planet, sub-human figures. Gradually, as analysis progresses, Shadow figures develop more human characteristics, frequently passing from animals and aliens to dark-skinned people (in the dreams of caucasians) and others seen as primitives by the psyche: negroes, arabs, Indians, etc. This tends to have no relationship to the person's degree of outer prejudice or lack of it; the images come from deep places in the human psyche (see Travis,1978).

> ... the more remote a complex is from consciousness, the more unusual, bizarre, mana-filled, grandiose, or grotesque a symbol is apt to be.
>
> (ibid:224)
>
> ... What lay furthest away from waking consciousness and seemed unconscious assumes, as it were, a threatening shape, and the affective value increases the higher up the scale you go: ego-consciousness, shadow, anima, self.
>
> (Jung,1959:28).

As an analysis continues, Shadow figures evolve past primitives to strangers, to casual acquaintances, to friends. The progression is from the unknown, feared, despised to the known, respected, comfortable. The progression is also from a vague, ill-defined "otherness" to a precise, accurate portrait of the dreamer's particular shadow personality.

> ... as the patient gains in strength, the symbol for the same complex changes its form, and the change will follow a design which is roughly and generally uniform.
>
> (Travis,1978:232).

Projection and Transference

Freud was the first psychologist to discover the process of transference and projection; i.e., the patient's tendency to transfer or project his own conflicts onto the analyst. His description was highly accurate and ran as follows: neurosis is a symptom of the patient's inability to acknowledge and deal with an inner conflict. As long as the conflict remains unresolved, it occupies more and more of the patient's attention. Since the patient is not able to consciously acknowledge the source of the conflict, he encounters the conflict wherever he turns.

Since, during the period of therapy, his relationship with the analyst is likely to be the most important relationship in his life, the patient projects his inner conflict onto the therapist and experiences the conflict with the therapist. Jung saw projection and transference as much broader and more complex than Freud (see Von Franz,1980), but the limited sense of projection is helpful here in understanding Shadow issues.

If a person cannot admit that he has certain desires, such as sexual desires unconnected with love, he blocks such desires from consciousness. In the unconscious, they actively organize into a personified whole, which the dreamer might be willing to admit into consciousness, because the personification seems so clearly to be other than himself. Perhaps the dreamer is willing to acknowledge that there are primitive people, like natives of the South Seas, who indulge in wild sexual orgies. That is an image that the dreamer's consciousness can accept because it is so far from the dreamer's view of himself:

> We do not like to look at the shadow-side of ourselves; therefore there are many people in our civilized society who have lost their shadow altogether; they have got rid of it. They are only two-dimensional; they have lost the third dimension, and with it they have usually lost the body.
>
> (Jung,1968:23).

If the dreamer engages his consciousness with the dream-image, a struggle for resolution of the problem can begin. For example, if the dreamer starts to wonder how the natives can be debased enough to indulge in indiscriminate sexuality, he will gradually arrive at the realization that he also has such desires. It will be a long, tortuous path to arrive at an honest admission of his desires, but once a dialog between conscious and unconscious has begun, the problem has a chance to be resolved.

However, if the dream image is dismissed as having nothing to do with the dreamer, the need for resolution of this conflict grows stronger, and increasingly more emotional energy is diverted to the Shadow figure. When the energy level is high enough, the person can no longer hold it back and it bursts into consciousness. But since the patient still can't acknowledge that he is in any way like that wild, sexually-depraved native, he projects it out onto someone it seems to fit.

> ... it is not the conscious subject but the unconscious which does the projecting. Hence one meets with projections, one does not make them.
>
> (Jung,1959:17)

> ... Projections change the world into the replica of one's own unknown face.
>
> (ibid:9).

The fit doesn't have to be very close if the energy is strong enough. He might see any dark-skinned person as a sexual pervert. Or he might see anyone who disagrees with him on the issue of sexual morality as the Shadow figure. Frequently the issue is projected or "transferred" onto the analyst. Freud felt that psychoanalysts should reveal as little of themselves as possible to the patient; in that way, they formed an ideal blank screen on which the patient could project his conflict. Jung felt less sure of the value of the transference.

> Practical analysis has shown that unconscious contents are invariably projected at first upon concrete persons and situations. Many projections can ultimately be integrated back into the individual once he has recognized their subjective origin; others resist integration, and although they may be detached from their original objects, they thereupon transfer themselves to the doctor.
>
> (Jung,1966:6).

> ... Anyone who thinks that he must "demand" a transference is forgetting that this is only one of the therapeutic factors, and that the very word "transference" is closely akin to "projection"—a phenomenon that cannot possibly be demanded. I personally am always glad when there is only a mild transference or when it is practically unnoticeable.
>
> (ibid:8f).

The Shadow figures produced in dreams by the unconscious exactly mirror the issue; therefore, to the extent possible, dreams are the ideal place to deal with Shadow issues. If the Shadow is instead projected onto someone in the outer world, the fit is less perfect; it's rare that we encounter someone who exactly fits our Shadow. However, it is an unusual person who can work up the emotional energy to confront the Shadow figures of dreams with the same intensity that they can deal with the Shadow projections they encounter in the world. Therefore, integrating the personal contents of the Shadow normally takes an interaction with the outer world as well as with the Shadow figures in dreams.

The Shadow as Archetype

Jung did not develop the concept of the Shadow theoretically. Jung had observed that, in most patients, early dreams in an analysis were filled with Shadow figures and that the problems which first emerged in analysis were what has been characterized here as Shadow problems. He watched the Shadow figures evolve as the patient sorted out the personal from the collective. Jung's key realization was that though the type and variety of these Shadow figures, and the concomitant conflicts, was wide and varied (in no way limited to a sexual issue such as I've used as my example above), the nature of the problem at this stage was the same for all patients: how to get the patient to acknowledge that the Shadow figures were part of his own psyche, that he had such thoughts and desires. The issue at this stage was not how to deal with the desires; the issue was merely to acknowledge that one had such desires. This required great courage on the patient's part.

> The shadow is a moral problem that challenges the whole ego-personality, for no one can become conscious of the shadow without considerable moral effort. To become conscious of it involves recognizing the dark aspects of the personality as present and real. This act is the essential condition for any kind of self-knowledge, and it therefore, as a rule, meets with considerable resistance.
>
> (Jung,1959:14).

Jung saw that there was a single collective entity underlying the multiplicity of Shadow figures that appeared in dreams. He termed this collective entity the Shadow; the images with which the Shadow clothed itself in dreams were personal to the dreamer. In the following quotation, Jung speaks of the personification of another archetype, that of the Anima/Animus, but his argument applies equally to the personification of the Shadow.

> I have often been accused of personifying the anima and animus as mythology does . . . the personification is not an invention of mine, but is inherent in the nature of the phenomena. It would be unscientific to overlook the fact that the anima is a psychic, and therefore a personal, autonomous system . . . The anima is nothing but a representation of the personal nature of the autonomous system in question. What the nature of this system is in a transcendental sense, that is, beyond the bounds of experience, we cannot know.
>
> (Jung,1957:61).

It is critical in dealing with archetypes to understand that the archetype is not the image it wears any more than a man is the clothes he wears. The archetypes are eternal principles that reside in the human psyche. As such, they are beyond any individual humans ability to integrate into their personality. When the author, and sometimes Jung, speaks of "integrating" the Shadow (or any other archetype), we really mean integrating the personal experiences and memories that have clustered around the archetype of the Shadow. The archetypes, as collective entities, cannot be integrated into our individual consciousness without doing great harm to that individual consciousness. Our personal experiences accumulate around the archetypes to flesh them out. As time passes, we encounter an archetype only through a penumbra of such personal experiences and images. Once we are able to differentiate the personal experiences which surround the archetype from the collective experience of the archetype itself, and integrate the personal into our consciousness, the archetype is once again reduced to the collective and beyond our ability to integrate.

> . . . Though the *contents* [Jung's emphasis] of anima and animus [author's note: and the other archetypes as well] can be integrated they

themselves cannot, since they are archetypes. As such they are the foundation stones of the psychic structure, which in its totality exceeds the limits of consciousness, and therefore can never become the object of direct cognition. . . . Hence they remain autonomous despite the integration of their contents, and for this reason they should be borne constantly in mind.

(ibid:20).

The Expanded EGO

The original appearance of the Shadow in our dreams, or its projection out onto the outer world, comes about because the ego has accepted too limited a view of itself. The fact that the Shadow appears at all is evidence of the fact that the human psyche seems to have some function that pushes the individual toward his potential. Now this might be viewed as nothing more than a homeostatic principle, like a thermostat. When the temperature in a room deviates too far from a reference temperature, the thermostat turns the heater or the air conditioner off or on to compensate. However, even if that were all which took place in the human psyche (and the human psyche is hardly that simple), it would at least imply that there existed a reference point with which the ego could be compared. This reference point is again what Jung termed the Self. If the ego deviates too far from its potential Self, compensatory mechanisms go into action and, in our initial example, the Shadow appears.

As we have already illustrated, Shadow figures initially appear as feared or despised creatures. As a person confronts the Shadow figures and regains the parts of the Shadow that are actually part of his (or her) own personality, the Shadow figures evolve, until they are represented by close friends or relatives. By regaining those previously denied character traits, the ego expands; its range of choices, of possible behaviors expands. When confronted by situations, which previously led immediately to a single behavior, much like the behaviorists' stimulus-response model, now the person has a choice. And, of course, while an increase in choices means an expanded healthier existence, it also means an increase in moral dilemmas. At such a point, a new archetype enters the picture: the Anima/Animus.

> ... the more we become conscious of ourselves through self-knowledge, and act accordingly, the more the layer of the personal unconscious that is superimposed on the collective unconscious will be diminished.
>
> (Jung,1966:178).

> ... the integration of the shadow, or the realization of the personal unconscious, marks the *first stage* [author's emphasis] in the analytic process, and that without it a recognition of anima and animus is impossible.
>
> (Jung,1959:22).

15

The Anima/Animus

Body, Soul, Mind, and Spirit

Jung's studies of his patients' dreams and behavior convinced him that each of us, male or female, contains both masculine and feminine characteristics. Since males rarely consciously accept and use their feminine characteristics (nor, of course, females their masculine characteristics), those characteristics remain unconscious. In the unconscious, they personify into females figures, just as the unacknowledged male sides of our personality form into Shadow figures. This female within Jung called the Anima; the male within a woman he termed the Animus.

Where the Shadow was the personified archetypal expression of our hidden "personal" character traits, the Anima/Animus was farther from our personal experience. The Anima/Animus was a personified archetypal expression of the connection between conscious and unconscious. We have already discussed in chapter 13 how archetypes from the unconscious accrete personal experiences to form complexes, and how the ego, as the center of consciousness, is the most important of such complexes. The Anima/Animus forms the connection between the ego and the unconscious. As such, it is obviously a complex psychological function. However, it was Jung's discovery that this complex function is personified in the psyche by contra-sexual archetypal figures.

> The autonomy of the collective unconscious expresses itself in the figures of the anima and animus. They personify those of its contents which, when withdrawn from projection, can be integrated into consciousness. To this extent, both figures represent *functions* [Jung's

121

emphasis] which filter the contents of the collective unconscious through to the conscious mind. They appear or behave as such, however, only so long as the tendencies of the conscious and unconscious do not diverge too greatly. Should any tension arise, these functions, harmless till then, confront the conscious mind in personified form and behave rather like systems split off from the personality, or like part souls.

(Jung,1959:20).

Jung felt that the connecting function between conscious and unconscious in a male was the soul, but he used the Greek term for soul, Anima, to separate it from the religious overlay which Christianity had put upon the concept of soul. Jung's soul was the connecting link between body and spirit that the Greeks, and most other ancient cultures, referred to in the tripartite separation of a human into body, soul, and spirit.

... She is not an invention of the conscious, but a spontaneous product of the unconscious. Nor is she a substitute figure for the mother. On the contrary, there is every likelihood that the numinous qualities which make the mother-imago so dangerously powerful derive from the collective archetype of the anima, which is incarnated anew in every male child.

(Jung,1959:14).

However, Jung drew a major distinction between the Anima and Animus. While Anima is Greek for soul, Animus is Greek for mind or spirit.

... I have called the projection-making factor in women the animus, which means mind or spirit.

(Jung,1959:14).

Thus Jung already differentiates between the male and female condition, and their concomitant paths toward individuation. A man's task in resolving the problem of the Anima is to integrate his soul; a woman's in resolving the Animus to integrate her spirit. Obviously, this is because the course of development has already forced a man to integrate his mind, a woman her soul. Thus, the goal of each, in integrating the

Anima/Animus, is the same as was the case with the Shadow, the restoration of a missing wholeness.

As this book has pointed out repeatedly, since the Renaissance there has been a great development of the mind, at the expense of the body and emotions. With the increase in man's role as an objective observer of physical reality, mind began to withdraw from its previous unconscious unity with nature. However, the masculine split between mind and body was already well underway long before the Renaissance. Christianity stressed the need for subjugation of the body, with its sinful temptations, to the spirit which served God. Christianity, Buddhism, and Islam, the three great modern religions, each sounded this new theme in its own manner. The idea that the body is inherently evil was not central to more ancient religions, such as Hinduism and Judaism.

In the Middle Ages, Christianity effectively brought an end to any speculative thought that went beyond the bounds of dogma. However, Christianity did cause an enormous increase in theological thought. Theology, during the Middle Ages, centered on the need for man to increase his spiritual connection with God at the expense of his physical connection with reality. The Renaissance further increased that separation of mind and body as the observing mind turned its power upon the physical world. Men turned increasingly to the physical world for proof of speculative thought instead of to religious dogma. As men relied less and less upon the authority of religion, they also believed less in the spiritual experiences that underlie religion. The period since the Renaissance has seen the further separation of mind from spirit, splitting the tripartite division of body-soul-spirit still further into body-soul-spirit-mind. Unfortunately, during this development, the role of the soul, with its emphasis on feeling, valuing, relating, has been largely ignored.

While the author feels the above to be a fair summary of the history of the psyche since the Renaissance, from the masculine viewpoint, a question remains as to what that same history would look like from the feminine side. Obviously, as revisionist histories are written which point out the hidden role of women (and blacks and other minorities), much could be added to the above. But there is a deeper issue when we are considering not just history but the history of the psyche. The role of women has been ignored in history because women have been subjugated to men in most cultures. If this is because the feminine principle itself was subjugated within the psyche of both men and women, then the masculine picture presented in this book (and nearly every other such book) is justified.

Jung himself felt that a major transition was taking place in the human psyche in our time. This transition involved an attempt to restore a psychological wholeness which had been absent since man developed an ego. This new "conscious" wholeness would include an integration of the feminine principle. Incomplete attempts at wholeness, such as the Christian trinity, needed the addition of the feminine to become true symbols of wholeness. Such a recognition was a great attempt at bridging the gap between masculine and feminine, at a time when few yet recognized the importance of such a reconciliation.

Mandalas

Jung's studies of dreams and mythology convinced him that three-part divisions of reality, such as body-soul-spirit or the Christian trinity, were incomplete attempts to model the wholeness of reality. At times of stress, when a patient badly needs to restore psychological wholeness, dreams abound with four-part, bi-polar arrangements. Jung later discovered, in his studies of oriental religious symbolism, a counter-point to the symmetric figures that appeared in his patients' dreams; these were the beautiful symmetric patterns called Mandalas, the most satisfying of which are normally four-sided. These were exactly the sort of patterns Jung's patients spontaneously produced in their dreams and visions.

In Edward Edinger's *Ego and Archetype*, he reports on Rhoda Kellog's studies of pre-school art:

> The mandala or circle image seems to be the predominant one in young

children who are first learning how to draw. Initially a two-year-old with pencil or crayon just scribbles, but soon he seems to be attracted by the intersection of lines and begins to make crosses. Then the cross is enclosed by a circle and we have the basic pattern of a mandala. As the child attempts to do human figures, they first emerge as circles, contrary to all visual experience.

(Edinger, 1972:8).

This seems clear evidence that the mandala pattern is archetypal. If Jung is correct in his interpretation that the Christian trinity and the ancients' model of body-soul-spirit are failed attempts at a mandala, then the period of human history since the Renaissance can be seen as an attempt to evolve a new picture of wholeness. This wholeness would reflect a balance of four parts of the human being: Body, Soul, Spirit, and Mind.

Regardless of our philosophical and religious beliefs, all of us know intuitively what is signified by each of these four terms. We know what it means to have body experiences that have nothing to do with emotion. We know when emotional experiences have touched us to our soul. We can separate purely mental experience from spiritual experience. And we have all had experiences in which all of these parts seem to be participating equally in a harmonious whole. In his work with the psyche Jung encountered physical, emotional, intellectual, and spiritual problems; all are part of our common lot as human beings, and none should be excluded from any psychology that purports to deal with the whole man.

Repression and Integration

Man's unique task is to find a harmonious balance between the four divisions. Modern man has learned far too well how to use the mind to hold the body, soul and spirit in check. Families teach children how to control instinctual needs. Society further demands that individuals be willing and able to subsume their individual needs within society's needs. The mind's ability to control the instinctual and spiritual needs was a necessary step in the evolution of consciousness, but one that has gone too far. In dealing with Shadow issues, we are effectively reversing that process, recognizing that the body, soul and spirit have needs that must be acknowledged, not repressed.

Consider the body as an example; the body operates as a whole, not as a collection of separate parts. Before the overdevelopment of the mind at the expense of the body, it was normal for men to be much more consciously aware of the body than we are now. The ancient Greeks, who we admire so much for the products of their minds, assumed that the body and mind formed a whole with each influencing the other. In contrast, modern man has subjugated body to mind, and the body's needs frequently go unnoticed, unless it produces something dramatic like an illness to call attention to itself.

The body's primary need is for harmony in all its parts. It won't tolerate a one-sided development which works to the benefit of a kidney at the expense of the other organs that connect with it, for example. Since most of us are no longer able to listen to the body, we presume that its needs are limited to the simple gross needs that are the only ones that still penetrate into our consciousness: the needs for food, water, sex, sleep. In actuality, each of the individual parts of our four-part division of body-soul-mind-spirit seem to contain the other three. We have grown incredibly adroit at containing the body, emotions, and spirit within intellectual paradigms.

There is nothing inherently wrong with such a containment; it is a powerful tool which was unavailable to our ancestors. But the body also contains the mind, soul, and spirit; the soul contains the body, mind, and spirit, etc. When we subjugate our physical, emotional, and spiritual needs to our intellect for too long a period, they protest at the imbalance. The goal of the Christian era has been perfection: further, higher, more! Such perfection always subjects the whole to one of its parts. Jung stressed that man's goal was the integration of the separate parts into the whole. As we saw in the previous chapter, in our discussion of the Shadow, this need for wholeness seems to be an inherent function of the human psyche. The Shadow appears in dreams when there is too large an imbalance between the ego and the Self.

Wholeness can only be achieved if each of the four parts can harmoniously contain and honor the other three. Millions of years of evolution have enabled our bodies to record and adjust for every sensation, thought or feeling. No matter how overly cerebral we become, our body still breathes, circulates blood, digests food, etc. If the mind is hard at work, the body sends more oxygen and food to the brain. If we are in emotional pain, the body manufactures tranquilizing chemicals to reduce the pain. In moments of spiritual transcendence, the body controls breathing and other autonomic functions in order to produce a feeling of oneness. In other words, the integration of mind, soul, and spirit into the body is a wonderful gift of our evolutionary heritage; we all possess it without further effort.

For a male, the integration of the contents of the Shadow into the conscious personality can be seen as the final step in the integration of body, soul, and spirit within the mind. An integrated whole demands both control and harmony. The archetype of the Shadow is originally activated because the ego has accepted a limited definition of itself, at the expense of undeveloped possibilities or denied desires, frequently those of the body. Jung said that "the body is very often the personification of this shadow of the ego"(Jung,1968:23). Once the personal characteristics represented by the Shadow personality are accepted as part of the whole personality, mind is once more willing to acknowledge the needs of the body, soul, and spirit.

Of course, such an integration doesn't happen once and for all. We spend a lifetime recovering the personal traits that the Shadow has accumulated. None of us is ever so whole that he doesn't deny healthy parts of his personality out of laziness or fear or a myriad of other reasons. Rhoda Kellog's previously reported research on children's art shows that the need for wholeness seems inborn. We have already seen in our discussion of the Shadow that it appears when the ego deviates too far from a reference point that Jung called the Self. In the above presentation, the author has tried to present the integration of the Shadow using the model of body-soul-mind-spirit. Jung was continually looking for models which could help illustrate the process of individuation. It is important to realize that the process of individuation is an observable psychological process; the models are attempts to picture that process without doing too much damage by over-simplification.

The Masculine/Feminine Syzygy

Successful integration of the personal contents of the Shadow enables a man to accept that there are other parts to his personality. Until the Shadow is acknowledged, he is like a cardboard figure with no depth; afterwards, he has more faces than the one he happens to present to the world. Until the Shadow is integrated into the personality, the world appears filled with opponents, adversaries, who are actually products of the unconscious; afterwards, people can be seen as individuals. Though the Shadow, as an archetype which appears in all men, is collective, the resolution of the problem that the Shadow presents is accomplished by accepting parts of our unique personality that have previously been unnoticed or rejected; most shadow issues are thus personal issues. Anima/animus issues are much more complex.

> ... the more we become conscious of ourselves through self-knowledge, and act accordingly, the more the layer of the personal unconscious that is superimposed on the collective unconscious will be diminished.
> (Jung,1966:178).

> ... the most accessible of these [shadow, anima, animus], and the easiest to experience, is the shadow, for its nature can in large measure be inferred from the contents of the personal unconscious.
> (Jung,1959:8).

> Those who do succeed [in integrating the personal contents of the anima or animus] can hardly fail to be impressed by all that the ego does not know and never has known. This increase in self-knowledge

is still very rare nowadays and is usually paid for in advance with a neurosis, if not with something worse.

(Jung,1959:20f).

Men have always been both fascinated and mystified by women (and, of course, women by men). Materialist psychologists would have us believe that it is only because of the physical pull of sexuality, but there is so much more than just sex that draws men and women together. Jung stresses that the syzygy between masculine and feminine is an archetypal fact of the human psyche.

> We encounter the anima historically above all in the divine syzygies, the male-female pairs of deities. These reach down, on the one side, into the obscurities of primitive mythology, and up, on the other, into the philosophical speculations of Gnosticism and of classical Chinese philosophy, where the cosmogonic pair of concepts are designated yang (masculine) and yin (feminine). We can safely assert that these syzygies are as universal as the existence of man and woman.
>
> (Jung,1969:120).

In our time, a fascination with the characteristics of the opposite sex has nearly become an obsession. The woman's movement has encouraged women to try on the hitherto masculine robes of power and achievement. In equal numbers, men have begun to try on the feminine garb of sensitivity and vulnerability. At the more experimental fringes of society, attempts at androgyny abound. But even in the vast middle-class of society, it has become accepted practice for a man to sometimes help with the kids and housework, and for a woman to have a job to help provide part of the family's income. Both practices were almost unheard of until very recently.

This attempt to discover and develop the contra-sexual elements within our personality has created a confusing time for most of us. Jung recognized this difficulty seventy years ago in his studies of the Anima/Animus. Shadow issues required courage to resolve, the courage to face the dark side of our psyche. But the actual personality traits which the Shadow possesses are known quantities. After we give up our protests, we recognize the face in the mirror. At base, all men share the same physical and emotional experience. However, a man does not consciously know what it is like to be a woman (nor a woman to be a man). The psychological worlds inhabited by men and women have been separate in nearly every culture and time. In almost every culture throughout history, women's roles have centered around the home and family, men's roles around the world outside the home.

Cultural or Biological?

In the first throes of the sexual revolution around us, it was common-place to profess that the only differences between men and women were cultural. Researchers in many fields began, for the first time, to study male/female differences. They have found that the differences are varied and deep. The study of the nature and origin of such differences has become a broad one that includes psychologists, sociologists, anthropologists, biologists, socio-biologists, ethologists, historians and practitioners in other sub-fields too numerous to name.

The author doesn't intend to examine any of this fascinating literature in this book. The point-at-issue here is merely that virtually all current scientific study indicates that there are distinct psychological and behavioral differences between men and women, and that those differences are not merely cultural. Further, a great deal of the literature supports Jung's point that, not only are men and women different, they also seem to possess the characteristics of the opposite sex in an undeveloped form.

> No man is so entirely masculine that he has nothing feminine in him
> . . . The repression of feminine traits and inclinations naturally causes these contrasexual demands to accumulate in the unconscious.
> (Jung,1966:297).

At the biological level, it is easy to see why men contain undeveloped feminine characteristics and vice-versa. A male is merely a female with a missing X-chromosome. The male sex organs develop as an add-on to the natural simplicity of the female sex organs. Without sufficient amounts of the male sex hormone, testosterone, at key points in development, the male would develop into the female. Both sexes have characteristic chemical and hormonal balances that vary within characteristic cyclic patterns. This biological picture of developed differences coupled with undeveloped similarities seems to be repeated in the psyches of men and women.

Anima and Animus

Jung discovered that the Anima/Animus was further away from consciousness than the Shadow. While the Shadow as archetype is collective and impersonal, its contents are largely personal. The Anima/Animus, as the bridge between conscious and unconscious, is much less personal. Because of that distance from personal awareness, Anima/Animus issues are much more complex to resolve. Throughout the ages, men and women have learned how to relate to each other without ever learning what the other's experience is like. The relationship between men and women is like a dance where each responds to the other's movements. Similarly, dealing with the contra-sexual elements within is also like a dance, where each shifts in response to the other. What seems to be archetypally contained within all of us is the experience of the opposite sex in myriads of different situations.

Dealing with Anima/Animus issues brings more of those archetypal experiences into consciousness where we can integrate the experiences into our personal lives. When a man integrates the contents of the Shadow, he integrates hitherto unadmitted masculine personality traits. In contrast, when a man integrates the contents of the Anima, he integrates the broadened possibilities of relating to the feminine. If a man is the stereotypical macho, dominating, unemotional type, he learns the experience of being responsive instead of dominating, caring instead of unemotional. But he learns these characteristics within the framework of being a male relating to a woman. He doesn't become a woman.

> ... We can see how it is possible to break up the personifications, since by making them conscious we convert them into bridges to the unconscious. ... They cannot be integrated into consciousness while their contents remain unknown. The purpose of the dialectical process is to bring these contents into the light; and only when this task has been completed, and the conscious mind has become sufficiently familiar with the unconscious processes reflected in the anima, will the anima be felt simply as a function.
>
> (Jung,1966:210).

Because Jung's concern with the Anima and Animus was in large part to help his patients, he wrote a great deal about the characteristics that the Anima and Animus exhibit when they "confront the conscious mind in personified form." Jung provided one short summary of their characteristics which is especially useful in this discussion.

> If I were to attempt to put in a nutshell the difference between man and woman in this respect, i.e., what it is that characterized the animus as opposed to the anima, I could only say this: as the anima produces moods, so the animus produces opinions.
>
> (Jung,1966:331).

What is a "mood"; how does a "mood" differ from a feeling, for example? The author would suggest that moods are collective, feelings are personal. Depression and elation are both examples of moods. Both are collective, independent of consciousness. In contrast, a feeling is relationship between a conscious ego and a thing or person. We say "I like you", or "I hate that". Without the conscious sense of identity, there is no feeling. A mood envelops the ego, swallows it. A depressed person has little or no sense of identity; they become the depression. Moods can be seen as unconscious collective substitutes for conscious feelings. Thus, to the extent that a man can learn to accept his feelings and relate to people and things through those feelings, there is no need for the Anima to project collective moods onto the outer world.

Opinions are analogous. We have strong, unyielding opinions on those issues we haven't really thought about. The strength of the opinion lies in its collective unconscious nature. A woman, in the grip of her Animus, cannot consciously examine the opinions she expresses, any more than a man, in the grip of the Anima, can feel the mood he's possessed by. Therefore, when the man is relating to a woman through his Anima, and the woman to the man through her Animus, we get a combination of the worst qualities of each.

> . . . when animus and anima meet, the animus draws his sword of power and the anima ejects her poison of illusion and seduction.
> (Jung,1959:15).

Though words like thoughts and feelings are poor substitutes for the fullness of the Shadow and Anima, they can help. Jung was continually trying to find ways to deal with the full complexity of the archetypes. In his early writings he used the Greek words Logos and Eros, instead of thoughts and feelings as has been used in this paper. But, in time, he rejected these terms as unsatisfactory, largely because they were too removed from the actual experience of the archetypes.

> . . . I do not, however, wish this argument to give the impression that these compensatory relationships were arrived at by deduction. On the contrary, long and varied experience was needed in order to grasp the nature of anima and animus empirically. Whatever we have to say about these archetypes, therefore, is either directly verifiable or at least rendered probable by the facts.
> (Jung,1959:14).

As we will see later in chapters 17 and 18, Jung eventually turned to alchemy as a source of symbols better able to picture the inner processes of the psyche. A famous alchemical picture in a fourteenth century text portrays the process of masculine psychic development as a tree sprouting from the genital area of a man wounded by an arrow in his side (see Jung,1968:357). In a sixteenth century alchemical text, a woman's developmental path is shown as a tree sprouting from the crown of the head of a fully erect, physically powerful woman (see Fabricius, 1976:133). These pictures express the complexity of the issues. The integration of the Shadow leaves a man fully a man, a woman totally a woman. The integration of the Anima/Animus is much more complex because it defines a man in relationship to the world, which he experiences through his relationship with women, and similarly for a woman.

The alchemical pictures portray the differences in the two journeys. The man has to be wounded, forced to turn in upon himself. The woman has to stand strong and erect. Obviously, both are stances unnatural to the sexes as we know them. The tree representing a man's process of individuation is shown growing from his sex organs, as a symbol of his instincts, the source of his deepest sensations and feelings, and of his creativity. The tree representing the woman's process of individuation grows from the top of her head, the source of rationality and judgement. Both paths of individuation are pictured as trees to symbolize the organic quality of the growth that has to take place. Clearly, the symbolic pictures describe more than can be captured by merely saying that the Anima represents a man's feelings, the Animus a woman's thinking.

However, regardless of the oversimplification involved in the statement, the integration of the personal contents of the Anima does enable a man to accept his feelings as a part of him. Such a man feels a sense of rootedness, of meaning; he is able to relate equally to the world outside him and the world inside through his deepest feelings. For a woman, integrating the personal contents of the Animus enables her to accept that rational thoughts are a necessary part of life. She is able to act in both the inner and outer world with the swiftness of thought. Freed from the need to be projected onto reality, the Anima/Animus can return to its psychological function of bridging the gap between conscious and unconscious.

> However, all these traits, as familiar as they are unsavoury, are simply and solely due to the extraversion of the animus. The animus does not belong to the function of conscious relationship; his function is rather to

> facilitate relations with the unconscious. : . . . the animus, as an associative function, should be directed inwards, where it could associate the contents of the unconscious.
>
> (Jung,1966:208f).

In both cases, to return to our earlier model of body-soul-mind-spirit, this integration marks the integration of body, mind, and spirit within soul. However, in considering such four-fold models, it is well to remember, as Jung always stressed, that while quaternities represent wholeness, wholeness can be represented by more than one such quaternity. It is also well to remember that the integration of the Anima/Animus, even more than the integration of the Shadow, is a life-long process to which we return over and over during the process of individuation.

> . . . a content can only be integrated when its double aspect has become conscious and when it is grasped not merely intellectually but understood according to its feeling value. Intellect and feeling, however, are difficult to put into one harness—they conflict with one another by definition.
>
> (Jung,1959:31).

> The shadow can be realized only through a relation to a partner, and anima and animus only through a relation to a partner of the opposite sex, because only in such a relation do their projections become operative. The recognition of the anima gives rise, in a man, to a triad, one third of which is transcendent: the masculine subject, the opposing feminine subject, and the transcendent anima. With a woman the situation is reversed. The missing fourth element that would make the triad a quaternity is, in a man, the archetype of the Wise Old Man . . . and in a woman the Chtonic Mother. These four constitute a half immanent and half transcendent quaternity.
>
> (Jung,1959:42).

Thus Jung recognized that there was still a further level of the individuation process, where the archetype of the Wise Old Man or the Chtonic Mother was activated. In the formulation I have presented earlier, this is the stage of the integration of body, mind, and soul into the spirit. In terms of Jung's three major archetypes of the process of individuation, the archetype that followed the Shadow and the Anima archetypes was the Self, which we have discussed very briefly in earlier chapters, and which will be our next topic of discussion.

16

The Self

Jung found that beyond the Anima/Animus archetype was an archetype of transcendence and wholeness he called the Self. By capitalizing Self, he meant to imply an entity that is both personal and transcendent. Today, many psychological paradigms talk of a Higher Self, a God within, etc.; these closely match Jung's concept of the Self. However, few of these modern paradigms as yet capture the complexity Jung found in the Self. The Self seemed to be the paradox from which all paradox originated.

Its representations in dreams reflected this paradoxicality. Sometimes, it appeared in god-like form to fit our human expectations; but sometimes it appeared as an animal, much like the gods who appeared in animal form to our ancestors. Sometimes the Self appeared as some natural force, as when God appeared to Moses as a burning bush, or even an abstract design that approached Spinoza's abstract view of God. Usually the Self could be identified beneath its masks by the incredibly powerful impact it had on the dreamer. But sometimes, like Zeus walking on earth in disguise, the Self appeared as some common-place figure one hardly noticed until much later.

The Self, as Jung experienced it, could not be limited by human expectations. More than either the Shadow or the Anima/Animus, the Self appeared to be beyond restrictions of space or time. In general, Jung found that at the deepest levels of the unconscious, there were no longer any such limits; dreams could roam over times hundreds or even thousands of years in the past; dreams could show occurrences years in the future. The Self could be the dreamer's deepest personality, the process of development, and the goal of the process, all wrapped up in one entity. Equally, the Self transcended all limits of personal morality, yet its ethics possessed a rightness at some deep level that could not be denied.

Clearly, a symbol of such complexity cannot be approached directly. One has to enter the domain of the Self by the side door, so to speak. Let us make an oblique approach by way of the "symbol", for Jung meant something deep and abiding when he called something a symbol. And to arrive at Jung's concept of the symbol, we must first consider his own confrontation with the symbolic world of the unconscious.

The Confrontation With The Unconscious

When Jung published *Symbols of Transformation* in 1912 (originally titled *Transformations and Symbols of the Libido*; extensively rewritten in the 2nd edition of 1952, which is published as Volume 5 of the Collected Works), he extended the symbolic interpretation of dreams far beyond the sexual interpretation Freud declared to be holy dogma for psychoanalysis. Jung examined the fantasies of a woman referred to as "Miss Frank Miller", which Theodore Flournoy had published in 1906. There is an oft-quoted cliche that Freudian patients have Freudian dreams and Jungian patients have Jungian dreams. Since Jung had no personal contact with "Miss Miller", this book stands as a document to the lack of validity of the above cliche.

In it, Jung traced the "transformations and symbols of the libido" from tiny seeds in the early fantasies to full-blown development in the later fantasies. In *Psychology and Alchemy* (volume 12 of the Collected works, published in 1952, based on lectures given in 1935 and 1936), Jung repeated this task with a series of four hundred dreams and visions of a patient with whom Jung had no personal contact. However, just as the early dreams and fantasies of a patient contain the seeds of later developments, Jung's earlier work contained the seeds of his later developments. Though Jung strove mightily to use

Freud's interpretations wherever possible, he ranged far beyond sexual reductionism.

Jung drew extensively on mythology to amplify images in "Miss Miller's" fantasies and show how her psyche was attempting to re-establish a psychic wholeness. Because "Miss Miller" was incapable of integrating the forces of the unconscious, and because her therapist also did not understand the process enough to help her integrate such forces, she eventually had a psychotic break. Jung carefully described how each element of the fantasies related to her on-going problems and showed the slow deterioration of the psyche due to the lack of conscious integration. The author had a patient in a similar situation, flooded with material from the unconscious in an attempt to restore psychic wholeness. She had already made one suicide attempt and was considering another. By helping her understand this strange material which bombarded her consciousness, the author reduced her fear. In under six months, she left therapy, totally transformed, not by therapy and not by conscious effort, but rather by her ability to integrate the material thrust upon her by the forces of the unconscious.

Freud selected Jung to be his successor. However, the price Jung had to pay for this honor soon proved too high; Freud wanted Jung to accept his views uncritically. Freud viewed Jung as his favorite son; Jung's new ideas seemed to Freud to represent the Oedipal desire of a son to destroy his father. Freud in turn disinherited his "son" and "cast him forth into the wilderness" [the author's biblical quotation, not Freud's]. Having published *Symbols of Transformation*, Jung became "persona non grata" to psychoanalysts everywhere. He was forced to resign all his positions in the psychoanalytic community; excommunication would be a fair term for what Jung experienced.

Jung had admired Freud deeply and found his exclusion a painful isolation. But he decided that if he was right, and Freud was wrong, then he would have to explore the unconscious forces within himself no matter where they took him. During the period from 1913 to 1917, a so-called "fallow period" where

Jung published little but in actuality laid the groundwork for most of his later publications, Jung did just that. Where before he had sometimes interposed Freudian theory between himself and the figures that appeared in his dreams, now he let himself sink deeply into dreams and visions, much like inducing a psychosis. In *Memories, Dreams, Relections*, Jung commented on his reaction to his split with Freud, and on his psychic state during this period.

> After the parting of the ways with Freud, a period of inner uncertainty began for me. It would be no exaggeration to call it a state of disorientation . . . I avoided all theoretical points of view and simply helped the patients to understand the dream-images by themselves, without application of rules and theories. Soon I realized that it was right to take the dreams in this way as the basis of interpretation, for that is how dreams are intended.
>
> (Jung,1965:170f).

> I lived as if under constant inner pressure. At times this became so strong that I suspected there was some psychic disturbance in myself. Therefore I twice went over all the details of my entire life, with particular attention to childhood memories [author's note: since, if Freud was correct, this is where the problem must lie]; for I thought there might be something in my past which I could not see and which might possibly be the cause of this disturbance. But this retrospection led to nothing but a fresh acknowledgement of my ignorance. Thereupon I said to myself, "Since I know nothing at all, I shall simply do whatever occurs to me." Thus I consciously submitted to the impulses of the unconscious.
>
> (ibid:173).

In order to keep stability in his life during this period, he kept regular office hours with patients, and spent a normal amount of time with his wife and children. When the energy from the unconscious grew too overpowering, he would do Yoga exercises, which helped to contain the energy. But the rest of the time, he allowed himself to journey into the strange land of the unconscious.

> An incessant stream of fantasies had been released, and I did my best not to lose my head but to find some way to understand these strange

things. I stood helpless before an alien world. . . . I was living in a constant state of tension; often I felt as if gigantic blocks of stone were tumbling down upon me. One thunderstorm followed another. My enduring these storms was a question of brute strength . . . when I endured these assaults of the unconscious I had an unswerving conviction that I was obeying a higher will, and that feeling continued to uphold me until I had mastered the task. . . . To the extent that I managed to translate the emotions into images—that is to say, to find the images which were concealed in the emotions—I was inwardly calmed and reassured. Had I left those images hidden in the emotions, I might have been torn to pieces by them . . . as a result of my experiment I learned how helpful it can be, from the therapeutic point of view, to find the particular images which lie behind emotions.

(ibid:176f).

From 1913 to 1917, Jung lived in this symbolic world. He explored every dream and vision. No image was ignored from fear or laziness. As time passed, and he weathered the storms that raged within him, he slowly developed a psychic center where there was always calm, even during the storms. Finally, "the stream of fantasies ebbed away" (ibid:206), and he could take stock of the world he'd explored. An unusually rich period of creativity followed.

If there was one thing Jung had learned during this trying period, it was the power of the images of the unconscious. Jung's split with Freud was caused by many differences, but primary was his disagreement with Freud's sexual reduction of dream images; e.g., a key is a penis, a cave is a vagina. In his work with patients, Jung had come to feel that dreams were far too complex for such easy translation. Now Jung had experienced the dream world first hand, and knew not only intellectually, but emotionally, that a symbol was far more than a sign.

The Symbol

In *Psychological Types* (volume 6 of the Collected Works), one of the first works written after Jung emerged from his isolation, Jung included a nearly hundred page long section of "Definitions". In reality, these were miniature essays on fifty-seven terms that Jung felt to be critical to any understanding of psychology. Almost a quarter of the section was spent on three terms: (1) fantasy, (2) image, and (3) symbol. Clearly Jung felt that these were central. His mini-essay on the "symbol" is not widely quoted, yet brings together many key concepts that appear nowhere else in his writing; it deserves the extensive quotation and discussion that follows.

> The concept of a symbol should in my view be strictly distinguished from that of a sign. Symbolic and semiotic meanings are entirely different things . . . so long as a symbol is a living thing, it is an expression for something that cannot be characterized in any other or better way. The symbol is alive only so long as it is pregnant with meaning. But once its meaning has been born out of it, once that expression is found which formulates the thing sought, expected, or divined even better than the hitherto accepted symbol, then the symbol is dead, i.e., it possesses only an historical significance.
>
> (Jung, 1971:814ff).

> An expression that stands for a known thing remains a mere sign and is never a symbol. It is, therefore, quite impossible to create a living symbol, i.e., one that is pregnant with meaning, from known associations. For what is thus produced never contains more than was put into it. Every psychic product, if it is the best possible expression at the moment for a fact as yet unknown or only relatively known, may be regarded as a symbol.
>
> (ibid:817).

Jung clearly distinguished symbols from signs here. A sign stands for something known; it is derivative, where symbols precede conscious understanding. Hence a symbol is reduced to a sign after the mystery it represented is fully understood. Consider the cross as a symbol. Jung commented that:

> . . . The way in which St. Paul and the earlier speculative mystics speak of the cross shows that for them it was still a living symbol which expressed the inexpressible in unsurpassable form.
>
> (ibid:816).

Though Jung never used the term "archetype" in this essay, there was a clear indication that he was discussing one of the two possible ways in which archetypes came into existence. In several contexts previously in this book, we have considered the other possibility; i.e., objects and events that have had meaning for a large number of people for a long period of time leave a record in the human psyche.

Though materialists would argue about where such a record is kept (occult literature refers to such material as Akasic Traces; i.e., a trace in the ether; to indicate clearly that such a record is not contained in matter), such a concept could clearly be assimilated into science as we know it. Biologist Rupert Sheldrake has recently postulated exactly such a premise; he calls the process "morphic resonance". He has drawn extensively on behavioral research with rats, probably the most materialistic branch of experimental psychology, to argue for this "morphic resonance" (Sheldrake,1981).

However, it is quite another thing to argue that the archetype comes first and the objects or events that mirror it follow afterwards. But how else to explain creativity? In Bateson's story of the highly creative dolphin, in Archimedes' "Eureka" experience, in von Kekule's dream of a chain of snakes, we have seen examples of the normal way in which creativity operates in our lives.

When conscious methods are insufficient to resolve an issue, emotional energy is diverted into the unconscious. The longer the issue remains unresolved, the more the pressure builds. Eventually, something bursts forth into consciousness that is the "best possible expression at the moment for a fact as yet unknown" (to use Jung's terms). If the problem that needs resolution is not confined to a single person, but rather engages most of humanity over a large period of time, then the emotional energy is correspondingly greater, as is the pressure, and as is the eventual symbol that emerges.

> . . . Since, for a given epoch, it [the living symbol] is the best possible expression for what is still unknown, it must be the product of the most complex and differentiated minds of that age. But in order to have such an effect at all, it must embrace what is common to a large group of men. This can never be what is most differentiated, the highest attainable, for only a very few attain to that or understand it. The

common factor must be something that is still so primitive that its ubiquity cannot be doubted.

(ibid:820).

In our era, where living symbols are in short supply, people turn to past symbols, like the cross or the flag, pretending that they still have energy. Those too honest to delude themselves in such a way frequently despair of any new meaning ever emerging. They delude themselves with litanies of despair, such as existentialism or nihilism, as if the pronouncement that all was meaningless itself possessed some inherent meaning. Both groups deeply yearn for meaning and purpose in their lives. Over sixty years ago, Jung discussed the role of the individual in bringing a new archetypal symbol into existence.

> . . . Only the passionate yearning of a highly developed mind, for which the traditional symbol is no longer the unified expression of the rational and the irrational, of the highest and the lowest, can create a new symbol.
>
> But precisely because the new symbol is born of man's highest spiritual aspirations and must at the same time spring from the deepest roots of his being, it cannot be a onesided product of the most highly differentiated mental functions but must derive equally from the lowest and most primitive levels of the psyche. For this collaboration of opposing states to be possible at all, they must first face one another in the fullest conscious opposition. This necessarily entails a violent disunion with oneself, to the point where thesis and antithesis negate one another, while the ego is forced to acknowledge its absolute participation in both. If there is a subordination of one part, the symbol will be predominantly the product of the other part, and, to that extent, less a symbol than a symptom—a symptom of the suppressed antithesis . . . But when there is full parity of the opposites, attested by the ego's absolute participation in both, this necessarily leads to a suspension of the will, for the will can no longer operate when every motive has an equally strong countermotive. Since life cannot tolerate a standstill, a damming up of vital energy results, and this would lead to an insupportable condition did not the tension of opposites produce a new, uniting function that transcends them. . . .
>
> From the activity of the unconscious there now emerges a new content, constellated by thesis and antithesis in equal measure and standing in

> a compensatory relation to both. It thus forms the middle ground on which the opposites can be united.
>
> ... The stability of the ego and the superiority of the mediatory product to both thesis and antithesis are to my mind correlates, each conditioning the other. . . .
>
> I have called this process in its totality the "transcendent function", "function" being here understood not as a basic function but as a complex function made up of other functions, and "transcendent" not as denoting a metaphysical quality but merely the fact that this function facilitates a transition from one attitude to another.
>
> (ibid:823–828).

Thus Jung explained exactly how the individual could help bring a new symbol into existence. It requires the "passionate yearning of a highly developed mind" as well as the acceptance of a "violent disunion with oneself". To the extent that a person avoids the tension by giving primacy to either the spiritual or the instinctual side of the problem, the emerging product is "less a symbol than a symptom." If one bears the tension, and does not yield to the pull of one side or the other, "the tension of opposites produces a new, uniting function that transcends them."

The thesis of this entire book has been that the twentieth-century is a time when the tension has reached the breaking point. We have seen the twin poles of spirit and instinct pull people in first one direction, then in the other. From the sixties to now, for example, we have seen the spokespeople for the sexual revolution avow the primacy of instinct; the followers of the "born again" movement the primacy of spirit. Back and forth the pendulum has swung, carrying people in its wake. But neither side of the pendulum's swing can contain a final answer.

The power and mystery of the unconscious can easily overwhelm. In his own five year struggle, Jung found of necessity that the ego had to be strong and vital in its turn. Only the equal and opposite pull of conscious and unconscious can produce a true synthesis. Too often, when one discovers the power of the unconscious, one discounts one's own power and yields abjectly to the unconscious. Or, alternately, one arrogantly assumes that all these strange new things belong to oneself. Many people of our time, no longer finding any meaning in traditional western symbols, are turning to eastern symbols, and therein lies a danger. In order to address this, we need to take a short detour through Jung's ideas on the Eastern spiritual traditions.

Eastern Spiritual Traditions

Eastern spiritual traditions have long examined the interplay of conscious and unconscious mind. Jung read widely in such traditions, but was forced sadly to reject them as offering guidelines for Westerners to use. Jung felt that Western tradition had developed the individual ego at the expense of the collective ego. Therefore, Westerners had first to deal with the Shadow that formed in the unconscious in opposition to the ego.

Jung saw that Easterners had the opposite problem. Their tradition had developed a collective ego at the expense of the individual ego. Therefore, Eastern spiritual paths start from their place of strength, the collective ego, and further dissolve the individual ego. This slowly forms a compensatory individual ego within the unconscious which only appears fully developed at the end of the spiritual journey.

Hindu, Buddhist and Sufi masters who have emerged from this training tend to be strong individualists who couple wisdom with personal idiosyncracies in an appealing whole. Jung realized that when Westerners try to dissolve their personal ego before they have resolved Shadow issues, Shadow issues grow to godlike proportions. Therefore, Jung felt that the Eastern paths were dangerous for Westerners, that a Western path must be found.

The Self as the Transcendent Function

This chapter has already ranged quite a distance without a direct discussion of the Self. We followed Jung's confrontation with the unconscious and saw how it led Jung to appreciate the strength and primacy of the images of the unconscious. We then examined Jung's thoughts on the concept of the symbol. We saw that a symbol is not merely a sign; that a symbol is an attempt to express something as yet not understood. We saw how, in times like our own, there is a desperate attempt to synthesize a new "living symbol" that can once more satisfy our mutual need for meaning. However, we saw that such a synthesis can only occur if the tension between opposites, such as instinct and spirituality, is accepted as necessary. If either instinct or spirituality is considered to have all the answers, no synthesis occurs. When only one side of the polarity is honored, Jung said that a "symptom", not a symbol, emerges.

The mystery, of course, is how such a "living symbol" does emerge. As Jung has carefully pointed out, such a symbol cannot be a product of consciousness alone; it can only be produced by the opposition of conscious and unconscious, and within that opposition, it is the unconscious which gives it birth. That seems to necessitate the existence of a function in the unconscious whose purpose is to restore wholeness in the organism, whether the organism is a person or a civilization. If there isn't such a function, how is it that creative solutions originate, how is it that new "living symbols" emerge that capture a person or even all the people of an epoch?

It is easy to see how such a function serves a causal, compensatory purpose. The organism is a whole of which consciousness is only a part. When consciousness becomes too one-sided for the organism's good health, some function is necessary to balance the one-sidedness and restore health. At this level, the function is little more than a complex version of a thermostat, cooling things down when they get too hot, heating them up when too cold.

> The self [author's note: this function will soon be presented as one aspect of the Self] could be characterized as a kind of compensation of the conflict between inside and outside.
>
> (Jung,1966:239).

But this function also seems to serve a teleological purpose. In *Symbols of Transformation*, and later in *Psychology and Alchemy*, Jung described how later developments were prefigured in early fantasy images. The resolution of Jung's personal crisis, which began with his "excommunication" by Freud, not only restored him to psychic health, but also produced a change of viewpoint which provided Jung with the material he developed more fully over the rest of his life. The author's patient, who felt in such psychic danger that she had to attempt suicide, was restored not merely to health; she was transformed into a new, far more creative woman than before.

The wholeness which emerges from the unconscious is not a return to the way things were before the crisis and is not contained in either side of the earlier, seeming dichotomy. This book opened with the discussion of the plight of twentieth-century man, who has had to watch all his vaunted institutions crumble around him. It seems clear that neither side of the many argumentative polarities we see around us has the final answer. Must art be abstract or must it mirror physical reality? Must music be harmonic or must it be atonal? Is light a wave or a particle? Is the purpose of religion to help the individual soul find spiritual awakening or to be the ultimate spokesman for the rights of all individuals? Must the American government protect people from the greed of business, or protect the rights of businesses since the success of business is necessary to the success of the economy? Any answer to such questions must transcend the form in which the questions are couched; the new synthesis must transcend such oppositions.

This "transcendent function", as Jung termed it (Jung, 1960:131–193), this psychic function which restores wholeness to the organism, is also the Self. We have already discussed this aspect of the Self in our discussion of mandalas in the previous chapter. However, since the ultimate goal is pre-figured in the original images, that goal is also the Self. We saw the necessity for such a pre-figured, individual goal in our discussion of the Shadow in chapter 14. Thus the Self is both process and goal. This is quite a paradox and paradoxes are usually not welcomed by scientists, but this paradox is not the result of metaphysical speculation but a simple description of how symbolic resolutions emerge.

> There is nothing mysterious or metaphysical about the term 'transcendent function'. It means a psychological function comparable in its way to a mathematical function of the same name, which is a function of real and imaginary numbers. The psychological "transcendent function" arises from the union of conscious and unconscious contents.
>
> (ibid:131).

[Author's note: interestingly, mathematicians originally resisted the mathematical concept of transcendent functions much the same as psychologists resist its psychological namesake].

Abraham Maslow and Self-Actualization

Jung was wise enough to recognize that such a function did exist in the human psyche, and to describe the symbolic forms it took and the way in which it manifested itself. In recent times, Abraham Maslow pointed out that we all seem to have a "hierarchy of needs", progressing from the need for such physical necessities as food and water to the ultimate need for self-actualizing; that is, becoming all that one can be.

Maslow identified men that others considered to be self-actualized. He listed the terms people used in describing such men. He actually enumerated fourteen such qualities these men seemed to exhibit: wholeness, perfection, completion, justice, aliveness, richness, simplicity, beauty, goodness, uniqueness, effortlessness, playfulness, truth, and self-sufficiency. Surprisingly, these same terms were used over and over in describing such men, an indication that there was a commonality that transcended their individual differences.

Maslow found that normal people exhibited these same qualities in their best moments, moments that he termed "peak-experiences". This convinced Maslow that these values were indeed transcendent values. Further, when self-actualized people were questioned as to the values they considered to be ultimate, one or another of the above values seemed to emerge. However, when they were closely questioned as to what that value meant to them, it quickly emerged that it contained all the other values as well. That is, truth was whole, perfect, complete, just, alive, rich, simple, beautiful, good, unique, effortless, playful, and self-sufficient. At this highest level, Maslow found all values seemed to merge into a single value that could not be described directly (see Maslow,1968).

The Self and the Mystical Experience

Jung had earlier discovered much the same as Maslow in his explorations of the Self. The pathways to the Self vary, but not infinitely; they definitely fall into categories much like Maslow's categories (though Maslow's attempt to enumerate exactly what such categories are does seem a little over-reaching). Yet all pathways, which are the Self, seem to lead to the same goal, which is also the Self. At that goal, all values seem to merge into a value that transcends description.

This has been the experience of mystics and saints throughout all history when they try to describe the mystical moment; that is, the moment of "peak-experience". Many have attempted to describe their essentially indescribable experience; most have described it in terms of their particular religious or spiritual value-system; i.e., in terms of an experience of Jesus or Buddha, etc. Yet to the extent that they truly had a transcendent experience, they all fall back on words that are much like Maslow's.

When the author has questioned schizophrenics about their experiences, they frequently describe the same sort of experience as the mystics or Maslow's Self-Actualizers; however, when the schizophrenics tried to integrate the experience into their lives, they failed and the "peak-experience" becomes a "nadir-experience" (to use a term invented by Maslow).

Finally, though this enumeration is properly endless, the same words are used over-and-over in the description of "trips" on LSD, mescaline, peyote, psilocybin, and other hallucinogenic drugs. The ubiquity of the descriptions of the experience points to an archetypal content. But since the primary quality of this experience is the transcendence of all other experiences and values, this archetype seems to transcend all other archetypes. That is, in fact, exactly what Jung found of the Self. In an effort to separate the personal experience of the Self, which was channeled through each person's unique qualities and experience, in his later writings, Jung termed the ground from which the Self emerged the Unus Mundus (i.e., unitary world).

Pascal, Lao Tzu, and Holograms

Blaise Pascal, a renowned seventeenth century philosopher and mathematician, said that God (or the universe, for he considered the two synonymous) is an infinite sphere whose center is everywhere and whose circumference is nowhere. Lao Tzu said the same thing two thousand years earlier. They, and Jung, were attempting to express the fact that everyday people in exceptional moments understand that they contain the entire universe. Since every person is capable of that same experience, the universe has an many centers as it has people. Maslow and Jung both said that exceptional people continually live a close approximation to that exceptional experience.

> ... the more numerous and the more significant the unconscious contents which are assimilated to the ego, the closer the approximation of the ego to the self, even though this approximation must be a never-ending process. This inevitably produces an inflation of the ego, unless a critical line of demarcation is drawn between it and the unconscious figures.
>
> (Jung,1959:23).

Jung described our lives as the "circumambulatio of the Self"; that is, as a spiral journey around this inner center. For Jung, life was not a straight-line progress toward some distance goal, higher or farther. Rather, it was a journey to find a center within ourselves which we could approach infinitely closely, but never fully reach. For Jung, the Self was transcendent, but each experienced the Self through the filter of his own unique existence. He saw the Self as the window each of us possessed into a single transcendent world.

Karl Pribram, one of the world's most respected neurophysiologists, also feels that the human mind contains the entire universe. Pribram has come to the conclusion that the universe is a hologram and individual human minds are each part of the hologram (Pribram,1981;Rossi,1980). A hologram has the unique quality that every part of it can reproduce the whole. If the part is small enough, like a single human mind in comparison to the universe, the reproduction can be fuzzy and indistinct. As more and more parts are added, the clarity increases; however, at each stage the whole is represented. This is merely a contemporary way to say, as Pascal and Lao Tzu said, that the universe is an infinite sphere whose center is everywhere and whose circumference is nowhere.

There is clearly no final way to describe or to delimit the Self. Jung's greatness lay in recognizing that it was not a metaphysical concept, but an objective fact of psychic existence. Because of the necessary complexity in approaching any of the three key archetypes of the individuation process; i.e., (1) the Shadow, (2) the Anima/Animus Syzygy, and (3) the Self; Jung searched for another description of this process which could better capture some of the complexity of this objective psychic experience. He found this further description in an unexpected place, the forgotten field of alchemy.

17

Alchemy as a Model of Psychological Development

Jung's Rediscovery of Alchemy

Jung's discoveries in the unconscious seemed strange, alien from what other psychologists were studying. In his spiritual autobiography, *Memories, Dreams, Reflections*, he says that:

> I had to find evidence for the historical prefiguration of my inner experiences. That is to say, I had to ask myself, "Where have my particular premises already occurred in history?" If I had not succeeded in finding such evidence, I would never have been able to substantiate my ideas. . . . Analytical psychology is fundamentally a natural science, but it is subject far more than any other science to the personal bias of the observer. The psychologist must depend therefore in the highest degree upon historical and literary parallels if he wishes to exclude at least the crudest errors in judgement.
>
> (Jung,1965:200).

After Jung discovered the collective unconscious, he patiently recorded what he found there. He found a number of archetypes which he discussed throughout the years. The archetypes of Shadow, Anima/Animus, and Self were of a different order, since they corresponded to psychological stages of development. Jung was never satisfied with this single presentation of the stages of development because it only captured part of the mystery.

For example, in order to resolve the problems presented by the Shadow, a joining of two previously opposed parts of the personality has to occur. What is the nature of the union and what steps need to be followed to create it? Jung's archetypes of development only presented the unconscious figure that represented the problem at each stage of development; they didn't speak to the nature of the union between conscious and unconscious.

The unconscious was much like the world Werner Heisenberg found in sub-atomic particles. Heisenberg said that one can observe either the momentum or the position of a particle, but not both (Heisenberg,1930:12–19,48–52). Similarly, if Jung froze the process of psychological development, he was able to discover the archetypes that were operative at each stage; these were the Shadow, Anima/Animus and Self. By way of analogy only, those would correspond to the position of the sub-atomic particle. Jung also wanted to find more about the process, the momentum. But he needed a different model to observe that. In *Memories, Dreams, Reflections* he discussed his search for such a picture.

> Between 1918 and 1926 I had seriously studied the Gnostic writers, for they too had been confronted with the primal world of the unconscious and had dealt with its contents, with images that were obviously contaminated with the world of instinct. Just how they understood these images remains difficult to say, in view of the paucity of the accounts—which, moreover, mostly stem from their opponents, the Church Fathers [author's note: Jung's study of Gnostic Christianity was, of course, long before the discoveries at Nag Hammadhi]. It seems to me highly unlikely that they had a psychological conception of them. But the Gnostics were too remote for me to establish any link with them in regard to the questions which were confronting me . . .
>
> When I discovered alchemy I realized that it represented the historical link with Gnosticism, and that a continuity therefore existed between past and present. Grounded in the natural philosophy of the Middle ages, alchemy formed the bridge on the one hand into the past, to Gnosticism, and on the other into the future, to the modern psychology of the unconscious.
>
> (ibid:200f).

Because alchemy was such an important discovery for Jung, an extended quotation from *Man and His Symbols* (Jung,1964) follows, wherein Jung described how he came to rediscover the value of alchemy. Before this passage, Jung discussed in general the reason for recurring dreams, which he felt were noteworthy attempts of the psyche to either compensate for some long-standing "defect in the dreamer's attitute to life" or to "anticipate a future event of importance."

> I myself dreamed of a motif over several years, in which I would 'discover' a part of my house that I did not know existed. Sometimes it was the quarters where my long-dead parents lived, in which my father, to my surprise, had a laboratory where he studied the comparative anatomy of fish and my mother ran a hotel for ghostly visitors. Usually this unfamiliar guest wing was an ancient historical building, long forgotten, yet my inherited property. It contained interesting antique furniture, and toward the end of this series of dreams I discovered an old library whose books were unknown to me. Finally, in the last dream I opened one of the books and found in it a profusion of the most marvelous symbolic pictures. When I awoke, my heart was palpitating with excitement.
>
> Some time before I had this particular last dream of the series, I had placed an order with an antiquarian bookseller for one of the classic compilations of medieval alchemists. I had found a quotation in literature that I thought might have some connection with early Byzantine alchemy, and I wished to check it.
>
> Several weeks after I had had the dream of the unknown book, a parcel arrived from the bookseller. Inside was a parchment volume dating from the 16th century. It was illustrated by fascinating symbolic pictures that instantly reminded me of those I had seen in my dream.
>
> As the rediscovery of the principles of alchemy came to be an important part of my work as a pioneer of psychology, the motif of recurring dream can easily be understood. The house, of course, was a symbol of my personality and its conscious field of interests; and the unknown annex represented the anticipation of a new field of interest and research of which my conscious mind was at that time unaware. From that moment, 30 years ago, I never had the dream again.
>
> (ibid:53f).

A Short History of Alchemy

Alchemy has generally been presented as a foolish, superstitious predecessor to chemistry. Few of us have any awareness of the practice of alchemy. We probably visualize solitary men working with beakers and flasks; that portrait would be partially accurate. We might be aware that the goal of alchemy was the production of the "philosopher's stone", but we have little idea what that might be. We are also probably aware that alchemists attempted, and sometimes claimed to have succeeded at, the transmutation of lead into gold.

This gives us a picture of the alchemist as either a greedy fool or a charlatan. Though alchemists included both fools and charlatans among their number, as have every other calling, most alchemists were neither. They were likely to be intelligent, religious, inquisitive, and necessarily solitary. In order to understand how alchemy could possibly offer anything of substance for depth psychology, we have to understand a little of the history of alchemy.

Alchemy and Christianity came into existence in the Western world at roughly the same time. Alchemy developed into a separate field during the first through the third century A.D. However, its roots can be traced to 330 B.C., when Alexander the Great conquered Egypt and founded the city of Alexandria with its great library. The library, which housed nearly half a million manuscripts, brought scholars from all over the world. Even though a great part of the library burned during Caesar's conquest of Alexandria in 80 B.C., it remained a haven for scholars (Stillman,1924:137).

During this period, commerce, warfare and Christianity all served to mix cultures that had hitherto gone their separate ways. John Stillman, in his history of alchemy and early chemistry, said of these times that:

> Greek philosophy, Egyptian arts, Chaldean and Persian mysticism met and gave rise to strange combinations not always conducive to improvement upon the relative clarity of the Greek foundation.
> (ibid:137).

Obviously, Stillman shared the views of alchemy as a naive pre-science that I've mentioned earlier. His views are typical of the histories of alchemy written from the viewpoint of Western science. Marie-Louise von Franz (to whom the author is indebted for much of this history of alchemy) felt otherwise; she commented that:

> The Greek philosophers who, as you all know, initiated rational thought regarding the problems of nature, of matter, space and time, etc., made practically no or very few experiments. Their theories are bolstered by certain observations but it never really occurred to them to actually experiment. On the other hand, in Egypt there was a highly developed chemical-magical technique, but in general the Egyptians gave it no thought, either philosophical or theoretical. It was simply the handing down by certain priestly orders of practical recipes, plus some magic religious representation but I should say without theoretical reflection. When the two trends of Greek and Egyptian civilization came together they united in a very fruitful marriage, of which alchemy was their child.
>
> (von Franz,1979:1).

The first great alchemists were also Gnostic Christians. Christianity was largely the religion of the simpler, less-educated members of society. The Gnostics tended to be more intellectual; they viewed Christianity as the newest and greatest of the "mystery religions", which held deep truths hidden beneath the innocent words preached to the masses. Gnostics wanted a personal experience of God, not merely a collective religion interpreted for them by priests. They could be viewed as early precursors of depth psychologists.

> The mystery of the structure of the universe was in themselves, in their own bodies and in that part of their personality which we call the unconscious, but they would say in the life of their own material existence. They thought that instead of taking outer materials you could just as well look inside and get information directly from that mystery because you were it.
>
> (ibid:8).

These men wanted to discover the deepest secrets of the universe. For them, that meant searching for the building blocks of both matter and psyche, for they saw no clear distinction between the two. For them, there was always a relationship between the experimenter and his experiment. An alchemical operation had to be conducted at a propitious time because they believed that the micro world of their experiments was connected with the macro world of the cosmos. The experimenter had to meditate deeply on both his own inner nature and the inner nature of the matter upon which he was experimenting. Similarly, a modern depth psychologist observes not only his patient's psyche but his own, for he realizes that the two are inextricably connected.

After the third century A.D., the alchemical tradition spread, as mathematics spread, to the Moslem world. There existed in Islam, as in Christianity, a split between the outer-oriented religion of the masses, and a more inner-oriented, mystical religion followed by the intellectuals. The latter eagerly adopted alchemy as one more avenue into the greater mysteries. Alchemy reached its peak in the Islamic world during the tenth century.

As the Moslem world became the center of intellectual achievement, it attracted European Christian scholars. In Spain, the mystery teachings spread to the Jewish mystics; the Kabala was the product. Whether directly from the Moslems, or by way of the Jews, alchemy spread again in the West at roughly the time of the Renaissance. It reached its peak in the fifteenth and sixteenth centuries, and still existed in some form during the seventeenth and eighteenth centuries. Goethe, for example, was still familiar with the alchemical writings and drew on them in *Faust*, much as other authors drew on the Bible or Shakespeare. However, by Jung's time, alchemy was largely unknown to the educated reader, and the alchemical allusions in Goethe meant nothing to Jung, when he read *Faust* with such fascination in his youth.

Bringing Order Out of Chaos
Jung had to discover Gnostic thinking largely through the writings of their opponents in the organized Church. Therefore, he wasn't aware of Gnostic alchemical writing until he had the dream we've quoted and began his alchemical research. What he found would have daunted most men. Alchemical writings were a mixture of philosophy, religion,

mysticism, scientific theory, and "cookbook" recipes for experiments. Both the early texts, written in Greek, and the later Latin texts were impossible to translate literally.

> ... sulphur is called theion and theion means also the divine. Then a material called arsenikon is often mentioned. Arsenikon simply means male, and in contrast to theion, which really means sulphur, you cannot define in old treatises what is mean by arsenikon; it might be anything.
>
> (ibid:9).

Jung had to go through the texts and list the words and their possible meaning in that text. He made concordances where he listed all the references to a given word in any alchemical text in order to sort out their meanings. This was the method used by the alchemists themselves.

> Even the alchemists had said: 'One book opens the other. Read many books and compare them throughout and then you get the meaning. By reading one book alone you cannot get it, you cannot otherwise decipher it'.
>
> (ibid:17).

Because of the translation problem, the alchemists differed frequently among themselves over the meaning of a word. This increasingly led them to ascribe deeper meanings to words than might originally have been intended.

> They themselves got mixed up by not being able to consult with their colleagues, because they were all lonely experimenters. Therefore, they spoke about an esoteric and exoteric language, and thus got into a completely Babylonian confusion of languages.
>
> (ibid:10).

Jung gradually began to make some sense out of the confusion. He saw that matter and psyche were not differentiated for the alchemists, that they could talk simultaneously of physical and psychic operations. Because of this lack of differentiation, he saw further that their unconscious issues were projected out onto matter, in much the same way as contemporary men and women project Shadow qualities onto the people around them.

If the projection of unconscious, and even archetypal, material onto matter seems strange, consider science itself. The existence of any spiritual reality has been consciously denied by modern scientists. However, the need for spiritual values seems to remain intact in the unconscious, where it is projected out onto matter. For example, the quest of a modern physicist for the ultimate building blocks of matter is hardly a disinterested scientific study. Similarly, the biologist's search for the language of life in DNA and RNA generates a zeal that is more spiritual than intellectual.

The emphatic insistence of scientists that everything can ultimately be reduced to physical properties is surely a projection. There is no objective need for such an emphasis. When a new theory threatens this "religious" viewpoint, such as Rupert Sheldrake's theory of morphogenetic fields, its author is considered a "heretic" to be "excommunicated".

Because alchemists were solitary men engaged in a quest of both outer and inner exploration, their writings documented the stages of this quest. Once Jung could make sense of the strange manner of writing, he was able to trace the paths of inner development represented symbolically by the alchemical operations. The later alchemists were themselves aware of the dual nature of their studies, but the early alchemists were blithely unaware and the symbolic material is correspondingly more useful.

Jung recorded his discoveries in this field in his later writings. These are collected in *Psychology and Alchemy* (volume 12 of the Collected Works), *Alchemical Studies* (volume 13), *Aion* (volume 9.ii), "The Psychology of the Transference" (contained in volume 16), and in his magnum opus *Mysterium Coniunctionis* (volume 14) (i.e., the title means the mysterious or miraculous union). A discussion of the latter volume in the next chapter will conclude our examination of Jung's alchemical studies.

18

The Mysterious Union

Mysterium Coniunctionis, volume 14 of the Collected Works, (Jung,1963) represented Jung's second great attempt to express the process of psychological development through the archetypes of the unconscious. His first was through the archetypes of development: the Shadow, Anima/Animus, and the Self. In *Mysterium Coniunctionis* he approached psychological development from a different direction. Rather than concentrating on the archetypes that represented each stage of psychological development, he centered instead on the psychic unions that formed as one stage gave way to the next.

With the completion of *Mysterium Coniunctionis*, Jung felt that he had said all that he had to say on alchemy. From its completion in Jung's eightieth year to the end of his life, he turned to more personal writings: his spiritual autobiography *Memories, Dreams, Reflections; Man and his Symbols*, which introduced the wider reading public to Jung; his correspondance with many of the other great thinkers of his time.

Jung's pre-alchemical work has been described thoroughly for the intelligent lay public by many later writers. In fact, many readers have only encountered Jung through his "translators". Unfortunately, the ideas in Jung's works on alchemy, especially the ideas in *Mysterium Coniunctionis*, have not yet been presented to a wider public. Marie-Louise von Franz and Edward Edinger, among others, have made noble attempts to spread Jung's late alchemical thoughts to a wider audience, but it's difficult to find a way to present such complex material (see von Franz:1959;1979 & Edinger:Summer 1978, Winter 1978, Summer 1979, Spring 1980, Spring 1981, Fall 1981, Spring

1982). There seems to be no way to make Jung's concepts simple, any more than there is a way to make quantum mechanics simple. Both are attempts to describe the ultimate nature of the universe and, therefore, lie beyond facile presentation.

In recent years, books such as *The Tao of Physics* (Capra,1975) and *The Dancing Wu Li Masters* (Zukav,1979) have spawned a wide variety of books that have successfully introduced quantum mechanics to a wider audience. These books cannot describe quantum mechanics itself, since that would require a mathematical language which is shared by very few. What they do present are analogies to quantum mechanics' view of the world, such as its similarities to the symbolic truths expressed in Eastern spiritual traditions. *Mysterium Coniunctionis* still awaits such a presentation. What follows is merely a tiny taste of the riches contained in Jung's great final work.

The Conjunction of Opposites

Mysterium Coniunctionis began at the point where most of Jung's writings ended. Time and again, throughout his writings, Jung described how the unconscious compensated for an overly narrow consciousness. This compensation produced a polarity, an opposition demanding resolution. The polarity between conscious and unconscious led in turn to a psychic attempt at mediation. Jung described in great detail the nature of the conflict at various stages of psychic development. However, in *Mysterium Coniuntionis* Jung went straight to the end-point of that process, the conjunction of opposites.

Deep conflicts cannot be resolved by "compromise", by splitting the issue down the middle. Instead, our attempts at mediation form a new opposition. Thus, the conjunction of opposites becomes a "quaternio"; i.e., a four-way opposition, not merely a polarity. Such a strange opposition naturally led the alchemists, as it later led Zen Buddhist masters, to the use of paradox as a way to express the inexpressible.

As we have discussed in the chapters on the archetypes of development, Jung had discovered that the human psyche inevitably personified psychic conflicts. In *Mysterium Coniunctionis*, Jung spent nearly 300 pages on his description of three such personifications of inner polarities which he had discovered in alchemical literature: (1) the Sun and the Moon, more often presented in alchemy as Sulphur and Salt; (2) King and Queen; (3) Adam and Eve.

Alchemists usually personified the mediator between these opposites as Mercurius, or Hermes Trismegistos, a legendary figure who was the Greek god Hermes made man, much as Jesus was god made man. Thus Mercurius represented perfectly the struggle between matter and spirit which we have come to consider our unique problem. The god Hermes was the messenger of the gods, thus admirably suited to going between the world of gods and the world of men; that is, the world of the unconscious archetypes and the world of consciousness.

He was a protean god who could be either a benefactor of man, or a dread enemy. As the god of thieves, he could assist man in recovering psychic treasure from the unconscious. As the god of borders, he could teach how to live on the border between polarities. Thus able to contain oppositions within himself, Mercurius formed the second polarity that combined with any of the other primary polarities to create a psychic "quaternio".

Though this sounds far removed from psychology, it is tremendously useful to the psychologist willing to put up with the difficulty of the material. Twentieth century man has reached an impasse. Rationality, taken to its logical extreme, has produced paradoxical conclusions in mathematics, physics, art, music, literature, and philosophy. We children of the twentieth century have all struggled to find some way to give meaning to disinterested fact, some way to rationally validate that in which we believe. None of us can any longer be indifferent to this problem. However, in earlier times, most men were able to remain blissfully unaware of the conflict. It was left to the lonely few who pushed into the depths of the psyche to be caught in this modern trap.

The Gnostic Christians knew of the conflict; they wanted to

experience their divine nature directly, not through the intercession of an organized body of religious beliefs. That inevitably led them to experience the problem of the opposition between spirit and flesh. They attempted to reconcile the two, not merely to subjugate flesh to spirit as the organized Church proposed. Thus they struggled unsuccessfully with the issue. Any knowledge of the nature of their struggle and their attempts at reconciliation are therefore enormously useful to us.

However, the Gnostic Christians fought their inner battles nearly two millenia ago; the alchemists were much closer to us in time and spirit. Coming into full flower with the Renaissance, alchemists struggled with the opposition between meaning and truth, between separation and harmony, in much the same way as we are now struggling. Because they were largely unconscious of the true nature of their inner conflict, at least during the early centuries of alchemy, it found symbolic representation in their alchemical experiments. Thus, by studying their records of these experiments, we can see our own struggle cleansed of the obfuscation of an over-developed rationality. If the alchemists talked of the opposition between Sun and Moon, King and Queen, Adam and Eve, it was because each of these polarities had some unique symbolic message to express about the nature of the inner conflict, and its possible resolution.

We stand at the end of the Christian era, an era wherein man has expanded upwards and outwards in an unprecedented fashion. But this incredible "progress" has created a polarity, an opposition in which we feel lonely and separated, cut off from our instinctual roots.

> The arcanum of alchemy is one of these archetypal ideas that fills a gap in the Christian view of the world, namely, the unbridged gulf between the opposites, in particular between good and evil . . . The alchemists sought for that effect which would heal not only the disharmonies of the physical world but the inner psychic conflict as well.
> (Jung,1963:674).

The Personification of the Opposites

For example, in the opposition between Sun (or Sulphur) and Moon (or Salt), the alchemists said much less about the Sun than they did about the Moon. It was as if the nature of the day, or consciousness, was clear to everyone, but the nature of the night, or the unconscious, needed clarification. In the opposition between King and Queen, the emphasis in the alchemical literature was on the King, and how a dying King could be regenerated into a new vital King. In the opposition between Adam and Eve, there was an explicit separation of the "old" Adam and the "new" Adam. The "old" Adam, the first man, was frequently represented as an enormous man as big as a mountain. The "new" Adam, however, was frequently seen as a wheel or a wheel with three legs. Thus the "new" Adam was an attempt at capturing a wholeness which transcended human personification.

Wherever possible, in bringing together this material, Jung tried to describe not only the alchemical symbols but their most probable psychological meaning. In an earlier book, *Psychology and Alchemy*, Jung traced the process of psychological development though the symbols of one man's dreams. There he showed how a modern man's dream symbols were pre-figured in alchemy. In *Mysterium Coniunctionis*, Jung once again traced the process of psychological development through the symbols of alchemy. But here Jung was dealing with the deepest oppositions in the human psyche, conflicts that have not yet been resolved by humanity.

The alchemical texts are therefore invaluable guides to the nature of the inner struggle at different points of development, but are necessarily incomplete in their ultimate resolution of the inner conflict. For if the issues had been totally resolved by the alchemists, we would not be struggling with them today.

The Nature of the Conjunction

The discussion of the personification of opposites, which we have mentioned so briefly above, occupies the first four hundred and fifty pages of *Mysterium Coniunctionis*. In the last and greatest part of *Mysterium Coniunctionis*, Jung discussed the three stages of the alchemical conjunction as models of the stages of psychological development. In approximately one hundred pages, Jung summarized all that he knew about the psyche. In this part, more than in any other of his works, with the possible exception of *Two Essays on Analytical Psychology* (Jung,1966), Jung brought these mysteries down to a very human level.

Jung began by summarizing the conclusions he'd reached in the earlier parts of the book. He described the conjunction of opposites as the "central idea" of alchemy. He reiterated that alchemists were not merely speaking of chemical experiments when they discussed combinations of various elements. Instead, they were projecting archetypes from the unconscious onto the matter of their experiments. Because these projections were archetypal, they were "numinous"; that is, they had an awe-inspiring effect on the alchemists. Since inevitably the human psyche personified its conflicts, the alchemists personified the material substances they dealt with. However, because they were trying to capture archetypal forces, there was no single way to personify these forces, and their projections took diverse forms.

> Henry Silberer [author's note: the first psychologist to point out the psychological nature of alchemy] rightly called the coniunctio the "central idea" of the alchemical procedure. . . . the adepts were ultimately concerned with a union of the substances—by whatever name these may have been called. By means of this union they hoped to attain the goal of the work: the production of the gold or a symbolical equivalent of it . . . even when he spoke of a union of the "natures," or of an "amalgam" of iron and copper, or of a compound of sulphur and mercury, he meant it at the same time as a symbol: iron was Mars and copper was Venus, and their fusion was at the same time a love-affair. . . . the substances they sought to combine in reality always had—on account of their unknown nature—a numinous quality which tended towards phantasmal personification.
>
> (ibid:654).

The Alchemical Creation Myth

The alchemists grounded their beliefs in a "creation myth"; they said that first there existed a primal quaternio of the four elements: Fire, Air, Water, and Earth. Fire acted upon Air and created Sulphur, Air upon Water to create Mercury, Water upon Earth to create Salt. Since there was nothing left for Earth to act upon, only three principles were created. Then the Sulphur and Mercury combined to create Male, Salt and Mercury to create Female. In each case, Mercury (i.e., Mercurius) was the mediating element. The goal of the alchemical process was then to join Male and Female into a new union that combined all the opposites from which they were created.

> The alchemical description of the beginning corresponds psychologically to a primitive consciousness which is constantly liable to break up into individual affective processes—to fall apart, as it were, in four directions. As the four elements represent the whole physical world, their falling apart means dissolution into the constituents of the world, that is, into a purely inorganic and hence unconscious state. Conversely, the combination of the elements and the final synthesis of male and female is an achievement of the art and a product of conscious endeavour. The result of the synthesis was consequently conceived by the adept as self-knowledge, which, like the knowledge of God, is needed for the preparation of the Philosophers' Stone. Piety is needed for the work, and this is nothing but knowledge of oneself.
> (ibid:657).

The Three Unions

Though the alchemists began with the idea of a single union between male and female, they found the issue was more complex in practice. Eventually three successive unions emerged: (1) the *Unio Mentalis*, or mental union; (2) the union of the mind with the body; and (3) the union of the mind and body with the *unus mundus*, or unitary reality. Over the same period of time that the concept of a single union developed into three successive unions, a deeper understanding of the underlying psychological principles also formed. The great sixteenth century alchemical writer, Gerard Dorn, commented that:

> We conclude that mediative philosophy consists in the overcoming of the body by mental union. This first union does not as yet make the wise man, but only the mental disciple of wisdom. The second union of the mind with the body shows forth the wise man, hoping for and expecting that blessed third union with the first unity.
>
> (ibid:663).

Quite obviously, the final union was less understood; it was difficult for the alchemists to separate themselves from the process in which they were engaged sufficiently to understand this final union. But all their writings discussed this "mysterium coniunctionis" in terms of a total unity of opposites in which all polarities vanished. Jung understood this to be a re-union of the individual with the "unus mundus"; that is, the ultimate ground of reality.

In more purely psychological terms, Jung described the "adept's" alchemical journey as beginning in unconsciousness, the original "unus mundus". Consciousness forced the dissolution of this original unity and left the adept in conflict, trying to reconcile elements previously united in the unconscious. A new union could only be formed when an original union has been destroyed and the individual elements carefully separated and purified.

The Unio Mentalis

> ... The *unio mentalis*, the interior oneness which today we call individuation, he conceived as a psychic equilibration of opposites "in the overcoming of the body," [Jung quoting Dorn here and in subsequent quotations] a state of equanimity transcending the body's affectivity and instinctuality.

> ... in order to bring about their subsequent reunion, the mind (*mens*) must be separated from the—body which is equivalent to "voluntary death"—for only separated things can unite. ... The aim of this separation was to free the mind from the influence of the "bodily appetites and the heart's affections," and to establish a spiritual position which is supraordinate to the turbulent sphere of the body. This leads at first to a dissociation of the personality and a violation of the merely natural man.

> ... Modern psychotherapy makes use of the same procedure when it objectifies the affects and instincts and confronts consciousness with them.
>
> (ibid:670ff).

As can be seen above, each union must be preceded by a conscious separation of elements from some original unconscious unity, followed by a now conscious re-union of selected elements. Before the mind can be one within itself, it must withdraw from its original unconscious union with the body and emotions. The mental union occurred when the adept was able to accept the unconscious, discarded parts of his personality. Once this was accomplished, the mind was one and could control the body.

Though this was the same stage Jung earlier characterized as the Shadow stage (ibid:707), the alchemical description explained much that is usually overlooked in discussing Shadow issues. Issues are undifferentiated in the unconscious; it is only consciousness that separates. Therefore, as long as the Shadow remained unconscious, it was merged with the urges of the body. This was clear in the alchemical symbolism, but rarely mentioned in discussions of the Shadow archetype. Once the Shadow was successfully integrated into consciousness, one could consciously acknowledge previously forbidden desires, but still choose not to act out those desires in reality. Thus conscious fantasy could prevent unconscious forces from overpowering consciousness.

The author used this technique in working successfully with a patient who sexually molested children. He was also receiving behavioral treatment under a court order. The behavioral treatment consisted of aversion therapy to make him lose sexual desire for young boys. The patient was growing more and more angry and frustrated under such treatment.

The author instead allowed him to fantasize without criticism. These fantasies revealed that his desire for young boys was because he himself had never developed emotionally past that age, due to many issues that are outside the scope of this discussion. Once the patient was free to acknowledge his desires, it became possible for him to honor them without acting them out. With the knowledge that he had the ability to control whether or not he acted on his desires, he gained a great deal of self-confidence. At that point, his desires began to slowly mature into the need for an adult sexual relationship.

However, the *unio mentalis* is only the first of the three stages of the conjunction. Jung commented that:

> Such an interior operation means a great deal, since it brings a considerable increase of self-knowledge as well as of personal maturity, but its reality is merely potential and is validated only by a union with the physical world of the body.
>
> (ibid:664).

The Union of the Mind and Body

> The second step on the way to the production of this substance [i.e., the "lapis" or Philosopher's Stone, which could heal all ills] was the reunion of the spirit with the body. For this procedure there were many symbols. One of the most important was the chymical [sic] marriage, which took place in the retort . . . already in the fourteenth century it began to dawn on them that the lapis was more than a chemical compound . . . in the individual was hidden that "substance of celestial nature known to very few."
>
> (ibid:677).

> The second stage of conjunction, the re-uniting of the *unio mentalis* with the body, is particularly important, as only from here can the complete conjunction be attained—union with the *unus mundus*. The reuniting of the spiritual position with the body obviously means that the insights gained should be made real. An insight might just as well remain in abeyance if it is simply not used. The second stage of conjunction therefore consists in making a reality of the man who has acquired some knowledge of his paradoxical wholeness.
>
> (ibid:679).

In their attempts to achieve this second union, alchemists re-discovered the technique that remains the core of all the mystery religions, all the mystical schools. That technique is what Jung termed "active imagination"; most of us are more familiar with it as meditation. Until recently, every school of spiritual development considered meditation a mystery open only to the chosen few. Now we live in a time when all the mysteries are available in the local bookstore (or perhaps even the supermarket) for the slight cost of a paperback book.

But it's important to realize that the alchemists considered meditation as the second stage of the conjunction, not the first. First came the *unio mentalis*, the stage of self-knowledge. In chapter 16, we discussed how Jung felt that Eastern spiritual techniques were inappropriate for Westerners because these techniques ignored the Shadow. Without a separation of the Shadow, with its largely personal garb, from the deeper, more exclusively collective parts of the unconscious, Shadow issues can achieve monumental stature. When we are forced to self-knowledge, we gain a place of solidity on which to stand and confront the strange symbols of the collective unconscious.

> . . . the coniunctio appears here as the union of a consciousness (spirit), differentiated by self-knowledge, with a spirit abstracted from previously unconscious contents. One could also regard the latter as a quintessence of fantasy-images that enter consciousness either spontaneously or through active imagination and, in their totality, represent a moral or intellectual viewpoint contrasting with, or compensating, that of consciousness.
>
> (ibid:736).

Meditation provides a method for by-passing consciousness in an attempt to directly obtain unconscious material. Jung's technique of "active imagination" should be considered in preference to many of the techniques which can produce violent reactions from the unconscious. For example, in many oriental techniques of meditation the meditator is instructed to ignore the visions and fantasies produced by the unconscious. The concept is that those are just empty fantasies thrown up by ego-consciousness; the acolyte should not be confused by these but should strive for direct union with God, Atman, etc. (i.e., the Self in Jung's terms). Ignoring the unconscious in this way is potentially dangerous without the self-knowledge gained by struggling with the Shadow.

> If the demand for self-knowledge is willed by fate and is refused, this negative attitude may end in real death. The demand would not have

come to this person had he still been able to strike out on some promising by-path. But he is caught in a blind alley from which only self-knowledge can extricate him. If he refuses this then no other way is open to him. Usually he is not conscious of his situation, either, and the more unconscious he is the more he is at the mercy of unforeseen dangers. . . . The unconscious has a thousand ways of snuffing out a meaningless existence with surprising swiftness.

(ibid:675).

Rather than ignoring the fantasy material produced by the unconscious, the alchemists recommended actively engaging with the fantasies. Jung described the process as follows:

. . . Take the unconscious in one of its handiest forms, say a spontaneous fantasy, a dream, an irrational mood, an affect, or something of the kind, and operate with it. Give it your special attention, concentrate on it, and observe its alterations objectively. Spare no effort to devote yourself to this task, follow the subsequent transformations of the spontaneous fantasy attentively and carefully. Above all, don't let anything from outside, that does not belong, get into it, for the fantasy-image has "everything it needs." In this way, one is certain of not interfering by conscious caprice and of giving the unconscious a free hand.

(ibid:749).

The light that gradually dawns on him consists in his understanding that his fantasy is a real psychic process which is happening to him personally. Although, to a certain extent, he looks on from outside, impartially, he is also an acting and suffering figure in the drama of the psyche. This recognition is absolutely necessary and marks an important advance. . . . if you place yourself in the drama as you really are, not only does it gain in actuality but you also create, by your criticism of the fantasy, an effective counterbalance to its tendency to get out of hand. For what is now happening is the decisive rapprochement with the unconscious. This is where insight, the *unio mentalis*, begins to become real.

(ibid:753).

Just as the mental union could be seen as another way of portraying the Shadow stage, so the union of mind and body could be viewed as the successful conclusion of the Anima stage, but the alchemical description has a richness separate and distinct from the image of the Anima.

The Union with the Unus Mundus

The third and final stage was the union of the individual with the *unus mundus*; that is, with his total environment, both inner and outer. This is the stage so often discussed in mystical literature.

> We could compare this only with the ineffable mystery of the *unio mystica*, or *tao*, or the content of *samadhi*, or the experience of *satori* in Zen, which would bring us to the realm of the ineffable and of extreme subjectivity where all the criteria of reason fail. Remarkably enough this experience is an empirical one in so far as there are unanimous testimonies from the East and the West alike, both from the present and from the distant past.
>
> (ibid:771).

Perhaps the best-known Western compilation of descriptions of this experience is Bucke's *Cosmic Consciousness*, first published in 1901 (Bucke,1923). In more recent times, several scientifically-trained individuals who have gone through the process have tried to record their experience. In 1973, Franklin Merrell-Wolff gave a step-by-step account of his experience, which had occurred thirty-seven years earlier, in a book called *Pathways Through to Space* (Merrell-Wolff,1973a). He tried to bring all the concepts together in a philosophic whole in a companion volume: *The Philosophy of Consciousness Without an Object* (Merrell-Wolff,1973b).

In 1972, John C. Lilly, M.D. gave his account of a similar, though perhaps less psychologically complete, experience in *The Center of the Cyclone: an Autobiography of Inner Space* (Lilly,1972). But as rich as both accounts are, they are conscious attempts at providing rational explanations for their experience [author's note: Merrell-Wolff, more than Lilly, attempts to describe without pre-judging]. The alchemical descriptions have the advantage that they come straight from the unconscious, unclouded by conscious rationalizations.

> ... if a union is to take place between opposites like spirit and matter, conscious and unconscious, bright and dark, and so on, it will happen in a third thing, which represents not a compromise but something

new. . . . For the psychologist it is the self—man as he is, and the indescribable and super-empirical totality of the same man. . . . Man himself is partly empirical and partly transcendental.

(ibid:765).

. . . The Self, in its efforts at self-realization, reaches out beyond the ego-personality on all sides; because of its all-encompassing nature it is brighter and darker than the ego, and accordingly confronts it with problems which it would like to avoid.

(ibid:778).

. . . we come to the conclusion that its most conspicuous quality, namely, *its unity and uniqueness* . . . presupposes a *dissociated consciousness* [Jung's emphasis]. For no one who is one himself needs oneness as a medicine—nor, we might add, does anyone who is unconscious of his dissociation, for a *conscious* situation of distress is needed in order to activate the archetype of unity.

(ibid:772).

If this begins to sound familiar to the reader, it should. In Chapter 16, we quoted Jung on the production of a new "living symbol" thusly:

. . . For this collaboration of opposing states to be possible at all, they must first face one another in the fullest conscious opposition. This necessarily entails a *violent disunion with oneself*, to the point where thesis and antithesis negate one another, while *the ego is forced to acknowledge its absolute participation in both* [author's emphasis in both cases].

(Jung,1971).

This quotation was from *Psychological Types*, first published in 1921, eight years before Jung encountered his friend Richard Wilhelm's translation of the Chinese alchemical text: *The Secret of the Golden Flower. Mysterium Coniunctionis* itself wasn't to be published until 1955 and 1956 [it was originally published in two volumes]. Jung was able to anticipate the information he would gain from the alchemists years later because Jung went through the same experience as the alchemists in his confrontation with the unconscious! He knew the necessity for a "violent disunion with oneself" because he had experienced just that. He knew that "the ego is forced to acknowledge its absolute participation in both" [matter and spirit, or the "empirical" and the "transcendental"] because he had been forced to do just that. Clearly, the alchemists, though writing hundreds of years in the past, had something of worth for modern man.

At this point, just as we are discussing the deepest mysteries of the human psyche, we must leave because we have passed beyond issues which the alchemists were able to solve. In *Mysterium Coniunctionis*, Jung drew on the work of the alchemists to present a symbolic description of the journey man has to take at this critical point in his history. For the alchemists, this attempt was largely unconscious and limited to the lonely few. For us, this must be a journey taken by all if we are to reach some new level of human consciousness.

Summary

Mysterium Coniunctionis cannot be briefly summarized, as has been attempted in these pages, without sacrificing most of its complexity. It was the culmination of Jung's work and the richest work in the Jungian canon. Much of its value lies in the incredible detail in which it described the elements of the alchemical process. Innumerable practical psychological problems are explicated by the symbols of alchemy. Even at five hundred and fifty pages of text, Jung was largely limited to summarizing the alchemical material, with an occasional explication of its psychological significance, just as this book's author has been limited to summarizing Jung's material, with an occasional explication of Jung's intention. As has already been mentioned, Marie Louise von Franz and Edward Edinger have done a yeoman job of extending Jung's work on alchemy. However, a full hermeneutic study of *Mysterium Coniunctionis* (as well as *Aion* and the shorter alchemical works) still lies ahead for future scholars. If it were ever done, it would be an invaluable aid to both clinical and theoretical psychologists. Jung has drawn the blue-print from which an imposing edifice can be built.

The description of Jung's psychology ends with this chapter

on *Mysterium Coniunctionis*. The author will next turn to an unlikely and seemingly unrelated field: mathematics. Mathematicians led the other sciences in their attempt to create a totally logical science. Twentieth-century mathematicians attempted to reduce all mathematics to arithmetic, then to prove that arithmetic was both complete and consistent.

If mathematicians had been successful in this attempt, it would have been the culmination of the Renaissance Ideal. However, a mathematician named Kurt Gödel brought them back to reality with a stunning mathematical proof that the world could *never* be reduced to mathematical logic. How he did so, and how this relates to the psychology of Carl Jung, is the topic of the third and final part of this book.

Part III:

Gödel's Proof

19

The Roots of Modern Mathematics

Philosophy From the Renaissance to Kant

Throughout this book, the author has tried to demonstrate that Jung was not an isolated thinker, expressing idiosyncratic ideas. Instead, Jung's ideas, though brilliant, developed out of necessity; the materialist/rationalist position was not adequate to deal with the facts available to Jung. Philosophers dealt with the contradiction inherent in a materialist position long before Jung.

In particular, we have seen that, over a hundred years before Jung, philosopher Immanuel Kant was forced to deal with the seeming paradoxes presented by Hume and Berkeley. The materialist position had found its clearest expositor in seventeenth century philosopher John Locke; never again would materialism seem so clear and reasonable. Locke said that, at birth, man's mind was a blank slate upon which the sensory experiences of a lifetime were later recorded. All ideas were merely memories or combinations of memories of sensory experiences.

Barely twenty years later, Bishop George Berkeley took Locke's ideas to their logical conclusion and demonstrated that the rationalist position led inevitably to idealism; i.e., the belief in the primacy of ideas. Berkeley pointed to the obvious fact that all that we have ever experienced, or can ever experience, are ideas; there is no necessary relationship between those ideas and the physical world.

In fact, since all we experience are ideas, there is nothing to prove that a physical world exists. Berkeley then restored the existence of the world by saying that it and we existed in the mind of God, but that accorded more with his theological occupation than his philosophical insight.

Another forty years passed, and eighteenth century philosopher David Hume demonstrated that our most basic beliefs about reality are open to question. In a justifiably famous example, Hume pointed out that there is no such thing as cause and effect. All we really observe is that two events occur contemporaneously in place and one precedes another in time. There is no necessity linking one event with the other; necessity can only be asserted with respect to the mental world of logic.

That was the cul-de-sac that philosophy had arrived at before Kant. It was in the late eighteenth century, nearly forty years after Hume published his major works, that Kant saw a possible way out of the dilemma. Kant wasn't solipsistic enough to really believe that the world only existed in his own mind as Berkeley had argued. Nor did Kant believe that Hume was right in denying cause-and-effect and other such seeming universals. Instead, Kant turned Hume's proof on its head and argued that there were indeed universal organizing principles, but these universal "categories" were within the human mind. These "categories" organized our experiences of physical reality into a form that could be mentally recorded and used.

The mind was not the blank slate that Locke asserted it to be; instead it was a complex unity of organizational principles which were capable of breaking the seamless reality of the physical world into parts that could be recorded and manipulated internally. Thus universal principles like cause-and-effect were restored; they were inherent structures of our psyches. There was a physical world accessible to our psyches, but it was only accessible because these psychic structures provided a way of imparting meaning to the inherently meaningless world outside. The particular psychic world of the individual and the collective physical world met in collective psychic categories.

The Problem Passes from Philosophy to Science

Scientists, however, went blithely along, unaware of either the dilemma which confronted philosophy or Kant's attempt at a solution to that dilemma. In our day, many physicists and chemists still implicitly assume a materialist position which would sound remarkably similar to Locke's if it were ever explicitly stated. But it isn't; instead it is implicit in their approach to the world. And implicit assumptions are beyond criticism.

Issues always seem to confront philosophy first, but inevitably those issues descend into other areas of human thought. Philosophy is arguably the highest expression of human thought. As such it deals with both truth and beauty, thought and feeling. Below philosophy arises the great split into the "two cultures" of science and art, as C. P. Snow has called them (Snow,1959). Both deal with philosophic issues at roughly the same time, but each in its own unique way. This book could trace the identical problem in either art or science; artists, musicians, and writers have been subject to the limits of the Renaissance ideal just as surely as scientists.

However, Jung's psychology was the response of a scientist to a problem, not an artist. One of the key moments in his life was the realization that his need to bring forth the contents of the unconscious and give them outer expression was not because he was an artist, but because he was a scientist. As part of his descent into the unconscious during those difficult years after his split with Freud, he had begun to spontaneously draw mandalas. Jung had a vision in which a female friend admired the beauty of these mandalas and tried to convince Jung that he was an artist. The idea was appealing because of its simplicity, but Jung finally rejected it (Jung,1965:195ff).

But, if not art, what was their purpose? In chapter sixteen, we have discussed Jung's eventual discovery that mandalas appear to be attempts by the psyche to produce symbols of the unity of opposites. Jung later called that unifying principle of the psyche the "transcendent function", and later yet the "Self". The existence of the "transcendent function", the

"Self", was his second great discovery after the discovery of the collective unconscious itself. The rest of Jung's work was an attempt to explain the relationship between the "Self" and the individual ego, and the developmental stages that led the ego closer and closer to the "Self". Thus it was Jung's realization that he was a scientist, not an artist, that led to his greatest achievements.

Happily, Jung was also able to give an artistically satisfying expression to his scientific thought, but that is more true than not of great scientists. For example, Newton, Darwin, and Einstein all wrote brilliantly. All three avoided jargon and felt that the essence of their discoveries could be understood by intelligent laymen. But their primary stance was as scientist, not artist. Their deepest concern was for the truth they presented, not its beauty.

In the remainder of this book the author will describe how one particular science, mathematics, was confronted with the limits of rationalism in much the same way as were Kant and Jung. Mathematics has been chosen for several reasons. Many previous works have described how twentieth-century physicists had to reject Newtonian absolutes in favor of relativity and quantum mechanics. But even physicists don't always understand the full implications of their discoveries. One who did was Werner Heisenberg. His famous Uncertainty Principle said that one can measure either the position or the momentum of a sub-atomic particle, but not both (Heisenberg, 1930).

This has led sophisticated commentators to realize that the observer, by the mere fact of observing, affects his experiment. But a deeper realization is that the observer and the observed are one, and that if observation becomes detailed enough it inevitably turns back upon itself. This is the problem of a self-referential system which will concern us greatly in the rest of this book. However, modern physics is such a hodge-podge of oddities that essential discoveries such as Heisenberg's tend to be lumped with others of less lasting significance. The issues are much more clearly drawn in mathematics. And, while relativity and quantum mechanics have been widely popularized, the even more significant discoveries of modern mathematics are largely unknown.

However, there is an even more significant reason for choosing mathematics to illustrate the fallacies inherent in materialism. Nineteenth century mathematician Carl Friedrich Gauss, arguably the greatest mathematician of all time, termed mathematics the "Queen of the Sciences" (reported in Bell,1937:xv). As the most abstract expression of scientific thought, it is the first of the sciences to deal with the deep issues of human intellect.

Problems first confront "pure" mathematicians; men who are proud of the fact that their field has absolutely no relevance to human affairs. However, once dealt with in "pure" mathematics, the issues are developed by "applied" mathematicians; men who are equally proud of the fact that their field contributes directly to the betterment of humanity. From "applied" mathematics, the issues descend into physics, and then beyond physics into chemistry and biology and the myriad of bifurcations of the sciences that are the norm in our day.

Analytic Geometry

In mathematics, the Renaissance ideal soon led to increasing abstraction. The greatest example of mathematical thought prior to the Renaissance was Euclid's geometry. This was the first, and for nearly two thousand years, the only known complete and self-consistent scientific system. Euclid's geometry defined the elementary objects with which it would deal; i.e., "points", "lines", "figures" and "angles". It defined the mathematical operations which it would perform on those elementary objects. Finally, it stated certain "axioms"; i.e., assumptions which were assumed to be self-evident.

It is important to realize that the axioms asserted nothing about the nature of the physical world; they were merely assumptions that would be used within this mathematical system. Until the nineteenth century even mathematicians didn't fully realize this. It was common to point to physical reality for proof of the self-evident truth of Euclid's axioms.

From those spare tools—elementary objects, operations, and axioms—a logically consistent set of proofs could be derived. Nothing derived from those axioms conflicted with anything else derived from those axioms. Thus the system was consistent. Further, anything that could be truly asserted about "points" and "lines" and "figures" and "angles" could be derived from those axioms. Thus the system was complete. Again, it awaited the nineteenth century to question whether geometry was truly complete and consistent.

Euclid's geometry provided a model on which other mathematical systems could pattern themselves. The first advance in mathematical abstraction beyond Euclid was made by the early-seventeenth-century mathematician and philosopher Rene Descartes. As a philosopher, Descartes' famous assertion: "Cogito, ergo sum (I think, therefore I am)" was the first clear expression of the Renaissance ideal.

As a statement about the whole man, Descartes' assertion is ridiculous. For millennia before man had any conscious awareness—which is clearly what Descartes means by "think"—he existed as a sensing, feeling animal. But as a statement that a new level of consciousness had come into existence, Descartes' assertion is a bold proclamation. However, it was far too early for men to realize that self-referential statements—in this case, the human mind discussing itself—are fraught with difficulty. The purpose of the remainder of this paper is to trace how one mathematician, Kurt Gödel, gave explicit mathematical expression to this difficulty.

Descartes' great advance in mathematics was of a piece with his advance in philosophy. Besides geometry, the other great mathematical tool prior to the Renaissance was arithmetic. It had drifted into the Western world by the same route as alchemy, from the Arabic world through the meeting place of East and West—Spain. Arithmetic was more abstract than geometry; even though geometry deals with abstractions called points and lines and angles, those abstract entities were derived from the points and lines and angles encountered in the physical world.

Numbers, the royalty of the kingdom of arithmetic, are something much different; there is no such thing as a number existing in physical reality. Our sense of numbers is relational; the thing common between my "two" eyes and my "two" ears and my "two" arms and my "two" legs is that there are "two" of each. A relationship doesn't exist as a "thing"; it is a statement about the connections between "things".

Arithmetic provides a system for formally dealing with numbers and the relationships between numbers, hence the relationships between relationships. We have said much about relationship previously in this book and will say more yet, but for now it is enough to realize that most of the thinkers who have found a way past the dilemmas of materialism have realized that relationships are primary and things are secondary, or even that both are secondary and derived from something nameless that transcends both categories.

For example, in Chapter seven, we observed how Gustav Fechner discovered that the primary unity of sensory perception is relational, not absolute. Fechner then concluded that there had to be a unity that underlay the physical world that was being perceived and the psychic world that was doing the perceiving.

Descartes asked if it wasn't possible to express geometry in terms of numbers and relationships between numbers rather than in terms of "things" like points and lines. In fact, it was possible; I am indebted to Eric Temple Bell for the following simple description of Descartes' solution to the problem, which appears in Bell's classic *Men of Mathematics*.

> The basic idea, like all the really great things in mathematics, is simple to the point of obviousness. Lay down any two intersecting lines on a plane. Without loss of generality we may assume that the lines are at right angles to one another. Imagine now a city laid out on the American plan, with avenues running north and south, streets east and west. The whole plan will be laid out with respect to one avenue and one street, called the axes, which intersect in what is called the origin, from which street-avenue numbers are read consecutively.

Thus it is clear without a diagram where 1002 West 126 Street is, if we note that the ten avenues summarized in the number 1002 are stepped off to the west, that is, on the map, to the left of the origin. This is so familiar that we visualize the position of any particular address instantly. The avenue-number and street-number, with the necessary supplements of smaller numbers (as in the '2' in '1002' above) enable us to fix definitely and uniquely the position of any point whatever with respect to the axes, by giving the pair of numbers which measure its east or west and its north or south from the axes; this pair of numbers is called the coordinates of the point (with respect to the axes).

Now suppose a point to wander over the map. The coordinates (x,y) of all the points on the curve over which it wanders will be connected by an equation, (this must be taken for granted by the reader who has never plotted a graph to fit data), which is called the equation of the curve. Suppose now for simplicity that our curve is a circle. We have its equation.

(Bell,1937:52f).

And, of course, we are not limited to circles; in fact, any geometric figure could be expressed with Descartes' system of coordinates. Mathematicians could then use algebraic techniques to develop relationships that were not readily apparent in the geometric figures. Because this provided a way of analyzing geometric problems, Descartes' discovery was termed Analytic Geometry. Of this discovery, John Stuart Mill said that:

> . . . [analytic geometry] far more than any of his metaphysical speculations, immortalized the name of Descartes, and constitutes the greatest single step ever made in the progress of the exact sciences.
> (quoted in ibid:35).

However, despite Mill's claim, there was a mathematical tool that far exceeded analytic geometry in the impact it had on "the exact sciences". That tool was the calculus of Newton and Leibniz.

Calculus

The next great advance in mathematics was the simultaneous development of calculus by Newton and Leibniz. Both men transcended the seeming dichotomy presented earlier between "pure" and "applied" scientists. Both tried to advance human thought and also to advance the applications of human thought to the physical world.

The great weakness that analytic geometry had in dealing with physical reality was that reality was in continuous flux, and analytic geometry had no way of expressing continuous change. Arithmetic can express any quantifiable physical relationship between objects, but it has no way of deriving changes in its own expressions. It can't lift itself up by its own bootstraps, so to speak. A new mathematical tool was needed: calculus.

Imagine an irregular closed figure drawn on a piece of paper; purely as an example, picture something like a lumpy circle. How could you find the area occupied by that lumpy circle? You might draw a rectangle that was as small as possible yet fully included the figure. Most of us learned in school that the areas of a rectangle is the product of its length times its height; so we can determine the rectangle's area. Since the rectangle is larger than the lumpy circle, you could consider the area of the rectangle to be an "upper limit" on the area of the figure; that is, by using the area of the rectangle as an approximation to the area of the lumpy circle, you would insure that the true area couldn't exceed your estimate.

If the lumpy circle was quite asymmetric, you could improve your estimate by drawing a line which split it in half, and constructing two rectangles of different sizes next to each other, meeting on the line, each just big enough to enclose its part of the figure. By calculating the area of each rectangle and adding the two, the "upper limit" would be smaller and closer to the actual area of the figure. If you increased the number of rectangles, your estimate would get better and better. The "limit" would get smaller and smaller, and approach the actual area more and more closely. With a thousand rectangles, the "limit" would be so close to the actual area that for all practical purposes, you could consider it to be identical. However, it's important to realize that it would still not be exact.

Now try and make a leap in thought. Imagine that you extended the number of rectangles endlessly. If you had some way of calculating the "limit" by adding up this infinite number of areas, this "limit" would now no longer be merely an approximation to the area of the figure; it would be exactly the area of the figure. That is just what calculus does. Descartes' analytic geometry provided a way of describing any geometric figure in terms of numeric coordinates, and then converting those coordinates to an algebraic function. Granted, if the figure was highly irregular, the function would be quite complex. Leibniz and Newton independently developed a method for calculating (hence calculus) the area contained within that figure. However, their discovery could be used for far more than the calculation of areas.

In effect, calculus provided a technique for breaking anything into an infinite number of pieces and summing the infinitely small sizes of each piece; therefore, change could be quantified. For example, assume someone told you that a rocket ship was accelerating at such-and-such a rate, a rate that could only be expressed as a complex algebraic formula. You could use calculus to derive what the velocity would be after any interval of time.

From the velocity you could further use calculus to derive the distance the rocket ship had moved. Or, proceeding in the opposite direction, calculus could just as easily be used to derive the acceleration from the velocity as the velocity from the acceleration. As long as something was changing continuously across time or space, and the something could be expressed in an algebraic terms, calculus could calculate the change.

The key insight that made calculus possible was the realization that infinity was not just an abstraction; infinity could be quantified. Consider the example given above of developing the area of an irregular figure by covering it with rectangles and calculating their areas. We referred to the sum of their areas as an upper "limit" on the sum of the figure. As the number of rectangles got larger and larger, the "limit" shrank and the approximation got better. No matter how close you wanted the approximation to be, say within a millionth of an inch, you could use a sufficient number of rectangles such that the difference would be less.

As you watched those successive upper "limits" shrink, they would seem to eventually approach some absolute "limit". There could only be one such "limit". If there was a second such "limit", the difference between the two "limits"—call it "d"—could be measured. Then a sufficient number of rectangles could be used such that the approximation to the true area would have to be less than "d/2". Since the distance between the two "limits" was d, and since we could make the difference between the actual area and the approximation less than "d/2", only one of the two limits could satisfy that condition. Whichever of the two it was, it must be the true limit. Thus, if a limit could be approached, the limit would be unique.

Calculus provided physical science, especially physics and astronomy, with a tool of incredible versatility. Bishop Berkeley, of whose philosophy we have already had much to say, claimed that:

> ... the method of Fluxions [author's note: Newton's term for calculus] is the general key by help whereof the modern mathematicians unlock the secrets of Geometry, and consequently of Nature.
> (quoted in ibid:90).

Even the most complex problems in physics and astronomy still require no mathematical tool beyond calculus or extensions of calculus such as tensor mechanics. Thus calculus marked the high water mark for mathematics as a tool of materialism. From that point on, having conquered the physical world with calculus, mathematicians turned backwards once more in order to make calculus still more abstract. As Descartes had reduced geometry to arithmetic, mathematicians now reduced calculus to arithmetic.

Having achieved this, which was a relatively minor accomplishment, mathematicians then turned their attention to the basis for arithmetic itself. They theorized that ultimately the physical world could be fully described by physics, and physics could be fully described by mathematics. After all, like Bishop Berkeley, they could see all around them the fruits of the applications of calculus. Since all of mathematics seemed to be reducible to arithmetic, if they could prove that arithmetic was both complete and consistent, then man would be able to fully explain the world. This pursuit of mathematical formalism is the subject of our next chapter.

20

Mathematical Formalism

For nearly two thousand years, Euclid's Geometry stood as the one great example of a seemingly complete and consistent mathematical system. However, as it stood, it was too "intuitive" for nineteenth century mathematicians. All this talk of points and lines and angles required far too much intuitive understanding of what a point or a line or an angle actually was. We've seen that as early as the seventeenth century, Descartes' analytic geometry translated geometry into the world of arithmetic, which made mathematicians much more comfortable. But no one had yet proved arithmetic to be both complete and consistent.

Late in the nineteenth century, David Hilbert became the champion of the attempt to put mathematics on a solid footing. He insisted that any mathematical system consist solely of a finite number of definitions of relevant terms, a finite number of axioms, and a finite number of operations. The definitions, axioms, and operations were all to be totally empty of content! Mathematics was assumed to concern itself only with the formal manipulation of empty symbols. Perhaps from all that has already been discussed in this book it will be apparent that this was an impossible goal. Symbols are not empty and, in fact, it is precisely because symbols produce deep feeling responses that mathematics is able to develop. The author of this book originally studied mathematics because of the power of the symbol of zero, of nothingness expressed.

In the second grade, a homework assignment introduced the concept of zero. There were a number of problems where zero was added to or substracted from various numbers. The answer, of course, was always the same number. Most of the other children in the class just regarded this as still another rule to be memorized and experienced no more difficulty than with any other such incomprehensible rule. But the author sat alone in his room that night, staring at the problems, in tears at their seeming senselessness.

How could you add something to a number and the number remained unchanged? And then, an understanding burst forth, and the author had the first mystical experience of his life. The immensity of the concept of nothingness overwhelmed him. The realization that mathematicians were brilliant enough to be able to capture that immensity in a symbol awed him. He determined on the spot that he would be a mathematician.

Hilbert was himself under the grip of a symbol, a symbol of unity. The new mathematical thought, like all the other outgrowths of the Renaissance, had grown in a piece-meal fashion, with no order or rigor. Hilbert saw the possibility of unifying all mathematical thought under a single formal method. This desire for unity was clearly the "living symbol" (to use Jung's term) for mathematics in Hilbert's era. Nearly all of the great mathematicians were striving toward this formal unity of mathematics. They were not able to stand outside their field and see that they were under the grip of a symbol. And, though their efforts were fore-doomed, the development of mathematical rigor was a necessary step in mathematics. Let us examine Peano's Postulates in an attempt to show the reader why such a seemingly cold, abstract goal could grip men like Hilbert.

Peano's Postulates

The first important product of this new formalism was Peano's Postulates, a system of axioms from which arithmetic can be derived. Giuseppe Peano was a mathematician and logician, and his postulates have a simplicity and an elegance that can be understood by non-mathematicians as well as mathematicians. Here are the five postulates (another name for axioms) as summarized in Reese's *Dictionary of Philosophy and Religion*:

(1) 0 is a number.
(2) The successor of any number is a number.
(3) No two numbers have the same successor.
(4) 0 is not the successor of any number.
(5) If P is a property such that: (a) 0 has the property P; and (b) whenever a number "n" has the property P, then the successor of "n" also has the property P, then every number has the property P.

(Reese, 1980:418f).

With the exception of the last axiom, which is what mathematicians refer to as "mathematical induction", the purpose of the axioms can be readily understood. (1) and (4) together imply that there is a first "number" (whatever a "number" might be, since all terms are understood to be empty symbols) which is called 0. (2) and (3) imply that there is a unique number that is the successor to 0; in normal arithmetic we call it 1.

In turn, using (2) and (3), 1 also has a successor; we call that 2, and so forth. Clearly there is no end to such numbers, since for any number there is a unique successor. However, though we have generated all the counting numbers, as yet we haven't given them any properties. E.g., a property of the integers might be that when you subtract any number from itself, the answer is zero. Another property might be that when you multiply two numbers together, that product is also a number. We need (5) in order to develop the properties possessed by the integers.

Let's look more closely at (5). As has been pointed out earlier, a scientific theorem is always provisional; experience might always contradict the theorem. But (5) implies that, in arithemetic at least, something can be proved once and for all. (5) says that in order to prove that all numbers possess some property P (which can be anything you like; the whole field of mathematical assertions about numbers is up for grabs) only two things need to be proved. First, 0 has to possess the property P. Second, if a number n possesses the property P, then n's successor, n + 1, also has to possess the property P.

Let's try an example. Let P be the property that any number added to itself is still a number. Does 0 possess property P? 0 + 0 = 0, and 0 is a number; therefore 0 does have property P. How about the second condition? If n + n equals a number q, then consider (n + 1) + (n + 1). Rearrange the terms so that (n + 1) + (n + 1) = (n + n) + 1 + 1. Now it's a given that n + n is a number q, so (n + n) + 1 + 1 is equivalent to q + 1 + 1. But (q + 1) is the successor to q, and (2) tells us that the successor to a number is also a number; let's call it r. Therefore, q + 1 + 1 = r + 1. But r + 1 is the successor to r, and (2) implies that it is therefore also a number, call it s. To summarize the steps:

$$(n + 1) + (n + 1) = (n + n) + 1 + 1 = q + 1 + 1$$
$$= (q + 1) + 1 = r + 1 = s, \text{ and s is a number.}$$

Therefore, we have just proved that, for any number n, if n + n is a number, so is (n + 1) + (n + 1); that is, if n has property P, so does n + 1. Since 0 also has property P, then (5) implies that all numbers have the property P. Therefore, the sum of any number with itself is also a number.

Why is it that this method of proof works? We've proved that 0 possesses the property. We've also proved that if n possesses the property P, so does n + 1. Therefore, let n = 0. Since it's true for n, it must be true for n + 1. So it's true for 1. Let n = 1; clearly then 2 also possesses the property, and so on. This is obviously a very powerful method of proof since it's quite a bit easier to prove an assertion is true in two circumstances than to prove it's true in any of an infinite number of circumstances. But notice that it gets involved in infinite processes; i.e., there is no way to demonstrate this is true in a finite number of steps. That is both the power of "mathematical induction" and its Achilles heel. For, as we will see later, infinite processes tend to involve us in self-referential systems, and self-referential systems cannot always be reduced to logical analysis.

Still, Peano's Postulates were a stunning example of the

possibilities of the new formalism. Using these five axioms, it was then at least theoretically possible to derive all the properties of arithmetic. Most colleges have a first-year mathematics course where the students derive all the major properties of arithmetic using Peano's Postulates, or some similar system of axioms. Note that there is absolutely nothing contained in the five axioms that points to the nature of those properties. It is undoubtedly true that there are properties of the integers that have never yet been discovered. Peano's Postulates only provide the starting point: an elegant axiomatic method for producing arithmetic.

Non-Euclidean Geometry

Now the question returns: how to prove that arithmetic, as developed using some axiomatic technique such as Peano's Postulates, is both complete and consistent? By complete, mathematicians mean that there are no true arithmetic statements that can be made that cannot be derived from the axioms of arithmetic. By consistent, mathematicians mean that if a statement can be derived from the axioms, then its opposite cannot also be derived; i.e., a statement cannot both be true and false at the same time.

As we will see later, Kurt Gödel was able to prove that, in fact, there are properties that cannot be derived from either Peano's Postulates, or any other finite set of axioms; that is, arithmetic is incomplete. More exactly, he was able to show that if arithmetic is assumed to be consistent, properties can be derived from the axioms which cannot be proved to be either true or false; i.e., if arithmetic is consistent then it's incomplete, if it's complete then it's inconsistent. Gödel proved that the only way out of the impasse was to use a system more powerful than arithmetic to prove arithmetic's consistency; but then how could you prove that system's consistency except with a still more powerful system, etc. However, we still have a considerable distance to travel before we can approach Gödel's Proof.

Until the nineteenth century, it seemed self-evident to mathematicians that an axiomatic system was inherently consistent and complete; after all, they had Euclidian geometry as a practical example. Euclid developed geometry from ten axioms, which all seemed self-evident to mathematicians. For example, if L is a line, then there exists a point not on L. One can readily draw a line on a paper and a point at some other place on the paper as an illustration.

However, the famous fifth axiom, commonly called the "parallel axiom", was not so self-evident. It said that for a given line L and a given point P not on line L, there existed one and only one line containing P that is parallel to L. This seemed to be so much less self-evident than all the other axioms that generations of mathematicians attempted to make it a theorem rather than an axiom and derive it from the other nine axioms. But to no avail; the only way to eliminate it was to give some other tenth axiom, equally un-self-evident, and derive the parallel axiom from it.

In the nineteenth century, mathematicians Janos Bolyai and Nikolai Lobachevski took another approach: they assumed the opposite of the fifth axiom—that more than one line could be drawn through the given point parallel to the given line. They hoped to derive a contradiction and thus prove the fifth axiom to be true. Instead they developed a strange geometry that was fully as consistent as Euclid's.

Still later Georg (sic) Riemann developed a geometry assuming that no line can be drawn through a given point parallel to a given line. This is the geometry of the surface of a sphere, if a line is defined to be a great circle of the sphere. On such a surface, there is indeed no such thing as a parallel line since any two great circles have exactly two points in common. This was the geometry that Einstein later drew on in his conception of general relativity. Scientist A. S. Eddington remarked that "a geometer like Riemann might almost have foreseen the more important features of the actual world" (quotation in Bell,1937:484).

Mathematicians were understandably surprised to find that new axioms produced new geometries rather than contradictions. However, that led them to a deeply disturbing realization. As long as Euclid's geometry could be assumed to be a self-evident picture of the world, one could turn to the world to show that no proposition could be both true and false. Once that was no longer possible, where could one turn for proof? This new mathematical world of formal systems could have no connection with physical reality. Bertrand Russell perfectly captured this world in a famous epigram: "mathematics may be defined as the subject in which we never know what we are talking about, nor whether what we are saying is true" (Russell,1956:1577).

As we have seen, Hilbert and others were able to reduce geometry and calculus to arithmetic, and Peano and others were able to develop formal axiomatic systems for arithmetic. But this just delayed answering the question: is arithmetic itself complete and consistent? Early in the twentieth century, Bertrand Russell and Alfred North Whitehead decided to shift the problem to a new domain. They attempted to show that arithmetic could be derived from logic and then hoped to prove that logic was complete and consistent. As we have seen, everytime the problem was answered by shifting to a different model, that model in turn had to be referred to still another model. The wonder is that there was ever a way out of this impasse. It took Gödel to find it, but first we need to discuss Russell's and Whitehead's attempt, and Cantor's remarkable attempt to quantify infinity.

21

Self-Referential Systems

The Barber Paradox

In the mid-nineteenth century, George Boole developed a symbolic representational system for logical syllogisms. These symbols could then be manipulated using a sort of algebra to determine the truth or falsity of complex logical relationships. In the latter part of the nineteenth century, Friedrich Frege demonstrated that arithmetic could be derived from a form of symbolic logic called set theory. At roughly the same time, Bertrand Russell read Peano's Postulates and determined to use the symbolic logic of Boole to develop similar axioms of logic, from which he could derive all of arithmetic.

Shortly after making this resolve, Russell discovered Frege's work which purported to do just what Russell intended. However, while studying Frege's work, Russell discovered a paradox, one seemingly so inconsequential that he thought initially it could be easily disposed of. But it proved intractable and, in 1902, Russell wrote to Frege describing the paradox.

The second and concluding volume of Frege's work was at the printer's when he received Russell's letter. Poor Frege was stunned to find his life's work destroyed by a single puzzle. He added a brief appendix to the work at the last minute, in which he said:

> A scientist can hardly encounter anything more undesirable than to have the foundation collapse just as the work is finished. I was put in this position by a letter from Mr. Bertrand Russell.
> (reported in Gardner,1982:16).

How could a paradox be so powerful that it could destroy a life's work? Most of us regard a paradox as a type of puzzle to amuse or annoy, but hardly a cause for deep concern. The word paradox has many meanings; for example, "an assertion that seems false but actually is true" or that "seems true but actually is false". Or "a line of reasoning that seems impeccable but which leads to a logical contradiction" (hence a fallacy).

However, the word paradox will be used in this paper to mean a statement that, if assumed to be true, leads to the conclusion that it is false. If assumed to be false, it implies that it is true. Hence, "an assertion whose truth or falsity is undecidable" (all quotes from ibid:vii).

Russell coined a popular version of the paradox which bedeviled Frege and called it "The Barber Paradox." Consider a village where the barber shaves every male villager if and only if the villager does not shave himself. That's clear enough—some of the villagers shave themselves and some let the barber do the shaving, but everyone gets shaved. The paradox arises when we ask whether the barber shaves himself. If we assume that he does, then, since the barber only shaves those who don't shave themselves, the barber cannot shave himself. Hence, if he does shave himself, he doesn't shave himself. If we assume that he doesn't shave himself, we get stuck in the circle again, since the barber shaves everyone who doesn't shave themself. Hence, if he doesn't shave himself, he necessarily does shave himself.

The version of the paradox which Russell described to Frege concerned Frege's theory of sets. This was a mathematical system which Russell used as the basis for his own system, which he called the theory of classes. A set is a collection of things of the same kind; e.g., the set of books about logic is composed of all the books about logic; the set of proofs for the existence of God is composed of all such proofs. Each item of the given kind is called a member of the set.

It's key to understand that the set itself is not the same as the members; the set is the collection, the assemblage, not the things assembled. Most sets are not members of themselves. For example, the set of all even numbers is not an even number; the set of left-handed tennis players is not a left-handed tennis player. Let's refer to such sets as normal. But, contrary to expectation, there are sets which are members of themselves. For example, the set of all concepts which can be imagined is itself a concept which can be imagined. Therefore, it is a member of itself.

Russell mentally constructed a higher level set, the set of all normal sets. In other words, the members of this set were themselves sets, sets which did not contain themselves. The paradox arose, just as it did in the "Barber Paradox", when Russell asked whether this set was normal. If he assumed that it was normal, then since it was defined as containing all normal sets, it must contain itself. However, by the definition of normal set, a set which contains itself is not normal. Hence, if it's normal, then it's not normal. Try it assuming the opposite, that it's not normal. Following a similar line of logic, we arrive at the conclusion that it must be normal. So, if it's normal, it's not normal and, if it's not normal, it's normal.

In March of 1985, the public television science program "Nova" had an episode on the history of mathematics. In that episode they gave a superbly simple illustration of Russell's paradox. They said to imagine that there was a central librarian for a state. He requested all the regional librarians to compile a directory volume which listed all the books in their particular library. When he received these directories, he found that some of the librarians had included the directory as one of the books in the library, and some had excluded it.

He separated the directories into two different groups on that basis. He then began to compile a master directory which listed all the directories in the second group; i.e., those directories which did not include themselves. However, when he had finished listing all the directories, he hit a snag. Should he list the master directory or not. And, of course, he was stuck just as Frege was stuck.

Self-Referential Systems

Why does such a paradox arise? The problem is because in both the "Barber Paradox" and in the paradox of the "set of all sets which do not contain themselves", we are dealing with self-referential systems. And self-referential systems quickly become too complex for logic. The self-referential system par excellence is the mind. The mind is the only tool that we have for thinking about anything. But that means that the mind is also the only tool which we can use to think about the nature of the mind. Jung constantly stressed "the fundamental fact that in psychology the object of knowledge is at the same time the organ of knowledge, which is true of no other science" (Jung,1964:1025).

As we will see, Jung was wrong in assuming that only psychology has the problem; if we think deeply enough about anything, we are led ineluctably to think about the process of thought. As an example which we have already discussed at some length, Kant ran up against the same issue in philosophy. Once the Renaissance ideal led men to separate themselves from nature in order to observe nature objectively, it was inevitable that they would turn that observation upon themselves. Berkeley and Hume were the first in the Western World to demonstrate the nasty little paradoxes that appear when the mind thinks about itself.

Gregory Bateson was fond of pointing out that all living creatures are complex feed-back systems. Feed-back systems provide information to themselves about their performance, which they in turn use to change their performance. That change leads to further feed-back, thus forming a continuous loop. The information, which the system feeds back to itself so that it can better adapt to reality, is of a higher order of reality than the behavior that it comments on. Hence, any theory that seeks to explain a living creature in terms of its behavior seemed to Bateson, and to the author, doomed to failure (see Bateson,1972;1979).

As physicist Werner Heisenberg discovered, even confining our observation to non-living systems is not sufficient to protect us from the problem. At the sub-atomic level, our observation changes the object under observation, which is another way of saying that the subject, the object, and the act of observation are actually a single system; the split between subject and object is artificial. Thus, even in physical experiments, the subject is once again involved in a self-referential system (Heisenberg, 1930).

There is no necessary paradox in self-referential systems as long as the systems are finite. Mathematicians have been able to successfully prove the consistency and completeness of many finite mathematical systems. If the system is small enough and simple enough, they simply develop every implication of the system for every member of the system.

Thus, if a man can be viewed independently from the world around him, and if he is, as the materialist position insists, nothing more than the finite amount of "things" that make up his physical composition, such as proteins and nucleic acid, etc., there is a way out of the problem of self-referencing. The mind is then reducible to the brain, and the problem of the brain thinking about itself eventually winds down since it is at most a finite process.

That is still the most popular scientific position. The point of this book is that such a position seems increasingly untenable as we dig deeper into any of the systems that explore the universe, from philosophy to mathematics to physics to psychology; in fact, to any field at all. All fields eventually involve themselves in infinite self-referential systems.

Principia Mathematica: Mathematics' Tower of Babel

One would have thought that, as the inventor of the paradox that proved that logic inevitably involved itself in self-referential systems, Bertrand Russell would have seen the limits of logic. Instead, Russell preferred to define the problem away and continue to believe that logic could still explain the universe. In order to dispose of the sets that were members of themselves, Russell invented the theory of classes. Classes were much the same as sets except that they were defined such that they couldn't be members of themselves.

A class was defined to be on a higher order than its members. Classes of classes were on a higher order than classes, and so forth. The problem wasn't in any way resolved; it was just pushed off to infinity. Russell was willing to do this because he felt that the mathematics of infinity, which we will examine shortly, was in better shape than other fields of mathematics.

This solution of shoving the problem out of sight, like an ostrich sticking its head in the sand, was the same that Russell and others used in their creation of a philosophy known as logical positivism. Logical positivism insisted that since the ultimate questions about reality, metaphysical questions, were not open to either logical or experiential verification, they were not questions at all. Logical positivists confined all questions about the ultimate nature of reality to the dust heap of non-sense; that is, they were not sensible questions. Their attitude was that if questions are too bothersome to fit into a theory, just define them away as non-questions.

Bertrand Russell and Alfred North Whitehead jointly worked on their attempt to derive all arithmetic from the theory of classes. The product of their work was eventually published in three massive volumes between 1910 and 1913 as the *Principia Mathematica*. It is often said among mathematicians and logicians that no one except Russell and Whitehead have ever read all of the *Principia*, and even they may not have read all of each other's work.

While it was a joint work, most of the more difficult mathematical proofs were Russell's. Whitehead was more interested in the philosophic import. Whitehead's later work went in a direction opposite to Russell; his philosophical position accords well with the viewpoints presented in this book, while Russell remained confident to his death that logic was sufficient to the solution of all of man's problems.

If Russell had been able to develop a consistent and complete arithmetic from the axioms of symbolic logic, then logic would indeed rule the universe. Logic would explain arithmetic, arithmetic would explain geometry and calculus, which would in turn explain physics and astronomy and the other sciences, and the sciences would explain the world. The universe would have been reduced to the manipulations of logical symbols.

That's why this section of this book was sub-titled 'Mathematics' Tower of Babel". Like the biblical tower, Russell and Whitehead were attempting to construct an edifice beyond man's capability. Like the biblical tower, it also collapsed because of the limits of language.

Since Russell got around the problem of the "Barber's Paradox" by his creation of an infinite chain of classes, we need to turn to the mathematics of infinity. This area is one of the great triumphs of twentieth century mathematics: Georg (sic) Cantor's discovery of transfinite numbers.

Transfinite Numbers

At approximately the same time that Frege attempted to reduce arithmetic to symbolic logic, and Hilbert derived geometry from purely abstract terms, Georg Cantor developed a new way of looking at infinity. Mathematicians had previously tried to avoid the infinite like the plague. The infinite summations of calculus were only accepted because they summed the infinitely small, which approached zero. For some reason, mathematicians thought that zero was more understandable than infinity; Zen masters could have taught them otherwise. In 1831, mathematician Carl Friedrich Gauss railed against infinity thus:

> I protest against the use of infinite magnitude as something completed, which is never permissible in mathematics. Infinity is merely a way of speaking, the true meaning being a limit which certain ratios approach indefinitely close, while others are permitted to increase without restriction.
>
> (reported in Bell,1937:556).

But Cantor's discoveries were over a half-century later, and much had been learned in that interim.

> ... [Cantor realized] that misuse of the infinite in mathematics had justly inspired a horror of the infinite among careful mathematicians of his day, precisely as it did in Gauss. Nevertheless he maintains that the

resulting 'uncritical rejection of the legitimate actual infinite is no lesser a violation of the nature of things . . . which must be taken as they are'.
(ibid:556f).

It was with the "legitimate actual infinite" that Cantor was concerned. For example, there is clearly no end to the integers; if a largest integer could be conceived, merely add one to it and it's no longer the largest. There is also clearly no end to the points on a line provided that a point is understood to be without dimension. On the surface, it seems that all one can safely assert is that there is an infinite number of positive integers, an infinite number of points on a line. But Cantor asked if these infinities were the same size. Lest this sound like the medieval scholastic arguments about the number of angels who could stand on the head of a pin, the reader should be aware that Cantor found a way of quantifying infinity, and thus answering his own question.

Let's return to Frege's and Russell's concept of a set or class. What does it mean to say that two sets have the same number of members? For example, what does it mean to say that the set of fingers has the same number of members as the set of toes? If we think deeply about it, it merely means that we can pair off members of each of the two sets and have no members left over in either set. In our example, we could place each of our ten fingers on one of our ten toes.

Notice that it wouldn't matter what finger we matched with what toe as long as we were careful not to pair any finger with two toes or any toe with two fingers. Further, we could define a "cardinal number", in this case "10", which would characterize the number of members of both sets. Having developed the cardinal number "10", it then can be used to describe the number of members of any set which can be paired off with the set of fingers. We would describe each as having the same "cardinality".

This method of counting by pairing the members of one set with the members of another is usually termed the "pigeon-hole" technique. Cantor found that the "pigeon-hole" technique produced surprising results with infinite sets. For example, he discovered that there were exactly as many even integers as there were both odd and even integers. He reasoned that for every integer "i" in the set of all integers, he could match "i" with the integer "2i" in the set of even integers. "1" in the set of all integers matched with "2" in the set of even integers, "2" with "4", "3" with "6", etc. No matter what integer you gave him in either set, he could tell you what integer it matched in the other set. Thus the "pigeon-hole" technique proved that the two sets had the same number of members.

Cantor could use the same logic to show that the set of numbers evenly divisible by three was also just as big as the set of all integers. In fact the particular multiple made no difference; the set of numbers evenly divisible by a billion is still just as big as the set of all integers. Going in the other direction produced the same result. The integers are a sub-set of the rational numbers; what non-mathematicians normally refer to as fractions.

For example, 2 can be expressed as 2/1 as a fraction; 3 as 3/1, etc. But think of all the other fractions: 1/2, 1/3, 357/962, etc. Surely there are more fractions than integers! Instead, Cantor proved that the set of rational numbers had exactly as many members as the set of integers. This was a very surprising result indeed! In fact, Cantor proved that any infinite sub-set of the set of rational numbers contains exactly the same number of members. All have the same cardinality, which Cantor termed "aleph-null".

Cantor then asked if every infinite set had cardinality "aleph-null"; i.e., was every infinite set the same size as every other infinite set. The answer to that was even more surprisingly a resounding "no"; e.g., the infinity of "real" numbers was found to be larger than the infinity of rational numbers. A "real" number is any number that can be expressed as a decimal. All "rational" numbers can be expressed that way; for example, 1/2 = .5, 1/3 = .3333. . .(the ". . ." means that the 3's go on indefinitely).

But there are other "real" numbers which can be expressed as a decimal number, but cannot be expressed as a fraction. For example, "pi" cannot be expressed as a fraction. Similarly the square root of 2, which describes the length of the diagonal of a square which is 1 unit on a side, cannot be expressed as a fraction. Still, it would appear that there's surely just a few such strange numbers, and that most decimal numbers could be expressed as fractions. Appearances can be deceiving.

The proof is a clever application of the "pigeon-hole" technique which can be followed by non-mathematicians. If it were true that the cardinality of the "real" numbers was the same as the cardinality of the "rational" numbers, we could pair up "real" numbers with integers (since both the "rational" numbers and the integers have cardinality "aleph null"), and there wouldn't be any "real" numbers left over.

As we saw earlier in pairing up our fingers with our toes, it doesn't make any difference what pairing technique we use as long as it pairs every member of one set uniquely with a single member of the other set. For purposes of illustration only, let's assume that such a pairing technique has been developed for pairing the "real" numbers with the integers, and let's assume further that, within that pairing, the integer "1" corresponds to the real number ".20357. . ."; "2" corresponds to ".053489. . ."; "3" to ".8693217. . .", etc. Any other pairing would be equally acceptable.

Cantor was able to construct a "real" number which was not paired off with any integer. Construct a "real" number which differs from the "real" number paired with the integer "1" in the first digit, from the "real" number paired with the integer "2" in the second digit, and so forth. Using our example above, this constructed number would contain anything other than a "2" in the first digit (.20357. . .), anything other than a 5 in the second digit (.053489. . .), anything other than a 9 in the third digit (.8693217. . .), etc.

This constructed number is not contained in the set which is paired off with the integers. If we insist that it is, all we have to do is ask which integer it pairs off with. Let's say it is assumed to pair off with the integer "529". By the method of construction, we can prove that it differs from the number actually paired with "529" in the 529th digit. Therefore, the "real" numbers cannot be paired-off with the integers. The cardinality of the "real" numbers, which Cantor termed "c" for the continuum, is greater than the cardinality of the integers.

At first all of this seems like some sort of a cheat, but upon deeper reflection it can be seen to be profound. It provides an unambiguous definition of infinity; i.e., an infinite set is a set which can be put in a one-to-one relationship (this is a formal mathematical way of expressing the "pigeon-hole" technique) with a sub-set of itself. A finite set is one where this is not true. However, as we have just demonstrated, not all infinite sets are of equal size.

Cantor was later able to prove that the set of all sub-sets of a set, which mathematicians term the "power set", is always of higher order of cardinality than the set, even if the set is infinite. Thus the "power set" of the "rational" numbers has a cardinality bigger than "aleph null", Cantor termed it "aleph one". The question whether "aleph one" is the same as "c", the cardinality of the "real" numbers (and of points on a line) was one of the great problems in mathematics, termed the "continuum problem". It was finally proved that it was unprovable, but any discussion of that proof is beyond the scope of this paper.

Cantor termed "aleph null", "aleph one", etc., "transfinite" numbers; that is, they transcended finite numbers. Clearly, there can be no largest "transfinite" number. If there was a largest "transfinite" number, say "aleph n", then the "power-set" of the set with cardinality "aleph n" would have a cardinality greater than "aleph n". It's nowhere near so obvious, but the set of transfinite numbers of the form "aleph n", for any n, has a higher cardinality than "aleph n" for any n. Thus there is no end to infinity, even though Cantor provided a method of quantifying it.

The reader can safely ignore all this seeming jabber-wocky

about "aleph null" and "power sets". However, it is essential for the reader to recognize that Cantor was able to quantify infinite numbers, and to show that there is no end to such numbers. At the time of writing *Principia Mathematica*, Bertrand Russell was under the misapprehension that it was possible for him to resolve the problem of the "Barber Paradox" by inventing his theory of classes because Cantor had rigorously quantified infinite numbers. However, brilliant as Cantor's new conception of infinity was, it did <u>not</u> resolve Russell's problem; mathematicians had to seek other ways to prove arithmetic complete and consistent. With that settled, we are now finally in a position to show how Gödel destroyed Russell's dream much as Russell destroyed Frege's.

22

Gödel's Proof

Summary: Mathematics Before Gödel

Let's begin by summarizing what we have already discussed about the history of mathematics. Euclidean geometry and arithmetic were the two great triumphs of mathematics prior to the Renaissance. Geometry was an example for all the sciences of how a seemingly complete, consistent axiomatic system could be developed. However, mathematicians felt geometry to be too "intuitive"; they felt more comfortable in the more abstract world of arithmetic (and its child algebra).

Modern mathematics began when, early in the seventeenth century, Rene Descartes discovered a method for "mapping" geometry onto arithmetic; that is, every geometric figure could be represented by an algebraic formula. In the latter part of the seventeenth century, Isaac Newton and Gottfried Leibniz vastly extended the possibilities inherent in such a mapping with their independent development of calculus. Soon afterwards, lesser mathematicians were able to map calculus onto arithmetic in much the same way as Descartes had mapped geometry.

The next jump in the move toward mathematical abstraction came two hundred years later. Late in the nineteenth century, mathematical "formalism" became the rage. David Hilbert led a movement to convert all mathematics to formal axiomatic systems. Giuseppe Peano demonstrated how arithmetic could be developed from a mere five abstract axioms. Friedrich Frege attempted to map arithmetic onto a new branch of mathematics called "set theory" as a preparatory step toward a proof of the consistency and completeness of arithmetic.

However, Bertrand Russell discovered a paradox inherent in set theory: does the set of sets which do not contain themselves contain itself? Russell tried to avoid the paradox by creating his "theory of classes" which put sets on a higher level than their members, sets of sets on a higher level than sets, etc. However, this merely postponed the problem rather than settling it. Russell considered this acceptable because he felt that the mathematics of infinity was on sound footing with the discoveries of Georg Cantor.

Gödel's Insight

Kurt Gödel saw deeper into the nature of the paradox than Russell. Russell had tried to define the problems of self-referential systems out of existence. Gödel saw that the formalists such as Russell were trying to resolve "meta-mathematical" statements about arithmetic within arithmetic. "Meta" means above, beyond, transcending, as in metaphysics, which is the field of philosophy which deals with ultimate questions, questions which transcend physical explanation.

Thus meta-mathematical statements are statements about mathematics which transcend mathematics. For example, the statement that "arithmetic is consistent and complete" is a meta-mathematical statement. Gödel recognized that this statement, which was the goal of the formalists in mathematics, was a statement which could not be resolved within arithmetic; it transcended arithmetic.

Further, Gödel recognized that Russell's paradox could not be defined away because in reality infinite systems actually do contain themselves as members; therefore, any formalized mathematical system will eventually have to confront the issue. Gödel discovered how to carefully map meta-mathematical statements about arithmetic onto arithmetic. Then the truth or falsity of the meta-mathematical statements could be established by determining the truth or falsity of mathematical equations.

In effect, a system could be made to talk about itself. This insight by Gödel is one of the great discoveries in mathematical history, perhaps the single greatest. In many ways, it is more important to the future of science than any of the better-known achievements of twentieth-century science, such as relativity and quantum mechanics in physics, or the discovery of the structure of DNA in biology.

Further Readings on Gödel

In the description of the proof that follows, the author is drawing extensively on Ernest Nagel's and James R. Newman's "Gödel's Proof". This is the best non-mathematical description of Gödel's Proof to date, and is contained in Newman's classic, four-volume *World of Mathematics* (Newman,1956). Douglas R. Hofstadter's Pulitzer Prize-winning book, *Gödel, Escher, Bach* (Hofstadter,1980), was the source of the author's later discussion of "twisted" paradoxes. A more rigorous mathematical presentation of the proof is contained in Andrzej Mostowski's *Sentences Undecidable in Formalized Arithmetic* (Mostowski,1952). A. A. Fraenkel's and Y. Bar-Hillel's *Foundations of Set Theory* (Fraenkel & Bar-Hillel,1958) contains material on Gödel's Proof and other proofs that extended Gödel's original proof [the author is indebted to David A. Moonitz for introducing him to both of the preceding volumes].

It will not be possible in this book to fully present Gödel's Proof. Instead, as has been done with analytic geometry, calculus, and formalized mathematics, the author hopes to point to the significant elements of the proof and to draw some conclusions from the proof that go considerably beyond mathematics. This seems appropriate in discussing the discovery that mathematics can itself settle meta-mathematical speculations.

Mapping Arithmetic and Logical Signs Onto Numbers

The key to Gödel's proof lay in the development of a method of mapping the elementary signs of arithmetic and logic onto arithmetic. When we discussed Peano's Postulates, we saw that arithmetic could be developed using only a few elementary signs: (1) "zero"; and (2) "successor".

In addition, symbolic logic required a few additional elementary signs: (3) "not"; (4) "or"; (5) "if . . . then . . ." (e.g., *if* all domestic animals have four legs, and a cow is a domestic animal, *then* cows have four legs); (6) "for every" or "there exists" (as in, "*for every* number x, such-and-such is true" or, alternatively, "*there exists* x, such that such-and-such is true."); (7) "equals"; (8) "such that"; (9) and (10) for a "left parenthesis" and a "right parenthesis".

He also added signs for variables which could be used in equations (e.g., "x", "y", & "z" in x = 3y + z; in this discussion, we will assign 11 to "x", 12 to "y", and 13 to "z"), and signs for logical variables called "sentential" and "predicate" variables.

Gödel was thus able to map all the elementary signs of arithmetic and logic onto a small number of numbers. On the surface this seems no different than what Boole, Frege, and Russell accomplished in reducing arithmetic and logic to a finite series of elementary signs. However, there is a tremendous advance in Gödel's decision to further map the signs onto arithmetic. The others had tried to reduce arithmetic and logic to signs, and manipulate the signs to prove the consistency and completeness of logic and arithmetic. In other words, shift the emphasis away from the area under discussion.

Gödel turned their method upside-down and mapped the signs of logic and arithmetic back onto arithmetic itself. In other words, he created a "snake that swallows its own tail". Jung was fascinated by this ancient symbol, which is called the "ouroboros"; he felt that it symbolized the primary unity that underlay all diversity. Gödel's Proof seems to demonstrate that it is just that. However, as we'll see later, Gödel gave the snake a few twists before he let it swallow its tail.

Having dealt with the elementary signs of arithmetic and logic, Gödel then had to find some way to convert arithmetic formulas into numbers. If we think about it, an arithmetic formula is nothing but a sequence of elementary signs; so all Gödel had to do was devise a method that assigned a unique number, now normally termed a Gödel number, to each unique sequence of signs. Thus, if a formula was given, a Gödel number could be calculated; if a Gödel number was given, it could be translated back into the formula. The mapping technique was clever, but the achievement was not in the technique, but in the recognition that some such technique could be developed.

In the discussion which follows, formulas will be expressed in words. Normally, formulas would be nothing but a sequence of mathematical signs. Words have been substituted for signs in an attempt to simplify the understandably difficult task of presenting mathematics for non-mathematical readers. Consider a formula, such as "there exists a number x, such that x is the successor to a number y". Each elementary sign of that formula has already had a Gödel number assigned to it above; e.g., "there exists" = 6; "x" = 11; "such that" = 8; "x" = 11; "equals" = 7; "successor" = 2; "y" = 12. Thus the seven signs that make up the formula correspond to a sequence of seven Gödel numbers: 6, 11, 8, 11, 7, 2, 12.

Gödel defined the Gödel number of the formula by taking the first seven prime numbers (i.e., a prime number has no divisors except 1 and itself), raising each to the power of the Gödel number for the elementary sign in its position, and multiplying them together. The first seven prime numbers are 2, 3, 5, 7, 11, 13, 17. Therefore, the Gödel number for our simple formula is (2 to the 6th power) times (3 to the 11th power) times (5 to the 8th power), etc.

This is a very big number, but Gödel wasn't concerned with its size. What interested Gödel was the fact that this number could be converted back into a unique sequence of signs. A basic mathematical proof demonstrates that any number can be expressed as the product of prime numbers in one-and-only-one way. The reader will have to take this on faith as the proof strays too far from our concern here.

The details above demonstrate the cleverness of Gödel's method of mapping, but are not in and of themselves significant. The point is that since formulas were nothing more than sequences of elementary signs, and elementary signs already had Gödel numbers, formulas could also be converted into Gödel numbers. The next step Gödel took was similar. Just as formulas were sequences of signs, proofs (or demonstrations; the words are used interchangeably in mathematics) are sequences of formulas. If a proof involved a sequence of 10 formulas, Gödel converted it into a Gödel number by taking the product of the first 10 prime numbers in order, each raised to the power of the Gödel number of the corresponding formula.

It is far beyond the capabilities of even the largest current computers to break such numbers down into their prime factors (though mathematicians have recently been making great inroads into the problem of factoring on a computer). But again, that's not the point. The Gödel number of a proof, large as it was, could still *theoretically* be converted to a unique sequence of Gödel numbers of formulas, each of which could be converted to a unique sequence of Gödel numbers of signs, each of which could be converted to its appropriate sign. Thus, the entire proof could lie hidden in a single Gödel number.

The Amazing Code

If this sounds impossible to the reader, consider the similar scheme which Martin Gardner described as "The Amazing Code" in *Gotcha: Paradoxes to Puzzle and Delight* (Gardner,1982:48). A scientist from another galaxy visits our planet. When he decides that it's time to return home, his host suggests that he take a set of the Encyclopedia Britannica back with him, since it provides an excellent summary of the knowledge of our planet. The alien scientist says that sounds like a good idea, but the weight is prohibitive. Instead, he takes out a metal rod and, measuring carefully, he inscribes a single line on it. He says that the mark records the entire Encyclopedia Britannica.

His host is astounded and asks him to explain. The scientist says that he examined the encyclopedia and found that it contained less than a thousand different letters and symbols. Therefore, he converted each letter and symbol to a three digit number, adding zeros on the left as necessary. Thus the entire encyclopedia could be expressed as an enormous string of three digit numbers. For example, the word "CAT" would equal 003001020 (assuming that A = 001, B = 002, etc.).

By putting a decimal point in front of the number, the alien scientist converted it to a decimal fraction. Then he carefully measured the rod and made a mark which split it into two parts, A and B, where A/B equalled the decimal fraction. Therefore, when he returned to his galaxy, he could re-measure the two parts of the rod, convert their ratio into a decimal, and convert the decimal number back into the information contained in the Encyclopedia Britannica.

Gödel's numbers aren't as big as this number, but the method is similar. In each case, non-numeric statements are mapped onto numbers. The only reason that the alien scientist's method won't work is because there is no measuring technique in the universe capable of such refinement. However, both his method and Gödel's are theoretically possible, though Gödel's is much more carefully designed.

Mapping Meta-Mathematics Onto Mathematics

With all arithmetic signs, formulas, and proofs mapped onto integers, Gödel was able to move on toward the point of this process: the mapping of meta-mathematical statements onto arithmetic formulas. And, of course, these formulas could then be converted into Gödel numbers in turn. Gödel came to the culmination of his magnificent proof by considering a very special case where the Gödel number of the formula was itself contained in the formula. This would involve him in a deliberately chosen self-referential system.

Gödel was very careful in the choice of the meta-mathematical statement in question. He wanted to prove that there was at least one arithmetic formula whose truth or falsity could not be demonstrated using the elementary signs of arithmetic, provided one assumed arithmetic to be consistent. If there was at least one such formula, then the goal of the formalists was impossible.

In chapter twenty, we saw how Cantor proved that the

infinity of "real" numbers was bigger than the infinity of integers by showing that, no matter what matching scheme was chosen, there was at least one "real" number that could not be matched with an integer. In chapter eleven, we described the "collective" memory of one of Jung's schizophrenic patients that the wind was created by the swinging of the sun's "penis". If that single memory was accepted as non-personal, it would prove the existence of the collective unconscious. Gödel went about the finale to his proof in the same way.

A formal expression of this meta-mathematical statement was "for every x, where x is the Gödel number of a proof, x is not the Gödel number of a proof for the formula whose Gödel number is z." Let's describe it more colloquially as "there is a formula which cannot be demonstrated" (and that formula has Gödel number z). Gödel had to devise a formula such that the formula would itself be the representation of this meta-mathematical statement within arithmetic. In other words, the formula would represent a statement that the formula itself could not be proved.

We can see that the formula in question must be a strange one. In order for a statement about a formula to map onto the formula, the formula must map onto a variable within itself. In effect, it has to contain itself as a variable. Therefore, the meta-mathematical statement that there is a formula which cannot be proved can be mapped onto the formula itself. The formula can in turn be mapped onto a variable within itself, and that variable is the Gödel number of the formula.

Let's recall the image of the "ouroboros", the "snake that swallows its own tail". Instead of a snake, imagine a good-sized length of ribbon. If we connect one end of the ribbon to the other, making a ring, we can color the top side of the ribbon one color, say red, and the bottom side another color, say blue. Take another length of ribbon and give it a twist before you connect the two ends into a ring. Such a construction is called a Moebius strip. If you try and color the top side red now, you'll find that there doesn't seem to be a top and bottom any more. In fact, you will have colored the whole ribbon red when you return to your starting point. Stage magicians use a variant on this (which is called "The Afghan Bands") as a startling effect. Rather than coloring the ring of ribbon, they cut it in half along its length. Instead of two rings of equal size, they end up with a single ring twice as big.

You could think of the simple version of the "ouroboros" with no twist as corresponding to the simplest paradox. One side would say: "the statement on the other side is true". The other side would say: "the statement on the other side is false." That's an endless loop. However, the Moebius strip corresponds to a more complex paradox, such as: "the statement that 'the statement is false' is false." The "untwisted" paradox merely forms a chain which asserts, then contradicts, then contradicts the contradiction, and so forth. The "twisted" paradox forms an assertion that it itself is false. In other words, it is self-referential.

The mathematics of Gödel's actual construction is beyond the scope of this paper, but, in effect, Gödel constructed an arithmetic formula which asserted that it was itself not demonstrable. The meta-mathematical statement that mapped onto this formula stated that the formula was not demonstrable. In other words, he constructed not an "untwisted" paradox, not a "twisted" paradox, but a paradox with two "twists". To correspond to our examples above, the "twice-twisted" paradox would assert that "the statement that 'the statement that [the statement is false] is false' is false".

It was thus a three-step process. There was a meta-mathematical statement that said: some formula is not demonstrable. The representation of that meta-mathematical statement was the formula that could not be demonstrated. It couldn't be demonstrated because the formula in turn asserted that its opposite was true. Quite perplexing!

Why all that work to make such a strange embedded statement? Gödel was convinced that attempts to prove arithmetic to be consistent and complete, within arithmetic, were futile. He knew that such statements were meta-mathematical statements, and therefore involved a higher order of reality than mathematics. When you try to fit something bigger into something smaller, something has to be left out. Remember how Bertrand Russell tried to avoid the paradox of the "set of all sets which do not contain themselves" by creating "classes of sets", then "classes of classes", etc. Each time he created bigger entities, thus avoiding the problem infinitely. Gödel did the reverse; in effect, he mapped "classes of classes" onto "classes", "classes of sets" onto "sets".

Recall what mathematicians mean by the word "consistent": simply that you cannot prove both the truth and the falsity of a given formula. By constructing the "twice-twisted" paradox, Gödel could map it onto an arithmetic formula that was still "twisted".

> . . . if a formula as well as its contradictory can both be derived from a set of axioms, the axioms are not consistent. Accordingly, if the axioms are consistent, neither the formula nor its contradictory is demonstrable. In short, if the axioms are consistent, the formula is undecidable—neither the formula nor its contradictory can be formally deduced from the axioms.
>
> Very well. Yet there is a surprise coming. For although the formula is undecidable if the axioms are consistent, it can nevertheless be shown by meta-mathematical reasoning to be true . . . in the first place, on the assumption that arithmetic is consistent, we have already established the meta-mathematical statement [author's note: Gödel's assertion that: "the formula is not demonstrable"]. It must be accepted, then, that this meta-mathematical statement is true. Secondly, the statement is represented within arithmetic by that very formula itself. Third, we recall that meta-mathematical statements have been mapped upon the arithmetical formalism in such a way that true mathematical statements [and Gödel's statement is now proved to be true] always correspond to true arithmetical formulas. . . . Accordingly, the formula in question must be true.
>
> (Newman,1956:1692f).

What does that mean? Well, we've already seen that if arithmetic is "consistent", then there is a formula which is undecidable; that is, it's truth or falsity cannot be determined. Now it's gotten worse. Mathematicians say that an axiomatic system is "complete" if all true statements within that system can be derived from the axioms. But Gödel's upstart of a formula has now been proved to be true, and it cannot be derived from the axioms: i.e., if it were, its opposite could also be derived. That means that there is a true arithmetic formula which cannot be derived from the rules of arithmetic, and, therefore, arithmetic is incomplete.

This is quite a lot for the reader to absorb. Please realize that it was equally strange to mathematicians when they were first confronted with it. New ways of viewing reality are always strange and puzzling. However, recall the Barber Paradox, which asked if the barber, who shaved everyone who didn't shave themselves, shaved himself. We saw that there was no way to answer that question; any answer implied its own opposite. Gödel's formula did exactly the same thing.

A close analogy to the paradoxical formula in Gödel's Proof is the Liar Paradox attributed to the sixth century Greek poet Epimenides. "Epimenides is reputed to have said 'all Cretans are liars.' Considering that he was a Cretan, did Epimenides speak truly?" (Gardner,1982:4). Gödel created a formula that said that it was itself a lie. Clearly such a formula could not be demonstrated within arithmetic, since no matter which way you turned it, it turned itself upside-down once again.

The reason Gödel's proof is taken so seriously, while paradoxes like the Liar Paradox are dismissed as plays on words, is because of the mathematical rigor of the development of the paradox. While Gödel's method of mapping was new to mathematicians, it was totally sound. His method couldn't be discarded without discarding all of logic and mathematics. Yet if his proof was accepted, then logic and mathematics were inherently flawed and incomplete.

> That completeness' price is inconsistency, for logistic systems rich enough to contain recursive arithmetic, including all set theories worth their name formalized as such systems, is a result which was doubly unexpected: first, for its content; second, for the fact that it could be proved according to standards of rigor which were the highest known, higher even than those customarily used in mathematical proofs.
> (Fraenkel and Bar-Hillel,1958:304).

The Significance of Gödel's Proof

Some mathematicians were quick to see the implications of Gödel's Proof. Alfred Tarski, J. B. Rosser, and Gödel himself all extended the original proof, to show that any logical system containing recursive number theory, including elementary arithmetic and calculus, is essentially undecidable (see Fraenkel & Bar-Hillel,1958). However, the mathematical formalists felt quite differently. They examined every aspect of the proof, trying to find some way of evading its consequences, but to no avail. With no other recourse open to them, they then behaved just like their counterparts in philosophy, the Logical Positivists.

The formalists said, all right, we'll accept that there is no ultimate proof of consistency and completeness. Therefore, mathematics is the field that develops all the conclusions that *can* be consistently derived from a rigorously defined, finite set of axioms. In other words, if problems get too big for us, let's pretend that they aren't there; the ostrich technique once more.

Essentially mathematics is a field where mathematicians agree among themselves on formal methods to deal with intuitive concepts. The core of the field is all intuition; that is, it comes from some non-logical source within us. This, of course, is the collective unconscious that we have been discussing from the first page of this paper. However, mathematicians, like the rest of us, are very uncomfortable about dealing with concepts like "intuition". Thus the formalists attempted to reduce intuition to logic. Andrzej Mostowski expressed the problem that confronted the formalists this way:

> ... until we succeed to build a formal system coinciding with the intuitive mathematics, there is no immediate connection between the problem of completeness of any proposed formal system and the problem of existence of essentially unsolvable mathematical problems.
> (Mostowski,1957:3).

[author's note: translations of mathematical texts are frequently like translations of Japanese instruction manuals].

The goal of the formalist was essentially a meta-mathematical goal, not a mathematical one, and thus doomed to failure. Gödel himself cast his fate with intuition. In *The Mathematical Experience*, Gödel is quoted as saying that:

> Despite their remoteness from sense experience, we do have something like a perception also of the objects of set theory, as is seen from the fact that the axioms force themselves upon us as being true. I don't see any reason why we should have less confidence in this kind of perception, i.e., in mathematical intuition, than in sense perception. . . . They, too, may represent an aspect of objective reality.
> (quoted in Davis & Hersh,1981:319).

Mathematician Rene Thom takes such speculations to their Platonic conclusion and says that:

> . . . everything considered, mathematicians should have the courage of their most profound convictions and thus affirm that mathematical forms indeed have an existence that is independent of the mind considering them.
> (ibid:319).

All science is based on logic and mathematics. Gödel's Proof implies that all science is inherently flawed and incomplete to the extent that it is limited to logic and mathematics. However, the issue is even more pervasive than that. Though Gödel's Proof addresses the foundations of all science, it is still only a partial formulation of the limits of the problem. The larger issue is the recognition that the world is a unity.

When, in the Renaissance, man began to separate himself from that unity in order to observe the world which lay outside him, he was creating an artificial distinction. He was playing a game, though he didn't realize it at the time. As an example of the game, look down at your hands and pretend that they belong to someone else. By doing so, you can learn a great deal about your hands that you wouldn't be aware of as long as you remained unconscious of their separate existence and merely used them as a part of your total body. But it would still be a game; your hands remain connected to your arms which are in turn connected to the trunk of your body. Your body remains a single, unbroken entity despite the fact that you can observe parts of it separately.

The rewards for playing such a game are obvious; they lay about us in mankind's intellectual and physical achievements. Clearly it was important for us to learn this game and learn to play it well. But eventually it ceased to be a game; the snake swallowed its tail again. As our observations of reality became more detailed, we found ourselves looking into a microscope and seeing ourselves looking back. Gödel's Proof is the twentieth century's greatest intellectual expression of this truth, but the truth transcends even Gödel.

The author has attempted to trace the development within mathematics of the chain of events that led from the base of arithmetic and geometry upwards, seemingly ineluctably, toward Gödel's Proof. By the time we climb to that peak, the air is cold and thin around us, and human issues seem small and remote. The world is thus demonstrated to be a necessary unity by mathematics, mankind's most abstract and powerful tool.

However, it is at the human level that such conclusions will have to be integrated into our lives. Logic's greatest achievement points to its own inadequacy to deal with the full extent of reality. It is consciousness that has shown us that we are each unique individuals, not merely parts of a unified whole. It is consciousness that has then led us back to realizing that we are also inseparable parts of a unified reality. It is consciousness that will have to integrate those two, seemingly irreconcilable facts into a new unity. The psychology of C. G. Jung is a unique attempt to discover how such a conscious reconciliation can be effected.

Gödel and Jung

The abstract world of pure mathematics may seem a very long way from psychology, but the distance is much closer than it may seem. Let us return briefly to some of the facts we have examined earlier to see just how Gödel's Proof relates to the psychology of C. G. Jung. Jung began his studies of the human psyche, under the influence of his mentor Freud, with the expectation that the causes for psychic conflicts in a patient could be traced back to traumatic events in the patient's childhood. Jung hoped to use unconscious material from the patient's dreams and fantasies to get past any conscious repression or distortion. Once the traumatic event was discovered and its consequences accepted by the patient, the therapy process should be completed.

Jung's early experiments with word association tests did buttress this position. Jung discovered that there were centers of energy in the unconscious which he called "complexes." If a patient had a "mother complex", for example, it was impossible to directly approach issues involving the mother. One had to slowly work one's way through a surrounding bees' nest of related memories and fantasies. Jung presented his results to Freud and this started their close but short-lived association.

However, as Jung continued to unravel the complexes in his patients, he discovered that the center of the complex did not appear to be personal memories. Instead, after all the emotionally laden personal issues were stripped off, there remained a core that had enormous energy and seemed totally impersonal, with no connection to the patient's personal life. The core tended to be personified in images that, strangely enough, were remarkably similar to images from mythology or fairy tales.

This was very different from what Freud's materialistic theories had led Jung to expect. Jung chose to record his patients' dreams and fantasies without pre-judgement, rather than forcing them to fit into Freud's theories. If the dreams had elements that closely resembled mythic themes, Jung mentioned it. If the dreams seemed to center around non-sexual themes, Jung recorded that. Freud would not tolerate such heresy and Jung was "excommunicated" from the small body of psychoanalysts.

Cut-off from his peers, with no precedents to guide him in dealing with this strange new world, Jung took a brave step. He felt that he couldn't take his patients somewhere he had never been himself. Therefore, Jung decided to explore his own unconscious and faithfully record what he found there.

This turned out to be a dangerous journey, but one that Jung survived, and drew on for knowledge and support in the years to come. In the course of this exploration, he discovered collective personified forces within his own psyche just as he had found collective images in the dreams and fantasies of his patients. However, having abstract knowledge of something is a much different thing than experiencing it oneself. Jung found that the unconscious forces were powerful enough to shake consciousness to its roots.

Because of this personal experience, Jung was never to prattle about a patient's "resistance"; he knew that there was a good reason to be afraid of the power of unconscious forces. Having made such a self-exploration, Jung was able to directly relate to his patients when they brought forth similar collective images in their own dreams.

Similarly, when he examined the great mythological stories of antiquity, he recognized the forces which the ancient poets had tried to capture because he had experienced those same forces. Every patient, every myth, could teach Jung something more about himself because he had experienced the same collective, emotionally-wrought issues. Or his own experiences could be drawn on to help his patients past a crisis, or to elucidate the psychic meaning of a mythic tale.

For almost forty years after he finished his personal voyage into the unconscious, Jung continued to develop ever-better models for the structure and dynamics of the psyche. Since he had personally experienced the fact that the psyche had an impersonal, collective core, any model which mirrored that core could contribute to "scientific" knowledge of the psyche.

This is such an important realization that it deserves to be repeated. In our interpersonal relationships, we can assume a certain amount of shared experience. If we all contain collective elements in our individual psyches, we also can draw on common psychic experience. When we read a poem, watch a play, look at a painting, we can be moved not only because the poet, playwright, and painter shared common life experiences, but also because they shared inner experiences that are common to all men in all times.

Thus, Jung's studies were "scientific" in the best sense of the term. If the psyche is collective, then one should observe and describe collective sources. If those same collective sources are available within one's own mind, one should explore one's own mind and describe its contents as well. Since the mind doing the exploring is also the object under observation, a self-referential system is involved, which is Kurt Gödel's territory.

Gödel used the most rigorous logic to prove that "logic" itself was insufficient to fully describe any system which was at least as complex as arithmetic. Gödel demonstrated that "metamathematics"—that is, statements about mathematics—could be mapped onto mathematics, thus involving mathematicians, and therefore all scientists, in a vicious circle. It seems safe to assert that the totality of the human mind is more complex than arithmetic, since arithmetic is only one tiny product of the human mind. Therefore, psychology, which describes the human mind, is necessarily involved in such a Gödelian paradox. That is, the comments which a psychologist makes about the human mind are themselves products of the human mind, and, therefore, part of what is being discussed.

Gödel's Proof left mathematicians, and all other scientists as well, if they had only realized the full implications of his proof, in a position where they had to find some way other than logic to deal with the profound questions in their fields. This is not to say that logic was revealed to be useless. Far from it, logic and rigor were just as important as ever; after all, Gödel's Proof itself employed rigorous logic. However, logic and rigor were revealed to be insufficient to handle "meta" problems.

The core of the difficulty lies in the static quality of logic. In chapter four, we saw how Leibniz differentiated between analytic and synthetic truths. The former, the world of logic, are final and irrefutable, but limited and static. Nothing new ever develops from analytic truth; logic merely unravels tautologies. On the other hand, synthetic truths speak of the world of experience, whether inner or outer. Synthetic truths are dynamic, growing, but also provisional. There are no final synthetic truths.

In effect, Gödel told mathematicians that meta-statements were synthetic, not open to logical proof. Logic could reveal many hidden mysteries, but all the real questions were meta-questions, and those were forever beyond the capabilities of logic. So where could science go from there?

As we've also discussed in chapter four, Immanuel Kant proposed that there was a third variety of truth, which was both synthetic and analytic. These truths were collective, organizing principles, which he called "categories", inherent in the human mind. Since these "categories" were timeless, they could reveal final truth. Since they organized the reality around us, they could deal with growth and change. Of course, these "categories" were the "archetypes" of the collective unconscious which Jung discovered in his patients and himself, and which he explored for most of his life.

Not only should Jung's work be considered scientifically acceptable, and worthy of examination by other scientists, it offers a unique example of a method for advancing past the wall that Gödel seemed to have erected for science. If logic is not sufficient to deal with the larger questions of science, then scientists have to realize that the human mind contains within itself final truths which can deal with ultimate reality because they mirror ultimate reality.

In this book, the author has tried to demonstrate that Jung's psychology, far from being a reversion to pre-scientific, primitive belief systems, is instead an example of how science can be conducted at the leading edge of human thought. To the author, Gödel's Proof stands as the greatest single achievement of Western science.

If so, Jung's total achievement is greater yet, because Jung's psychology offers the possibility of a new reconciliation between man and nature. The Renaissance ideal has led to many wonderful achievements, but only at the price of man's alienation from the universe. It's time for peace and harmony once more, but they can be purchased only at the cost of giving up our splendid but arrogant separation from the reality around us.

> . . . Yet there is so much that fills me: plants, animals, clouds, day and night, and the eternal in man. The more uncertain I have felt about myself, the more there has grown up in me a feeling of kinship with all things. In fact it seems to me as if that alienation which so long separated me from the world has become transferred into my own inner world, and has revealed to me an unexpected unfamiliarity with myself.
>
> (Jung,1965:359).

Bibliography

Aiken, Henry D. (ed.). *The Age of Ideology: the 19th Century Philosophers.* New York: Mentor Books, Houghton Mifflin Co., 1956.
Section on Immanuel Kant especially useful.
Appignanesi, Richard and Zarate, Oscar. *Freud for Beginners.* New York: Pantheon Books, Random House, 1979.
As with most of the books in this series, surprisingly useful once the sophormoric humor is overlooked.
Asimov, Isaac. *Asimov's Guide to Science.* New York: Basic Books, 1960.
Material on nature of waves and on wave-nature of the human mind.
———. *Fact and Fancy.* New York: Discus Books Edition, Avon Books, 1962.
On the relationship of intuition to creativity.
———. *The Human Brain.* New York: Mentor Books, New American Library, 1965.
Current scientific information on the nature of the human brain.
Axelrod, Robert. *The Evolution of Cooperation.* New York: Basic Books, 1984.
Uses computer projections to demonstrate that cooperation emerged because it is evolutionarily the best mode of behavior. Fits well with Jung's models.
Bateson, Gregory. *Cybernetics and Mind.* N. Hollywood, California: Audio-Text Cassette #CBC972, n.d.
Lecture contains anecdote about creativity of dolphins.
———. *Steps to an Ecology of Mind.* New York: Ballantine Books, 1972.
Bateson's classic book that uses information theory to show how the human mind operates on successive meta-levels.
———. *Mind and Nature: a Necessary Unity.* New York: E. P. Dutton, 1979.
Bateson's last book. A deeply moving attempt by a great thinker to discover ultimate truth.
Bell, Eric Temple. *Men of Mathematics.* New York: Simon and Schuster, 1937.
Reads like a detective novel as Bell traces mathematics' history through its greatest mathematicians. Unfortunately, stops short of Gödel.
———. *Development of Mathematics.* New York: McGraw-Hill, 1940.
Excellent companion to *Men of Mathematics.*
Berlin, Sir Isaiah (ed.). *The Age of Enlightment: the 18th Century Philosophers.* New York: Mentor Books, Houghton Mifflin Co., 1956.
Berlin introduction provides clear history of how Locke's, Berkeley's, and Hume's ideas led to Kant's great synthesis. Sections on Hume, Berkeley, and Locke were drawn-on for this book.
Bohm, David. *Wholeness and the Implicate Order.* London: Ark Paperbacks, 1980.

Quantum physicist on the nature of reality. Accords well with Jung, as well as Pribram and Sheldrake among other seminal thinkers in contemporary science.

Boring, Edwin G. *A History of Experimental Psychology*, 2nd ed. New York: Appleton-Century-Crofts, 1950.
An especially valuable history. Boring belies his name.

Brill, Dr. A. A. (ed.). *The Basic Writings of Sigmund Freud*. New York: Modern Library, Random House, 1938.
The Interpretation of Dreams was used in this book.

Brown, Barbara B. June 18, 1983 speech. Association for Transpersonal Psychology, 11th Annual Conference.
Tells how behavioral psychologists reduced bio-feedback research to trivialities.

Brown, J. A. C. *Freud and the Post-Freudians*. Baltimore: Pelican Original, Penguin Books, 1964.
As with most such histories, totally dismisses Jung's work after he broke with Freud. Useful in describing all the followers who broke with Freud.

Bucke, Richard Maurice, M.D. *Cosmic Consciousness*. New York: E. P. Dutton, 1923.
Classic study of men who seem to have attained a "cosmic consciousness".

Bylinsky, Gene. New Clues to the Causes of Violence. 1973. In *Annual Editions, Readings in Psychology '74/'75*. Guilford, Connecticut: Dushkin Publishing Group, 1974.
Discusses Harry F. Harlow's experiments with substitute mothers for baby chimpanzees.

Campbell, Joseph. *The Hero With a Thousand Faces*. Princeton: Princeton University Press, Bollingen Series, 1949.
Superb study of the "hero" archetype.

———. (ed.). *The Portable Jung*. New York: Penguin Books, Viking Press, 1971.
Contains useful chronology to Jung's life and works.

Capra, Fritjof. *The Tao of Physics*. Berkeley: Shambhala Publications, 1975.
Already a classic. Draws explicit connections between modern physics and Eastern philosophy.

Davis, Philip J. and Hersh, Reuben. *The Mathematical Experience*. Boston: Houghton Mifflin, 1981.
Contains fascinating quotes from Gödel and Rene Thom about the archetypal nature of mathematical thought.

De Santillana, Giorgio. (ed.). *The Age of Adventure: the Renaissance Philosophers*. New York: Mentor Books, Houghton Mifflin Co., 1956.
Introduction and sections on Da Vinci, Michelangelo, and Copernicus used in this book.

Edinger, Edward F. *Ego and Archetype*. Baltimore, Maryland: Penguin Books, 1972.
Explores relationship between individual ego and collective unconscious.

———. Psychotherapy and Alchemy, I & II. *Quadrant*. Summer 1978.
Introduction to alchemy as a psychological model; section on alchemical operation of Calcinatio.

———. Psychotherapy and Alchemy, III. *Quadrant*. Winter 1978.
Section on alchemical operation of Solutio.

———. Psychotherapy and Alchemy, IV. *Quadrant*. Summer 1979.
Section on alchemical operation of Coagulatio.

———. *Psychotherapy and Alchemy, V. Quadrant.* Spring 1980.
Section on alchemical operation of Sublimatio.
———. *Psychotherapy and Alchemy, VI. Quadrant.* Spring 1981.
Section on alchemical operation of Mortificatio.
———. *Psychotherapy and Alchemy, VII. Quadrant.* Fall 1981.
Section on alchemical operation of Separatio.
———. *Psychotherapy and Alchemy, VIII. Quadrant.* Spring 1982.
Section on alchemical operation of Coniunctio.
Einstein, Albert. *Brain/Mind Bulletin.* June 18, 1984.
Eliade, Mircea. *The Sacred and the Profane.* New York: Harvest/HBJ Book, Harcourt Brace Jovanovich, 1959.
Eliade's thoughts on the history of religion correspond closely to Jung's.
———. *No Souvenirs: Journal, 1957–1969.* San Francisco: Harper & Row, 1977.
In these journals, the reader is privileged to watch Eliade's key ideas emerge across time.
Erickson, Milton H. *The Collected Papers of Milton H. Erickson on Hypnosis.* Edited by Ernest L. Rossi. Volume I: *The Nature of Hypnosis and Suggestion.* New York: Irvington Publishers, 1980a.
Especially interesting material on the induction of trance.
———. *The Collected Papers of Milton H. Erickson on Hypnosis.* Edited by Ernest L. Rossi. Volume II: *Hypnotic Alteration of Sensory, Perceptual and Psychophysiological Processes.* New York: Irvington Publishers, 1980b.
Interesting material which complements experimental work on perception.
———. *The Collected Papers of Milton H. Erickson on Hypnosis.* Edited by Ernest L. Rossi. Volume III: *Hypnotic Investigation of Psychodynamic Processes.* New York: Irvington Publishers, 1980c.
Articles on general history of hypnosis parallel material from Boring quoted in this book.
———. *The Collected Papers of Milton H. Erickson on Hypnosis.* Edited by Ernest L. Rossi. Volume IV: *Innovative Hypnotherapy.* New York: Irvington Publishers, 1980d.
Contains "Hypnotic Psychotherapy", perhaps Erickson's key early essay on the nature of hypnosis as a therapeutic tool. Quotation from this essay in chapter 12.
Evans, Richard I. *Konrad Lorenz: the Man and his Ideas.* New York: Harcourt Brace Jovanovich, 1975.
As with all the books in this series, a superb combination of a dialog with the subject, a summary of his central ideas, and key selections.
Fabricius, Johannes. *Alchemy: the Medieval Alchemists and their Royal Art.* Copenhagen: Rosenkilde and Bagger, 1976.
A monumental attempt to present actual alchemical writings and describe their psychological significance.
Fraenkel, A. A. and Bar-Hillel, Y. *Foundations of Set Theory.* Amsterdam: North-Holland Publishing Company, 1958.
More than most math texts moves in-and-out between Gödel's Proof and its philosophical implications.
Franz, Marie-Louise von and Hillman, James. *Jung's Typology.* Zurich, Switzerland: Spring Publications, 1971.
Especially valuable work on Jung's theory of types, which was largely omitted in this book.

Franz, Marie-Louise von. "An Introduction to the Symbolism of Alchemy." Lecture Notes. n.p., 1959.
Lecture notes on very early alchemical texts.

———. *Number and Time*. Evanston: Northwestern University Press, 1974.
Remarkable book which extends Jung's late idea that number was the primary archetype.

———. *C. G. Jung: His Myth in Our Time*. New York: C. G. Jung Foundation for Analytical Psychology, 1975.
Ideal companion work to Jung's own *Memories, Dreams, Reflections*. No one knew Jung and his work better than von Franz. This is written as a biography both of his life and psychic development.

———. *Alchemical Active Imagination*. University of Dallas, Irving, Texas: Spring Publications, 1979.
Valuable material on history of alchemy.

Fremantle, Anne. (ed.). *The Age of Belief: the Medieval Philosophers*. New York: Mentor Books, Houghton Mifflin Co., 1954.
Summary of scholastic philosophy.

Freud, Sigmund. *Three Essays on the Theory of Sexuality*. reprint 4th ed. of 1920, New York: Basic Books, Harper Colophon Books, Harper & Row, 1962.
Arguably Freud's greatest book. Discussed in some detail in this book.

Fromm, Erich. *Sigmund Freud's Mission*. New York: Harper Colonphon Books, Harper & Row, 1959.
Excellent description of Freud's personality and "idee fixes".

Gardner, Martin. *Gotcha: Paradoxes to Puzzle and Delight*. San Francisco: W. H. Freeman and Company, 1982.
As always with Gardner, both playful and serious. Many of these paradoxes are relevant to the issue of self-referential systems.

Grinder, John & Bandler, Richard. *The Structure of Magic I: a Book about Language & Therapy*. Palo Alto, Calif.: Science and Behavior Books, Inc., 1975.
First text on Neuro-Linguistic Programming (NLP). Draws heavily on Chomsky for theory and Milton Erickson for clincial techniques.

———. *Patterns of the Hypnotic Techniques of Milton H. Erickson, M.D., Vol. 1*. Cupertino, Calif.: Meta Publications, 1975.
Grinder's and Bandler's analysis of why Erickson's techniques work is frequently exasperating, alternately brilliant and naive.

———. *The Structure of Magic II*. Palo Alto, Calif.: Science and Behavior Books, Inc., 1976.
Less useful book than "Magic I" because too wed to its own rather doubtful theoretical base. Grinder and Bandler are most useful as describers of techniques, least useful as theorists.

———. *Frogs Into Princes: Neuro-Linguistic Programming*. Moab, Utah: Real People Press, 1979.
One of the most useful of the NLP books, since it consists entirely of transcribed workshop sessions filled with practical advice.

———. *TRANCE-Formations*. Moab, Utah: Real People Press, 1981.
Sophomoric presentation, but contains some practical applications of Ericksonian hypnosis.

———. *Reframing: Neuro-Linguistic Programming and the Transformation of Meaning.* Moab, Utah: Real People Press, 1982.
Totally Ericksonian hypnotic techniques, though not always credited.

Grun, Bernard. *The Timetables of History: a Horizontal Linkage of People and Events.* New York, Touchstone Books Edition, Simon and Schuster, 1982.
Useful companion to traditional histories which often present a field in a vaccum.

Hall, Calvin S. *A Primer of Freudian Psychology.* New York: Mentor Books, New American Library, 1954.
Very good short summary of Freudian psychology, much better than his comparable summary of Jung's psychology.

———. *Psychology: an Introductory Textbook.* Cleveland: Howard Allen, Inc., 1960.
Contains material on Freud not in the *Primer.*

Hall, Edward T. *The Silent Language.* Greenwich, Conn.: Fawcett Premier Book, Fawcett Publications, 1959.
Is language inborn or learned? The answer is key to the conception of the human mind.

Hampden-Turner, Charles. *Maps of the Mind.* New York: MacMillan Publishing, 1981.
Compendium of models of the human mind.

Hampshire, Stuart (ed.). *The Age of Reason: the 17th Century Philosophers.* New York: Mentor Books, Houghton Mifflin Co., 1956.
Section on Leibniz especially useful.

Harding, M. Esther. *Psychic Energy: its Source and its Transformation.* Princeton: Princeton University Press, Bollingen Series, 1947.
Expands Jung's concepts of psychic energy.

———. *The "I" and the "Not-I": a Study in the Development of Consciousness.* Princeton: Princeton University Press, Bollingen Series, 1965.
Much on what has been discussed in this book as the "archetypes of development".

Heidbreder, Edna. *Seven Psychologies.* New York: Appleton-Century-Crofts, 1933.
The battle between behavioral psychology and gestalt psychology is presented well.

Heisenberg, Werner. *The Physical Principles of the Quantum Theory.* Trans. Carl Eckart and Frank C. Hoyt. Chicago: University of Chicago Press, 1930; reprint ed., New York: Dover Publications, 1949.
Based on lectures delivered at the University of Chicago. Covers not only his own contributions but those of his fellow physicists.

Hilgard, Ernest R. *The Experience of Hypnosis.* New York: Harvest Book, Harcourt Brace Jovanovich, 1965.
Best representation of the materialist position on hypnosis.

Hofstadter, Douglas R. *Gödel, Escher, Bach: an Eternal Golden Braid.* New York: Vintage Books, 1979.
Justly famed Pulitzer Prize-winning book on self-referential systems. However, Hofstadter's conclusions differ somewhat from those reached in this book.

James, William. *The Principles of Psychology* (in two volumes). reprint 1st ed. of 1890, New York: Dover Publications, 1950.
Classic work. Especially useful on implications of physiological psychology.

Jastrow, Joseph. 1969 *Freud: His Dream and Sex Theories.* reprint 1st ed. of 1932, New York: Pocket Books, 1969.
A highly opinionated book which has to be read with discretion.

Jeans, Sir James. *The Growth of Physical Science*. Greenwich, Conn.: Premier Books Edition, Fawcett World Library, 1961.
In many ways, goes beyond Capra or Zukav in its conception of the nature of the physical world. Closely matches Jungian concepts.

Jung, C. G. On the Psychology and Pathology of So-Called Occult Phenomena. 1902. In *Collected Works, Vol. 1*. (2nd ed.) Princeton: Bollingen Series, Princeton University Press, 1970.
Discusses trance phenomena with a young country girl who achieved brief local fame as a medium.

———. Paracelsus the Physician. 1942. In *Collected Works, Vol. 15*. Princeton: Bollingen Series, Princeton University Press, 1966.
Discusses how Paracelsus saw physical and psychic, micro and macro worlds as connected.

———. The Psychology of the Transference. 1954. In *Collected Works, Vol. 16*. Princeton: Bollingen Series, Princeton University Press, 1966.
Uses alchemical symbolism of marriage of king and queen to examine nature of all relationships, whether between patient and analyst, man and woman, or ego and Self.

———. The Theory of Psychoanalysis (2nd edition). 1954. In *Critique of Psychoanalysis*. Princeton: Bollingen Series, Princeton University Press, 1975.
Jung's disagreements with Freudian and Adlerian theory.

———. Commentary on *The Secret of the Golden Flower*. (5th ed.) 1957. In *Collected Works, Volume 13*. Princeton: Bollingen Series, Princeton University Press, 1967.
When Jung read his friend Richard Wilhelm's translation of *The Secret of the Golden Flower*, a Chinese book of alchemy, in 1929, it was the first time he had come across ancient material that prefigured his own discoveries in the unconscious.

———. *Collected Works, Vol. 9ii: Aion, Researches into the Phenomenology of the Self*. Princeton: Bollingen Series, Princeton University Press, 1959.
One of the most complex books in the Collected Works.

———. *Collected Works, Vol. 8: The Structure and Dynamics of the Psyche*. Princeton: Bollingen Series, Princeton University Press, 1960.
Contains three key essays: "On Psychic Energy", "The Transcendent Function", and "Synchronicity: An Acausal Connecting Principle".

———. *Collected Works, Vol. 10: Civilization in Transition*. Princeton: Bollingen Series, Princeton University Press, 1964.
Contains a wide variety of articles and essays.

———. *Memories, Dreams, Reflections* (Vintage Books Ed.). New York: Vintage Books, Random House, 1965.
A unique document: an auto-biography of Jung's spiritual progress. Invaluable for clinical work because it discusses Jung's personal experiences at various stages of psychic development.

———. *Collected Works, Vol. 7: Two Essays on Analytical Psychology*. Princeton: Bollingen Series, Princeton University Press, 1966.
Seminal essays on the nature of Shadow, Anima/Animus, and Self. Because Jung describes how each archetype is experienced at various stages, is particularly useful for practical clinical work.

———. *Analytical Psychology: Its Theory and Practice* (Vintage Books edition 1970). New York: Vintage Books, 1968.

Commonly known as the Tavistock Lectures, a series of five lectures given in London in 1935. Excellent presentation of Jung's thought at mid-career.

———. *Collected Works, Vol. 12: Psychology and Alchemy* (2nd ed.). Princeton: Bollingen Series, Princeton University Press, 1968.

Traces the evolution of individual and archetypal images in dreams of a single patient. Extremely useful in clinical work, as it describes and explains representative dream images at various stages of analytic process.

———. *Collected Works, Vol. 9i: The Archetypes and the Collective Unconscious*. Princeton: Bollingen Series, Princeton University Press, 1969.

The largest collection in the Collected Works of Jung's ideas on archetypes in general and on specific archetypes. Sections on Mother archetype and Child archetype are especially useful for clinical work.

———. *Collected Works, Vol. 6: Psychological Types*. Princeton: Bollingen Series, Princeton University Press, 1971.

The first book written after Jung's confrontation with the unconscious. Contains section of key definitions, including "symbol".

Koestler, Arthur. *The Act of Creation*. New York: Dell, 1964.

The most exhaustive attempt at delimiting creativity.

———. *The Roots of Coincidence*. New York: Vintage Books, Random House, 1972.

Explores the areas Jung subsumed under his concept of synchronicity.

———. *Bricks to Babel*. New York: Random House, 1980.

Selections from his entire body of work. Notes added just for this book contain much private material on the nature of creativity.

Köhler, Wolfgang. *Gestalt Psychology*. New York: Mentor Books, New American Library, 1947.

The classic presentation of gestalt psychology. Contains description of experiment with perception of chickens.

Kuhn, Thomas S. *The Structure of Scientific Revolutions*. Chicago: University of Chicago Press, 1970.

Considered a classic. Shows difference between practice of "normal" science and development of scientific revolutions.

Laughlin, Tom. *Jungian Psychology, Volume 2: Jungian Theory and Therapy*. Los Angeles: Panarion Press, 1982.

Book attempts to prove that Jung believed in the biological roots of archetypes. This degree of insistence is strange since this is commonly accepted among analytical psychologists.

Lauzun, Gerard. *Sigmund Freud: the Man and His Theories*. Greenwich, Conn.: Fawcett Premier Book, Fawcett Publications, 1962.

Describes much of what went on "behind the scenes" between Freud and his followers.

Lilly, John C. *The Center of the Cyclone: an Autobiography of Inner Space*. New York: Bantam Books, 1972.

A record of dolphin researcher John Lilly's personal experiments with altered states of consciousness.

Linden, Eugene. *Apes, Men, and Language*. New York: Pelican Books, 1976.

One of many books to explore whether animals can speak and, hence, think as men do. This body of research supports Jung's ideas on psychological development.

Lorenz, Konrad. *King Solomon's Ring*. New York: Crowell, 1952.

Delightful book. Contains the story and pictures of Lorenz' baby goose who "imprinted" the Mother archetype onto Lorenz.

Maslow, Abraham H. *The Psychology of Science.* Chicago: Gateway Edition, Henry Regnery Co., 1966.
Critically examines the nature of the scientific method.

May, Rollo. *Love and Will.* New York: Laurel Edition, Dell, 1969.
Discusses how types of clinical problems varied in different eras; how Freud's emphasis on sexual problems was sign of his time rather than inherent.

McLuhan, Marshall and Fiore, Quentin. *The Medium is the Massage.* New York: Bantam Books, 1967.
McLuhan's ideas on how our perception of reality affects our development closely approximate many of Jung's thoughts.

———. *Understanding Media: the Extensions of Man.* New York: Signet Books, New American Library, 1964.
Perhaps McLuhan's greatest book.

Merrell-Wolff, Franklin. *Pathways Through to Space: a Personal Report of Transformation in Consciousness.* New York: Warner Books, 1973.
Probably the best account in Western literature of the mystical experience.

———. *The Philosophy of Consciousness Without an Object.* New York: Julian Press, 1973.
Companion volume to the above. Tries to place his experiences into a spiritual and philosophical framework.

Mostowski, Andrzej. *Sentences Undecidable in Formalized Arithmetic: an Exposition of the Theory of Kurt Gödel.* Amsterdam: North-Holland Publishing Company, 1952.
For mathematicians only; carefully constructed proofs of Gödel's Theory.

Mussen, Paul H. (ed.). *Carmichael's Manual of Child Psychology, Third Edition.* New York: John Wiley & Sons, 1970.
Massive compilation on child psychology; contains much by non-Jungians which supports Jung's views on development.

Nagel, Ernest and Newman, James R. Gödel's Proof. n.d. In James R. Newman (ed.) *The World of Mathematics,* New York: Simon and Schuster, 1956.
Best popular explanation of Gödel's Proof.

Neumann, Erich. *The Origins and History of Consciousness.* Princeton University Press, Bollingen Series, 1954.
Detailed study of evolution of the archetypes of the collective unconscious.

Newton, Sir Isaac. *Opticks.* reprint of 4th ed. of 1730, New York: Dover Publications, 1952.
Still readable, contains Newton's concept of light as composed of atoms, the reaction to which eventually led to quantum mechanics.

Piaget, Jean. *The Language and Thought of the Child.* New York: Meridian Book, World Publishing, 1955.
Is not a Jungian, but his work can be seen as corroborating much of Jung's ideas on developmental psychology.

Pribram, Karl. The Brain. In Alberto Villoldo and Ken Dychtwald (eds.) *Millennium: Glimpses Into the 21st Century.* Los Angeles: J. P. Tarcher, 1981.
Neuro-physiologist Karl Pribram on the holographic nature of the brain.

Price, Lucien. (recorded by). *Dialogues of Alfred North Whitehead.* New York: Mentor Books Edition, New American Library, 1956.

Whitehead's philosophical ideas pre-figure those of scientists Pribram, Boehm, Sheldrake and Prigogine.

Prigogine, Ilya. *Order Out of Chaos: Man's New Dialogue with Nature*. New York: Bantam Books, 1984.
Nobel prize winner whose idea of dissipative structures in chemistry has marked similarities to Jung's work.

Reese, W. L. *Dictionary of Philosophy and Religion: Eastern and Western Thought*. Atlantic Highlands, New Jersey: Humanities Press, 1980.
Mammoth one-volume encyclopedia of philosophy. Entry on Kant especially useful.

Richter, Jean Paul. *The Notebooks of Leonardo Da Vinci* (two volumes). New York: Dover Publications, 1970.
Contains Da Vinci's actual notes and drawings. Many quotes capture the Renaissance ideal.

Rose, Steven. *The Conscious Brain*. New York: Vintage Books, Random House, 1976.
Especially good in pointing out need to transcend a brain-mind dualism.

Rossi, Earnest Lawrence. As Above, So Below: the Holographic Mind. *Psychological Perspectives*. Fall 1980.
Describes Pribram's theory of the holographic mind and relates it to Jung's ideas and ideas of mystics.

Russell, Bertrand. *Wisdom of the West*. New York: Premier Books, Fawcett World Library, 1959.
Author's favorite one-volume history of philosophy.

———. Mathematics and the Metaphysicians. n.d. In James R. Newman (ed.) *The World of Mathematics*. New York: Simon and Schuster, 1956.
Delightfully captures the young Russell's conviction that recent mathematical discoveries would enable man to fully explain the universe.

Saunders, J. B. deC. M. and O'Malley, Charles D. (translators). *The Illustrations from the Works of Andreas Vesalius of Brussels*. New York: Dover Publications, 1950.
Detailed drawings of human anatomy are early product of Renaissance ideal of man as observer.

Schultz, Duane P. *A History of Modern Psychology*. New YorK: Academic Press, 1969.
Written from the materialist/rationalist position. Contrasts with Boring and Heidbreder, whose presentation is less limited by theory.

Sheldrake, Rupert. *A New Science of Life: the Hypothesis of Formative Causation*. Los Angeles: J. P. Tarcher, 1981.
Uses data from behavioral psychology to support concept of morphogenetic fields, which closely correspond to Jung's archetypes.

Snow, C. P. *The Two Cultures and the Scientific Revolution*. Cambridge, England: Cambridge University Press, 1959.
Delivered as the Rede Lecture for 1959. A fascinating commentary on the necessary bridge between the two cultures of science and art.

———. *Science and Government*. Cambridge, Massachusetts: Harvard University Press, 1961.
Delivered as the Godkin Lecture for 1960. Interesting account of a real-life struggle between the "two cultures" during WWII.

Stillman, John Maxson. *The Story of Alchemy and Early Chemistry*. reprint of ed. of 1924, New York: Dover Publications, 1960.
Materialist history of alchemy.

Strachey, James. (ed.). *Josef Breuer and Sigmund Freud: Studies in Hysteria.* reprint ed., New York: Basic Books, Harper Colophon Books, n.d.
   The classic early works written with Breuer, especially "Anna O.".
Talbot, Michael. *Mysticism and the New Physics.* New York: Bantam Books, 1980.
   Extends speculations in Capra's *Tao of Physics.*
Tart, Charles T. *States of Consciousness.* El Cerrito, California: Psychological Processes, Incorporated, 1975.
   Perhaps best contemporary work on altered states of consciousness.
Travis, Julius C. The Hierarchy of Symbols. In *The Shaman from Elko.* San Francisco: C. G. Jung Institute of San Francisco, 1978.
   Unusual article tracing the order in which symbols appear in dreams over the course of an analysis.
White, Morton. (ed.). *The Age of Analysis: the 20th Century Philosophers.* New York: Mentor Books, Houghton Mifflin Co., 1955.
   Nothing on Whitehead is easy, but the section on Whitehead contained herein is a lucid summary.
Whitmont, Edward C. *The Symbolic Quest: Basic Concepts of Analytical Psychology.* Princeton: Princeton University Press, 1969.
   One of the best general books on Jung's analytical psychology.
Wilson, Colin. *Inside the Outsider (I)* N. Hollywood, California: Audio-Text Cassette #36049, n.d.
   How can man break-through from the mundane world into the supra-personal world? Discussion of "Eureka" experience of creativity.
Zukav, Gary. *The Dancing Wu Li Masters: An Overview of the New Physics.* New York: Bantam Books, 1979.
   Especially good on paradoxes implicit in quantum mechanics.

Index

a posteriori judgement. *See* synthetic judgement
a priori judgement, *See* analytic judgement
acausal order. *See* synchronicity
Act of Creation, the, by Arthur Koestler, 96
active imagination. *See* meditation: active imagination
Aion, by C. G. Jung, 160
Akasic Traces, 143
Alchemical Studies, by C. G. Jung, 160
alchemy, 1, 2; Chinese, 174; coniunctio. *See* coniunctio; creation myth. *See* coniunctio: creation myth; difficulty of translation, 159; heaven above, heaven below, 48, 158; Kabala, 158; mixture of Greek philosophy and Egyptian technique, 157; as model of psychological development, 153–176; in Moslem world, 158; philosopher's stone, 156; pictures of male/female psychic development, 133f; precursor of depth psychology, 156; projection of unconscious onto matter, 157, 160; summary of Jung's conclusions, 166
Alexander the Great, 156
Alexandria, library of, 156
"Amazing Code, the", in *Gotcha: Paradoxes to Puzzle and Delight*, by Martin Gardner, 216f
analytic judgement, 23, 24f, 227
analytic psychology, *See* Jung, C. G., psychology of
ancients, 18, 64

Anima/Animus, 121–136, 153, 161; alchemical pictures, 133f; biological roots of, 130f; bridge between conscious and unconscious, 131; contemporary history, 129; contrasexuality of, 121, definition of, 121; divine syzygies, 129; following integration of Shadow, 119; function of relationship to unconscious, 121; Logos & Eros, 133; moods & opinions, 132f, soul, 122; *Also see* coniunctio: union of mind and body
animal magnetism. See hypnotism: animal magnetism
archetype, 2, 38, 67, 101; Anima/Animus. *See* Anima/Animus; artists, as experienced by, 90f; biological roots of, 82, 85f; of development, 113, 153, 161; ego, 104; etymology of, 38; example of baby goose imprinting Mother archetype, 66; example of baby's development, 103f; example of behavior of parmecium, 103; forms without content, 102, 103; Jung's schizophrenic patient, 89–91; Mother, 66, 102ff, 106; need for integration of personal experiences into consciousness, 117; ontology of, 142–146; personification of, 117; Platonic, 38; primordial images, 101f; relation to complex, 104f, 225; relation to instincts, 44; religious symbols, 66; Self. *See* Self; Shadow. *See* Shadow; sun's penis creating winds, 89; world axis, 66

241

Archimedes, 96, 143
Aristotle, 15, 23
associationism, 32f, 34, 51
astrology, 1

Bar-Hillel, Y., 213
Barber paradox. *See* mathematics: Barber paradox
Bateson, Gregory: anecdote about dolphins, 95, 143; life as complex feed-back system, 202
behaviorism. *See* psychology, behavioral
Bell, Eric Temple, 185
Berkeley, Bishop George, 7, 16, 24, 26, 27, 31, 58, 59, 179, 202; appreciation of calculus, 189, 190
Bernheim, Hippolyte, 37
bio-feedback, 37, 40f
Bohm, David, 3f, 102, 192
Boole, George, 199
Boring, Edwin G., 32
Braid, James 49f, 55, 58, 97
Breuer, Joseph, 62, 70
Brown, Barbara, 40f
Brown, Dr. Thomas, 32, 34
bubble chamber, 79
Bucke, Richard Maurice, M.D., 173
Buddhism, 123

Caesar, 156
Cantor, Georg, 197, 205–210, 217f
Capra, Frijof, 4, 162
categories, Kantian, 7f, 9, 26, 27, 31, 34, 38, 58, 67, 180, 228
causality, 5, 7, 24f, 31, 180
cause-and-effect. *See* causality
Center of the Cyclone, the: an Autobiography of Inner Space, by John C. Lilly, M.D., 173
Charcot, Jean Martin, 2, 37, 55f, 57, 58, 61, 62, 70, 97
Chomsky, Noam, 65, 67
Christianity, 13, 123; as era of progress, 164
Chtonic Mother. *See* Self

clinical psychology. *See* psychology, clinical
clocks, accurate, 15
collective unconscious. *See* unconscious: collective
colors, Newton's theory of, 18
complex: ego as complex, 106; Jung's discovery of complexes 105, 225; Mother, 225; relation to archetype, 104f, 225
Concerning the Revolutions of the Heavenly Bodies, by Nicholas Copernicus, 48
Concerning the Structure of the Human Body, by Andreas Vesalius, 48
coniunctio, 162–176; Adam and Eve, 163, 164, 165; creation myth, 167; King and Queen, 163, 164, 165; meditation. *See* meditation; Mercurius as mediator. *See* Mercurius; personification of opposites, 163, 164, 165; quaternio, 162, 167; Sulphur and Salt, 163; Sun and Moon, 163, 164, 165; three unions, 167–175; *unio mentalis* (mental union), 167, 168ff; *Also see* Shadow; union of male and female, 167; union of mind and body, 167, 168, 170ff; *Also see* Anima/Animus; union of mind and body with *unus mundus*, 167, 168, 173–175; *Also see unus mundus; Also see* Self
consciousness: boundary condition, 111; emergence from unconscious, 77, 83ff, 93; personal, 82; relation to ego, 106f
Copernicus, Nicholas, 13ff, 21, 48
Cosmic Consciousness, by Richard Maurice Bucke, M.D., 173
creative synthesis, John Stuart Mill's, 34f
Critique of Pure Reason, by Immanuel Kant, 25

da Vinci, Leonardo, 13f, 14, 21, 57
Dancing Wu Li Masters, the, by Gary Zukav, 162

242

Darwin, Charles, 77, 182
"das ding an sich". *See* categories, Kantian
depth psychology. *See* Jung, C. G.; and Freud, Sigmund
Descartes, Rene, 21, 24, 27, 57, 71, 184–186, 189, 191, 211
development, psychosexual, 68f
Dictionary of Philosophy and Religion, by W. L. Reese, 193
Dieterich, Albrecht, 89
DNA/RNA, 109f, 160, 213
dogma, religious, 13, 15, 123
dolphins, 95, 143
Dorn, Gerald, 167
dreams: author's experience with, 64f; Freudian interpretation of. *See* Freud, Sigmund: dream interpretation; Jungian interpretation of. *See* Jung, C. G.: dream interpretation; von Kekule's "ring-of-snakes" dream, 96, 143

Eastern philosophy/mysticism, 3, 156; not appropriate for Westerners, 146
Eddington, A. S., 196
Edinger, Edward, 82; alchemy as psychological model, 161, 175; mandalas, 124f
Ego and Archetype, by Edward Edinger, 124
ego: as archetype 104; as complex, 106; collective, 146; emergence of, 104; expanded, 118; potential of, 109; relation to consciousness, 106f
eighteenth century, 8, 35, 49
Einstein, Albert, 15, 41, 182; mystery of mathematics, 59
Eliade, Mircea, 66, 67
empiricism, 20, 24, 32
energy: Freud's concept of. *See* libido: Freud's concept of; Jung's concept of. *See* libido,: Jung's concept of; law of conservation of, 41f; nature of, 42; psychic. *See* libido; relationship to matter, 3; von Helmholtz' concept of, 41

entropy, law of, 41
Epimenides, 221
Erasmus, 13
Erickson, Milton, 50f; author's use of Ericksonian techniques, 97ff; concept of hypnotism 97
Euclid. *See* mathematics: Euclidean geometry
Euclidean geometry. *See* mathematics: Euclidean geometry
Eureka effect, 96, 143
experiment, scientific. *See* scientific method
experimental psychology. *See* psychology, experimental

Faust, by Johann Wolfgang von Goethe, 75f, 158
Fechner, Gustav, 37–41, 44, 60, 103, 185; early work, 38; spiritual crisis, 38
fifteenth century, 6
figure/ground relationship, 40
Fliess, Wilhelm, 62
Flournoy, Theodore, 138
Foundations of Set Theory, by A. A. Fraenkel and Y. Bar-Hillel, 213
fourteenth century, 6, 13
Fraenkel, A. A., 213
Franz, Marie-Louise von, 82; alchemy, history of, 156–158; alchemy as psychological model, 161, 175; Jung's love of nature, 75
free-association. *See* Freud, Sigmund: free-association
Frege, Friedrich, 199–201, 206, 210, 211
Freud, Sigmund, 56f, 60, 61–72, 224; and Jung. *See* Jung: split with; Freud, "black mud of occultism", 71; Breuer's "talking cure", 62; comparison to scholastic philosophers, 69; dream censor, 64, 71; dream interpretation, 2, 63–67, 70, 141; early work, 61–63; free association, 62, 70; Jung's concept of complexes, 105; last great rationalist, 2; libido. *See* libido: Freud's

243

concept of; race memories, 78; repression, 84; sexuality, 62, 67–70; split with Jung, 138–141, 148; super-ego, 112; theorist, 61; theory of psychosexual development, 68f, 71; transference, 113–116; unconscious. *See* unconscious: Freudian concept of

Galileo, 15, 20f
galvanic skin response, Jung's experiments with, 37
Gardner, Martin, 216
Gauss, Carl Friedrich, 183, 205
genetic predisposition, 109
geometry: Euclidean. *See* mathematics: Euclidean geometry; non-Euclidean. *See* mathematics: non-Euclidean geometry
Gilson, Etienne, 6
Gnostic Christianity, 21; early alchemists, 157; precursor of depth psychology, 154, 157, 163
God: nature of relationship to man, 5, 8, 13f, 24
Gödel, Escher, Bach, by Douglas R. Hofstadter, 213
Gödel, Kurt, 4, 8, 10, 176, 184, 195, 197, 210, 211–229; belief in mathematical intuition, 223; Gödel numbers, 214–216, 217; and Jung, 224–229; limits of logic, 223; mapping technique, 213–215; meta-mathematical mapping, 212, 217–221; meta-mathematical statements are synthetic judgements, 228; reaction of mathematical formalists, 222; significance of Gödel's Proof, 222–224; twice-twisted paradox, 213, 219f
Gödel's Proof. *See* Godel, Kurt
"Gödel's Proof", in *World of Mathematics*, by Ernest Nagel and James R. Newman, 213
Goethe, Johann Wolfgang von, 158
Golden Age of Greek philosophy, 16
Goodall, Jane, 86

Gotcha: Paradoxes to Puzzle and Delight, by Martin Gardner, 216
gravity: Aristotle vs. Galileo, 15; Newton's theory of, 18

Hall, Calvin S., 69
Hall, Edward T., 66, 67
Hampden-Turner, Charles, 101
Harlow, Harry F.: experiment with chimpanzees, 70
harmony between man and nature. *See* holistic viewpoint
Hartley, David, 32
heaven above, heaven below. *See* alchemy: heaven above, heaven below; *Also see* mind/body problem: relationship between macro- and micro-worlds
Hegel, Georg Wilhelm Friedrich, 76
Heisenberg, Werner, 154, 182, 202
Helmholtz, Hermann von, 37, 41f
Hermes. *See* Mercurius
hierarchy of needs, 149
Hilbert, David, 191f, 197, 211
Hillman, James, 82
Hinduism, 123
Hobbes, Thomas, 21
Hofstadter, Douglas R., 213
Hohenheim, Philippus Aureolus Bombast von. *See* Paracelsus, Theophrastus
holistic viewpoint, 1, 5, 33, 71; expressed in fringe phenomena, 58
holographic brain model. *See* Pribram, Karl
Hopi Indians: sense of space/time, 26
Hume, David, 7, 24f, 26, 27, 28, 31, 32, 34, 58, 59, 179, 180, 202
"Hypnotic Psychotherapy", paper by Milton Erickson, 97
hypnotism: animal magnetism, 49, 58; author's use of Ericksonian techniques, 97ff; behavioral view as simulation or delusion, 51; Charcot's conception of, 55; Erickson's concept of, 97; fixation, 50; Freud's use of, 61f; fringe phenomenon, 1,

71; history of, 47–53; Janet's concept of, 56; suggestion, 50
hysteria: Charcot's concept as exclusively female condition, 55f; Janet's concept as splitting of personality, 56; *Also see* neurosis

idealism, philosophical, 7, 24, 27, 31, 179
ideas, Locke's concept of. *See* Locke, John
Implicate Order. *See* Bohm, David
individuation. *See* Jung, C. G.: individuation; *Also see* Self
instinctual behavior of animals, 111
"interesting times", 8, 17, 18
Interpretation of Dreams, by Sigmund Freud, 63–67
introspectionism, 42, 45
Islam, 123

James, William: negative opinion of Fechner's research, 40
Janet, Pierre, 37, 56f, 58
Judaism, 123
Jung, C. G., 75–176, 179, 192; alchemy as model of psychological development, 153–176; Anima/Animus archetype. *See* Anima/Animus archetype; archetypes, discovery of, 105; archetypes of development, 81; background for ideas, 75–80; biological roots of archetypes, 82, 85; categories of psyche, 82; Chinese alchemical text, 174; collective unconscious. *See* unconscious, collective; complex, 105, 225; confrontation with unconscious, 138–141, 225f; descriptive scientist, 2, 61, 78f, 181; difficulty of interpreting Jung, 81f; dream interpretation, 2, 138–141, 148; dream of unknown annex of his house, 155; earthy quality, 75; experimental psychologist, 37; "fallow period", 139; Freud, split with, 70, 79, 138–141, 148, 181, 225; Gödel's Proof, significance of, 224–229; Goethe's *Faust*, 75f, 158; importance to science, 227ff; individuation 81; *Also See* Self; individuation, comparison to particle physics, 154; mind as self-referential system, 8, 202, 227; myths and fairy tales, 101; models of reality, 2, 61, 77, 226; occult phenomena, 76f; ouroboros, 214, 218f; personal consciousness, 82; personal unconscious, 82, 84f; philosophical and literary roots, 37, 75; psychology of, 3, 10; psychological dynamics, 35, 101–107; schizophrenic patient's collective memory, 111, 218; Self archetype. *See* Self; Shadow archetype. *See* Shadow; summary of development of his psychology, 224–227; support from animal research, 86; Tavistock lectures, 78; transference, 113–116; word association tests, 225; writing style, 76

Kabala, 158
Kant, Immannuel, 8, 9, 16, 24, 25–28, 31, 33, 34, 35, 38, 58, 59, 60, 87, 179, 180, 202, 228; categories. *See* categories, Kantian.
Kekule, Friedrich August von: "ring-of-snakes" dream, 96, 143
Kellog, Rhoda, 124f, 127
Koestler, Arthur: von Kekule's "ring-of-snakes" dream, 96
Kohler, Wolfgang, 51
Kuhn, Thomas, 9, 87

L' Autoisme Psychologique, by Pierre Janet, 56
Lao Tzu: definition of God/universe, 151, 152; *Aslo see* Pascal, Blaise
Lashley, K. F., 51
last universal man. *See* Leibniz, Gottfried
Lauzun, Gerald, 65

Leibniz, Gottfried, 23, 25, 87, 211, 227; fluxions (calculus), 186–190
Liar paradox, 221
libido: as cause of inner pressure 143; Freud's concept of, 42; Jung's concept of, 42, 84, 138
light, Newton's theory of, 18
Lilly, John C., M. D., 173
Lobachevski, Nikolai, 196
Locke, John, 7, 20, 23, 24, 27, 32, 51, 58, 179, 181
logic, 23; *Also see* Leibniz, Gottfried; *Also see* Gödel, Kurt
Logical Positivists, 222
Lorenz, Konrad, 66, 67, 85, 102f; story of baby goose, 66
love, as connecting principle of universe, 48
Luther, Martin, 13

Man and his Symbols, by C. G. Jung, 154, 161
man the observer. *See* Renaissance
mandala, 181; *Also see* coniunctio: quaternio; body, soul, mind, spirit, 123, 125–128; four-way nature of, 124f
Maps of the Mind, by Charles Hampden-Turner, 101
Maslow, Abraham 149f, 151; hierarchy of needs, 149; peak experiences, 149; self-actualization, 149f; self-actualized people, qualities of, 149f
materialism. See rationalist/materialist position.
Mathematical Experience, the, by Philip J. Davis and Reuben Hersh, 223
mathematics: aleph null, 207, 209; aleph one, 209; analytic geometry, 183–186, 191, 211, 213; applied, 59, 183, 189; axiomatic development of arithmetic, 192–195; author's second-grade experience of concept of zero, 191f; Barber paradox, 199–201, 205, 210, 221; before Gödel, summary, 211f; calculus, 18, 186–190, 211, 213; cardinality, 206; complete and consistent, 191, 220f; *Also see* Gödel, Kurt; continuum, 209; coordinates, 185f; Euclidean geometry, 183, 191, 195, 211; fear of intuition, 191; first science, 59; formalism, 191–204, 211, 213, 222; induction, 193f; infinite set, definition of, 209; infinity, 188, 205–210; intuition, 191, 211, 222, 223; limits, 187ff; logic, 23, 223; *Also see* Frege, Gottfried; *Also see* Gödel, Kurt; *Also see* Russell, Bertrand; mapping, 216f. *Also see* Gödel, Kurt: mapping technique, non-Euclidean geometry, 195–197; paradox. *See* paradox; parallel axiom, 196; pigeon-hole technique, 206, 208, 209; power set, 209; *Principia Mathematica*. See *Principia Mathematica*; proof, nature of, 86ff; pure, 59, 183; "Queen of sciences", 183; rational numbers, 207; real numbers, 207–209; *reductio ad absurdum*, 217f; self-referential systems. *See* self-referential systems; spherical geometry, 196; transcendent function, 149; transfinite numbers, 209
matter/energy, 3
medieval man. *See* Middle ages
meditation, 170f; active imagination, 170, 172, dangers of, 171f
Memories, Dreams, Reflections, by C. G. Jung, 140, 153, 154, 161
Men of Mathematics, by Eric Temple Bell, 185
Mercurius, 163, 167
Merrell-Wolff, Franklin, 173
Mesmer, Friedrich Anton, 49, 58
mesmerism. *See* Mesmer, Friedrich Anton
Michelangelo, Buonarroti, 13, 57
Middle Ages, 5, 6, 8, 13, 16, 18, 123
Mill, John Stuart, 34f; appreciation of Descartes' analytic geometry, 186
Miller, Miss Frank: fantasies of, 138f
mind as mirror of reality. *See* mind-/body problem: limits of observation; *Also see* self-referential systems

mind/body problem, 1; *Also see* alchemy; *Also see* coniunctio: three unions; *Also see* Self; *Also see* self-referential systems; Chomsky's concept of "deep structures" of language, 65; development over Christian era, 123; Eliade's discovery of common religious symbolism, 66, 67; Fechner's solution, 38–41; Heisenberg's uncertainty principle, 182; imprinting, 66; Kant's solution, 26–28, 31; limits of logic, 4, 223; *Also see* Gödel's Proof; limits of observation, 6, 7, 15f, 21, 223f; need for levels of organization, 94f, 95f, 110; non-verbal language, 66; parallelism, 32f; philosophical history, 5; Piaget's concept of inborn motor skills, 65, 67; relational nature of perception, 39; relationship between macro- and micro-worlds, 48, 58; solution expressed in fringe phenomena, 58; unitary reality as resolution, 3, 9; *Also see unus mundus*
Mithraic ritual, 89f
models of reality, 10
Moonitz, David A., 213
morphic resonance. *See* Sheldrake, Rupert
morphogenetic fields. *See* Sheldrake, Rupert
Mostowski, Andrzej, 213, 222
Mother, Chtonic. *See* Self
Mysterium Coniunctionis, by C. G. Jung, 160, 162–176
mystery religions, 157
mystical experience, 150

nadir-experience, 150
Nagel, Ernest, 213
neurosis: culturally dependent, 57; Jung's concept as shift of energy, 57, 78; *Also see* hysteria
Newman, James R., 213
Newton, Isaac, 3, 7, 17–21, 27, 28, 57, 182, 211; calculus, 186–190
Newton's Laws, 18–20, 28, 58

nineteenth century, 1, 28, 31, 34, 37, 43, 49, 79, 199
normal science. *See* paradigms: scientific
Nova: episode on history of mathematics, 201

observer/observed, problem of. *See* mind/body problem
ouroboros, 214, 218f

Paracelsus, Theophrasus, 47f, 49, 58, 71; importance of love, 48
paradigms, scientific, 2, 9f, 19, 87f, 228; example of hypnotism, 50f
paradox: definition of, 200; "Liar", 221; twisted, 218f
parallelism, 32f
particle/wave polarity, 3, 18
Pascal, Blaise: definition of God/universe, 151, 152; *Also see* Lao Tzu
Pathways Through to Space, by Franklin Merrell-Wolff, 173
peak experiences, 149
Peano, Giuseppe. *See* Peano's Postulates
Peano's Postulates, 192–195, 211, 213
perception, sense. *See* sense perception
philosopher's stone. *See* alchemy: philosopher's stone
philosophy: mind/body problem. *See* mind/body problem: philosophical history; mother of sciences, 58ff, 181
Philosophy of Consciousness Without an Object, by Franklin Merrell-Wolff, 173
physics: particle, 79; relationship with depth psychology, 41; twentieth century, 1, 2, 16, 28
Piaget, Jean, 65, 67
Plato, 28, 38
Pope, Alexander, 17
pre-paradigm times. *See* paradigms, scientific
Pribram, Karl: holographic brain, 3; world as hologram, 152

247

Prigogine, Ilya, 4
primordial images. See archetypes
Principia Mathematica, by Bertrand Russell and Alfred North Whitehead, 203–205, 210
probability theory, 28
projection, psychological, 113–116
Protestant movement in religion, 13
psyche: Also see Jung, C. G.; computer model of, 93ff; dynamics of, 101–107; levels of, 94; models of, 101; nature of. See mind/body problem; reflex-arc model of, 93
Psychological Types, by C. G. Jung, 141, 174
Psychology and Alchemy, by C. G. Jung, 138, 148, 160, 165
psychology, behavioral, 34, 53, 93, 95; supporting Sheldrake's hypothesis, 143
psychology, clinical, 2, 28, 37, 53; founders of, 55–60; importance of patients' subjective experience, 52
psychology, experimental, 1, 28, 33, 37–45, 53, 58; Fechner's pioneering work, 40; imitating the sciences, 43ff; precursors of, 31–35; Wundt's concept of, 42f
psychology, Gestalt 40; classic experiment with relational sense perception of chickens, 51
"Psychology of Transference, the", by C. G. Jung, 160
psychophysical threshold. See sense perception: threshold of
Ptolemaic system. See Ptolemy
Ptolemy, 13f

quantum mechanics, 213

Rank, Otto, 65
rationalism. See rationalism/materialism
rationalism/materialism, 1, 2, 8, 27; limits of in scientific method, 51; philosophic limits of, 58

reductio ad absurdum, 86ff
Reese, W. L., 193
reflex-arc, 34
Reid, Thomas, 31, 34
relationship, figure/ground, 10
relativity, theory of, 59, 213; Also see Einstein, Albert
Renaissance, 1, 5, 8, 13–16, 17, 20, 21, 27, 47, 57, 58, 71, 123, 164, 181, 211, 223
Renaissance Ideal. See Renaissance
Renaissance man. See Renaissance
repression, Freudian. See Freud, Sigmund: repression
Riemann, Georg, 196
Rosser, J. B., 222
Russell, Bertrand, 197, 203f, 206, 210, 212, 220; Barber paradox. See mathematics: Barber paradox; destruction of Frege's work, 199–201; epigram on nature of mathematics, 197

scholastic philosophy, 13, 16
science: development of, 1, 6; disavowal of philosophy, 59f; hypothesis, nature of, 4f; levels of, 110; limits of, 87f; normal. See paradigms, scientific; paradigms. See paradigms, scientific; philosophy's children, 58ff, 181; projection of scientists' spirituality onto matter, 160; twentieth century, 1, 3, 35
scientific method, 6f, 15, 16, 17–21, 21; limits of, 51
Scottish School of philosophy, 31f
Secret of the Golden Flower, the, translated by Richard Wilhelm, 174
Self, 81, 137–152, 153, 161; Also see coniunctio: union of mind and body with unus mundus: after integration of Anima/Animus, 135f; beyond restrictions of space/time, 137; circumambulatio of, 151; compensatory function of, 147; goal, 138, 148, 150; Jung's concept of, 33; paradoxicality of, 137, 148f; poten-

248

tial of ego, 111; presupposing dissociative consciousness, 174; process of individuation, 138, 148, 150; psychic center, 141; spiral path, 151; surrounding ego, 174; teleological function of, 148; transcendent function, 145, 146–149, 148, 149, 151, 174, 181f; window onto *unus mundus*, 151f; wholeness, 137, 148
self-actualization, 149
self-referential systems, 8, 194, 199–210, 227; *Also see* Gödel, Kurt; finite, 203; problems with, 202f
sense perception, 7, 20; organization, 27f; relation nature of, 39, 51, 185; threshold of, 38f, 44
Sentences Undecidable In Formalized Arithmetic, by Andrzej Mostowski, 213
seventeenth century, 1, 7, 15, 17, 28, 33, 35
sexuality: Freudian view as central problem of neurosis, 62, 67–70; Freudian view of perversions, 67f; Freud's concept of polymorphous perverse, 69, 71
Shadow, 81, 109–119, 146, 153, 161, 171; *Also see* coniunctio: *unio mentalis*: as archetype, 116f; dreams, 112f; evolution of, 113; integration of, 117, 127; personification of, 117, 118; projection of, 114–116; regulatory nature of, 112, 118; relation to ego and Self, 112, 118
Sheldrake, Rupert, 4, 143; morphogenetic fields, 160; use of behavioral rat studies, 104
Silberer, Henry, 166
sixteenth century 6, 47, 167
Snow, C. P., 76, 181
socio-biology, 86
space/time: absolute, 18f; Hopi Indians's sense of, 26
Spinoza, Baruch, 33, 34, 35
Stekel, Wilhelm, 65
Stillman, John, 156
Structure of Scientific Revolutions, the, by Thomas Kuhn, 9, 87
subject/object, problem of. *See* mind/body problem
subjective experience, value of, 52f
super-ego, 112
Sutcliffe, J. P., 50f
symbol, 138; example of cross, 142; Freudian reduction to sexual signs, 65; "living", 143ff, 147, 174, 192; Jung's definition of, 142; not a sign, 141, 142; reduced to signs, 144; reduced to symptom, 145, 147; transcendent function. *See* Self: transcendent function
symbolic logic, 199–201, 203–205
symbols, collective. *See* archetypes
Symbols of Transformation, by C. G. Jung, 138f, 148
synchronicity, 5
synthetic judgement, 23, 24f, 26, 227

tabula rasa, mind as, 32, 39, 70, 102, 180
talking cure. *See* Freud, Sigmund: free-association
Tao of Physics, the, by Frijof Capra, 162
Tarski, Alfred, 222
theories, great, 19f
Thom, Rene: belief in reality of mathematical forms, 223
Three Essays on the Theory of Sexuality, by Sigmund Freud, 67–70
three-body problem, 28
Tichener, Edward, 43
transcendent, experience, 150; comparison with schizophrenic experience, 150; comparison with experiences on hallucinogenic drugs, 150f
transcendent function. *See* Self; mathematical, 149
transcendent reality. *See unus mundus*
transference, psychological, 113–116
Transformations and Symbols of the Libido. *See Symbols of Transformation*.

249

tripartite division: body, soul, spirit, 122
twentieth century, 1, 8f, 34, 57, 79, 107, 145, 176
"two cultures", 76, 181
Two Essays on Analytical Psychology, by C. G. Jung, 166

uncertainty principle. *See* Heisenberg, Werner
unconscious: collective, 3, 82, 85, 88; comparison to particle physics, 79; continuity of, 80; creativity of, 93–99; fear of concept by early psychologists, 43f; Freud's concept of, 2, 44, 57, 62, 63; Jung's concept of, 57; Jung's proof of existence of collective unconscious, 89–91; personal, 82, 84f; scope of, 79, 80; source of consciousness, 77
unus mundus, 34; alchemical concept of, 48; coniunctio with mind and body. *See* coniunctio: union of mind and body with *unus mundus*; Fechner's concept of, 38, 40;

Jung's concept of, 33, 151; Spinoza's concept of, 33

Van Helmot, 49, 58
Vesalius, Andreas, 48

Weber, Ernst Heinrich. *See* Weber's Law
Weber's Law, 38–40, 49–51
Whitehead, Alfred North, 197, 204, 210
Whorf, Benjamin, 26
Wilhelm, Richard, 174
Wilson, Colin: "Eureka effect", 96
Wilson, Edward O., 86
Wise Old Man. *See* Self
World of Mathematics, by Ernest Nagel and James R. Newman, 213
Wundt, Wilhelm, 37, 42f, 58

Yoga, 140

Zeitgeist, 20, 44
Zukav, Gary, 4, 162

Duran, Eduardo

ARCHETYPAL CONSULTATION
A Service Delivery Model for Native Americans

American University Studies: Series 8, Psychology, Vol. 2
ISBN 0-8204-0082-3   167 pp.   pb./lam.   US $ 16.85

Recommended prices - alterations reserved

This theoretical model uses Jung's theoretical constructs as they are relevant to the Native American psyche. Jung's notions are then integrated with traditional or indigenous concepts of illness and therapy in order to make Jung's ideas more meaningful toward the delivery of cross-cultural psycho-therapy to Native Americans.

Contents: This work deals with issues and problems in the area of cross-cultural psycho-therapy with Native Americans.

PETER LANG
New York · Berne · Frankfurt am Main · Paris